Broken Bangles

Hanifa Deen

ANCHOR

Sydney   Auckland   Toronto   New York   London

BROKEN BANGLES
AN ANCHOR BOOK

First published in Australia and New Zealand
in 1998 by Anchor

National Library of Australia.
Cataloguing-in-Publication Entry.

Deen, Hanifa.
  Broken bangles.
  ISBN 0 86824 721 9.
  1. Muslim women–Pakistan–Social conditions. 2. Muslim
  women–Bangladesh–Social conditions. I. Title.
305.4869710549

Anchor books are published by

Transworld Publishers (Aust) Pty Limited
15-25 Helles Ave, Moorebank, NSW 2170

Transworld Publishers (NZ) Limited
3 William Pickering Drive, Albany, Auckland

Transworld Publishers (UK) Limited
61-63 Uxbridge Road, Ealing, London W5 5SA

Bantam Doubleday Dell Publishing Group Inc
1540 Broadway, New York, New York 10036

Cover design by Guy Mirabella
Cover photo by Hanifa Deen
Polaroid transfer by Lynette Zeeng
Author photo by Hans Versluis
Typeset in 11.5/14pt Adobe Garamond by Midland Typesetters, Victoria
Printed by McPherson's Printing Group

10 9 8 7 6 5 4 3 2 1

For Yasmeen Akhter and Zainab Noor

COPYRIGHT ACKNOWLEDGMENTS

✳   ✳   ✳

CONTENTS

*   *   *

ACKNOWLEDGMENTS

*   *   *

It is impossible to mention by name all the women and men who have helped me. Some, but not all, appear in the text. I would like to thank everyone for their trust and generosity in educating me and sharing their visions of the future.

Firstly in Bangladesh: my good friends Selina Hossain and Maleeka Begum; Hameeda Hossain, Ayesha Khanam, Tarana Halim, Tasmima Hossain and Razia Khan. I am also indebted to Farah Ghuznavi for the stories she shared and her painstaking translations.

I also wish to thank the following (Bangladeshi) organisations: Bangladesh Mahila Parishad, Ain O Salish Kendra, Saptogram, PROSHIKA, BRAC, UBINIG, Naripokkho, Community Aid Abroad and my good friends at Probe Newsagency.

In Pakistan my gratitude to the following people and organisations: Jocelyn Saeed, Moneeza Hashmi, Aisha Ghaznavi, Serenidad Lavador, Mr Sidiqqi from the Human Rights Commission and Mariam Habib from the All Pakistan Women's Association, Bedari, Nageen Hyat from the Women's Action Forum in Islamabad and the Centre of Excellence for Women's Studies at the University of Karachi.

Nearer to home, thank you to my agent Christine Nagel who stops me from going insane, Zubaida Begum for her advice, my good friend Ann McGuire who reads with a stern but loving eye and my partner Franz Oswald who suffers quietly and supports me in hundreds of different ways. I am also indebted to my editor Katie Stackhouse for her incredible patience and sensibility.

The following publications were particularly useful: Ain O Salish Kendra, *Attack on Fundamentals* (ASK 1995); Shirkat Gah and Women Living Under Muslim Laws, *Chart of Customary Practices in Pakistan in Comparison with Statutory Law* (Shirkat Gah 1995); N.S. Khan (ed.), *Unveiling the Issues* (ASR Publications 1995); and poems by Taslima Nasreen translated by Carolyne Wright with Farida Sarkar, Mohammad N. Huda and Subharanjan Dasgupta, *The Game in Reverse* (George Braziller 1995).

AUTHOR'S NOTE

* * *

I started my journey to Bangladesh and Pakistan in late 1995 with the idea of writing a book about women's lives which might go beyond many of the usual accounts of women in Islamic societies. Time, I thought, to question the myth of the 'Muslim Woman'. I'd long been critical of this view based on a single definition of Muslim womanhood and a homogeneous Muslim world. It seemed to me that most books on women in Islamic societies were centred on the Middle East, yet there are more Muslims in South Asia and South East Asia than anywhere else in the world. Besides religion is just one of many building blocks that shape women's lives: colonialism, history, nationalism, economics, class, gender, culture and patriarchal values make up a litany of influences embedded in the psyche of each country.

My need was to reach out and explore the lives of women at a personal, yet political level—that old feminist slogan of the sixties and seventies. Emancipation is also about private matters, sirens' voices from thirty years ago reminded me: gender roles, family relations, sexuality—the 'private' needs to be a part of the political agenda, too.

How did women see themselves? I knew there must be a

diversity of experiences out there waiting for me. It only remained for me to listen, to heed the solutions women proposed to their own problems.

The women I met do not see themselves as victims to be pitied: most are actively engaged in an uphill battle of renegotiation and struggle, working hard at self-emancipation in the face of oppression from men and other women.

They are under pressure on two different fronts. Firstly they confront criticism and oppression from inside their communities and often their families for not being good, decent women; for not following the Islamic code as interpreted by men for fourteen centuries. Secondly they face stereotyping by an outside world that seems increasingly Islamophobic. Many are shocked by the anti-Islamic sentiments they hear and read about when overseas, and by the intentions of well-meaning Westerners who want to 'save' them. Even women who are not particularly religious find their identities constructed for them by strangers and begin to feel defensive.

The book has certainly changed directions more than once, for there were times when I became side-tracked and even lost. But I remained engrossed with how women in Pakistan and Bangladesh were doing daily battle against forces and constraints which I had never experienced, or had managed to keep at bay, or had even vanquished (or perhaps merely postponed) many years ago. But when stories of violence towards women crept into the different narratives, I was struck with the universalism of the suffering. There were times when I felt deeply depressed, but in the face of so much energy and commitment, to remain downcast seemed an insult to the women I met. They are all remarkable women. And nothing prepared me for the friendship, the understanding and the acceptance I discovered in the company of these women from Bangladesh and Pakistan.

Broken Bangles is the story of how I found a place in a corner of their lives for a short while, of the wonderful and terrible things I witnessed, and of the stories and experiences they shared with me. We had never met each other before and I expected to be treated as a stranger—perhaps a half stranger if I was lucky; after all, in spite of my 'Australianness', when they heard my name and when we looked at each other, there were certain things we shared. I was wrong however, for they accepted me as a sister.

For all sorts of sound practical reasons I have tried half-heartedly to loosen the ties binding me to my friends in both countries, but this has proven impossible. Intimacy can't be turned on and off just because of distance and other problems. The Sindhi woman poet, Malika, expresses this so well:

I am not
A song on life's tape recorder
Which you can
Rewind again and again
And erase from your heart.

So my silly idea that I would write a book and that would be the end of that—on to another project, another place—has proven completely wrong. I return almost every year to the company of women who refuse to surrender to the 'circles of protection' surrounding them in the guise of customary laws, religious traditions and patriarchal and family values.

Friends have asked me why I chose Pakistan and Bangladesh to write about. Why not Indonesia or Malaysia?

I chose Pakistan because of my own blood ties, that much was obvious. But why Bangladesh as well? And then slowly I began to understand that this was no random selection but something I'd carried around with me for quarter of a century.

I remember following the news from Australia; I remember the quarrels and the shouting in my father's house—until my mother banned any further discussion and we subsided into two resentful, ugly factions.

The two former wings of Pakistan were now enemies and Bangladesh, after a terrible war in 1971, threw off the domination of West Pakistan to become the free nation of Bangladesh. As I followed the news I felt enormous shame and grew quiet.

Bangladeshi women paid a terrible price which went beyond losing family and friends in war. Little has been written in the official histories of how they were targeted, and even today people prefer not to talk about what happened. Mass inter-country adoptions were hastily organised by international agencies in the aftermath of the war for many newly born Bengali-Punjabi babies.

While this is not my story to tell, I have remained deeply shamed by what took place. Many Pakistani women feel the same and reconciliation between women activists of the two countries has recently been forged at an unofficial and individual level.

Broken Bangles is a work of non-fiction with real characters and events although occasionally pseudonyms are used to protect confidentiality. The people I met along the way and the discussions I recorded are woven together with my own observations and occasionally my own imagination.

The reader should assume that only when I moved outside Dhaka did I occasionally use interpreters, although for the most part, even in the rural areas, women spoke to me directly in their own language which I had translated later.

The title *Broken Bangles* came to me before I even sat down to write. Bangles are the most common item of female adornment in this part of the world and anyone who has ever been to Bangladesh, India or Pakistan will recall the bazaars and the stalls where hundreds of glass bangles of every imaginable colour are on display. They dazzle, they distract—and they bind.

The ceremonial breaking of a widow's glass bangles is an important Hindu ritual often performed by another widow and signifies that the woman's life is over. It is also observed by Muslim women in the region although, unlike their orthodox Hindu sisters, they are allowed to remarry. Middle-class widows, who as brides received gold bangles from their husbands, may have them removed from their wrists by their mothers-in-law.

These rituals of widowhood became a jumping-off point for my imagination. The more I thought about bangles, the more fascinated I became, but the images flooding my mind were not traditional: they were of rebellion and dissent.

I imagined a new freedom where a woman metaphorically 'breaks her bangles', stepping outside the circle of protection provided by family, society and the silent laws of tradition to free herself from customs that oppress and deaden.

Her life is not over—quite the opposite.

PART ONE

Bangladeshi Voices

* * *

I do not believe we are poor; we have been kept poor and this word 'poverty' has been thrust upon us. We have tremendous wealth in the way of natural resources and hard working people; we have an incredible richness in our literary traditions—a tradition of a thousand years. But politics here is about power and not about people. Our poet Bharat Chandra wrote, 'May our children flourish in milk and rice'; that is the world I long for.

—Selina Hossain, contemporary Bangladeshi
writer, novelist and a Deputy Director
of the Bangla Academy

CHAPTER 1

The Mona Lisa

* * *

For as long as anyone can remember, Saleem Sultan, devout Muslim and Head Cook extraordinaire, has never once breached his pact with the Almighty God—unless it was absolutely necessary. Every morning without fail, he slips through the green gates of the Mona Lisa Guest House and with a look of pious resolve stamped on his face makes his way along the drowsy streets of Dhaka to the Pearl Mosque—his favourite mosque in a city famous for its mosques—just in time for the dawn prayer.

At the start of each new day the persuasive voices of the *muezzin* calling to the faithful filter through his dreams, pulling him gently awake. Almost without thinking, he picks up his sandals and clean praying clothes, rubs the sleep from his eyes and makes his way towards the door, taking care not to disturb his less religious friends huddled on pallets on the hard floor.

'I am a considerate man,' he tells himself as he steps over silent figures in the half dark. 'It is only proper that a man on his way to pray should think of others.'

3

Bodies wrapped up in the loneliness of sleep, covered with odd bits of mosquito netting and scarves, look more like untidy bundles than sleeping men. And if the truth be known, after all these years, his colleagues at the Mona Lisa hardly stir as he steps over them. Both sides have silently reached an understanding that if Saleem will stop trying to persuade them to join him in communal prayer, then they in turn will make no complaints when the sound of a squeaking door, a sneeze or a cough, disturbs their sleep.

By now everyone knows that Saleem, more than most men, has good reasons for his devoutness—not that anyone would dare utter this aloud, for the Head Cook is a force to be reckoned with; a man worthy of respect. Without Saleem there would be no guest house and a berth as agreeable as their beloved Mona Lisa is not easy to find. The prospect of joining the millions of unemployed in Dhaka is something to be taken seriously.

An hour later Saleem returns once more and sits quietly reading the Qur'an with the sleeping house for company. Religious verses and recipes become confused in his head although he tries hard to maintain a sombre concentration. Now and then he drifts into the past, reminiscing over some exotic feast or other he might once have prepared for wealthy employers in Kuwait and Sri Lanka in the good old days. Travelling overseas used to mark him as someone special and now he feels nostalgic. But those magical menus—finger food for British cocktail parties and mountains of steaming, fragrant biryani rice for wealthy Saudi palates—have gone forever. The future had seemed rosy, with dreams of one day opening his own restaurant. But fate was unkind and here he is back in Bangladesh, waiting for the Mona Lisa to come alive and his working day to begin. Saleem's dreams are temporarily on hold.

The cook's face did not give much away and his habit of peering at you demurely from under his eyelids, as if waiting to test your mood before he spoke, gave him an odd flirtatious air. Above all he was a keeper of secrets. His voice was low and sometimes his words were difficult for foreign ears to follow. Barking orders and yelling at subordinates was something Saleem could never bring himself to do. While not as modern in his ways as his rival Shamu, the 'so-called' Assistant Manager whom he despised, Saleem was fastidious with his appearance. He changed clothes twice a day, not counting morning and afternoon visits to the mosque. Not a stain, not a splash, not a hint of ghee marred his trousers. His appearance was all the more remarkable because he refused to wear an apron, another of his harmless little affectations. The delicious, but oh so oily, Bangladeshi curries were always left for Mr Hashmi, his Assistant Cook, to prepare; of course it helped that young Abba the kitchen boy chopped and cleaned without complaint. Watching Saleem at work, elegantly stirring a pan, showed mind, body and ingredients in perfect harmony. With four silver rings on each hand—some set with tiger eye and black agate—and an expensive-looking watch, wrists turned and saucepans spun gracefully. His clean-shaven face perspired slightly even now in the cold season when daytime temperatures hovered around 26 degrees.

Saleem preferred to concentrate on the Western dishes for which the Mona Lisa had a certain reputation. In a land where stomach complaints were exacted from foreigners as though in penance for past colonial sins, the cook was worth his weight in gold and Mr Habib, the owner, was prepared to overlook some of Saleem's more 'eccentric' habits. The Mona Lisa boasted that no guest had ever been struck down with the dreaded Bangla belly. If guests foolishly chose to eat outside, well then, the Mona Lisa could hardly be held responsible, could it? Saleem's supervision was unrelenting: his kitchen was spotless, with floors mopped thrice daily, rubbish whirled away instantly and fresh food bought each day at the local market. Cockroaches, mice and ants were in permanent exile, banished to guest bedrooms. Word of mouth kept a steady flow of visitors through the gates of the Mona Lisa, prepared to put up with a lot in return for safe food and safe water, immaculate linen and interesting company.

At 6.30 young Abba begins his own daily ritual of setting the breakfast table in the old wing of the guest house. He nods at Rashid, the morning *chowkhidar*, a slight, serious man, who guards the green cast iron gates but who also finds time to deliver the papers. Yawning and still half-asleep, Abba sets out six cups and saucers, six plates, sugar, jam, salt and pepper. No use protesting that this is not really his job, for not even Saleem can force Kumar Gupta to change his ways. Unlike the other men, the senior house servant lives outside the gates with his family and this gives him more freedom to bend the rules and carve out small fiefdoms of privilege for his pleasure.

The 'old fox', as he is known to guests, always arrives well after seven. Dismounting from his bicycle he swaggers into the lounge, black hair gleaming with oil, Chaplin moustache bristling and plastic briefcase under his arm. His eyes, like shiny black buttons, are alert, ready for combat. He always arrives too late to set the table and serve breakfast, but just in time to receive a daily blast of complaints from guests about anything from cockroaches and sagging mosquito nets to overflowing bogs and sluggish ceiling fans.

As usual everyone has rehearsed their litany of woes and worked out new ways to ambush the fox, for he has a knack of disappearing when tension mounts and a groundswell of rebellion seems about to boil over. But today everyone is determined:

this time they will not be fobbed off with a gentle smile and a few muttered words in soft, inept English. Guests soon discover that Kumar's English is very good when it's to his advantage. The look of pitiful bewilderment is a total sham.

'Action!' mutters Erik through his teeth. He stares hard at the fork in his hand and tightens his grip. Poor Erik has been without hot water for four days now.

At breakfast everyone dissects eggs and munches toast while they listen attentively to one another's complaints—it is part of the breakfast ritual, for the guests also have their own morning ceremony. Molly McPherson, or Molly Mac as she prefers, is the veteran; the 'foreign expert' who has seen it all. Guests come and go, but Molly has been living at the Mona Lisa for over two years now and is well versed in the art of the possible. Everyone comes to her for advice—and on a good day Molly Mac can give sound advice. It may not yield much, but after all it has been tested and people feel better for having asked her ...

'What should I do Molly? My lamp fused last night and nearly set the mosquito net on fire. Any chance of our friend Kumar fixing it, do you think?'

She shrugs her shoulders and, grimacing, reaches for the toast and honey and chews over the problem. 'Tell him when he comes in. Make him look at it straight away; tell him he must call the electrician or you'll tell Jahangir.'

Telling Jahangir is an idle threat—the guests know it and Kumar Gupta knows it—but it remains part of the game which must be played. Jahangir is the 'absentee' Manager at the Mona Lisa. He smiles and soothes our injured spirits, listens attentively to complaints and pretends to be sympathetic. But Jahangir (unlike his namesake, the famous warrior of early Islam) is an absolute coward when it comes to taking a stand—he is a diplomat, not a soldier.

Jahangir comes and goes like the monsoons. 'Have you seen Jahangir?' everyone asks. Kumar smiles innocently, giving nothing away ... The only time you know for sure Mr J will appear is on the day you are due to leave. Then he bounces up and presents the bill, giving an awkward half-bow and smiling his heart out. Everyone at the Mona Lisa has a dream and Jahangir wants to work in a real hotel, not an unregistered guest house with no office, no fax and one telephone shared with fourteen or so guests of uncertain pedigree. An unspoken question hovers in the air: why don't we stay at the five star Sonargaon Hotel, like proper foreigners?

Shamu, the sulky-faced, dubious Assistant Manager, always has the final accounts worked out beforehand, somehow fitting them in between combing his hair in front of the mirror, noisily hawking mountains of phlegm from some internal cavern and spitting his tonsils out in the front garden. Fond of watching Bollywood movies on the guest TV in the new wing, he only holds down the job, or so we hear from Saleem, because he can add up figures and because he is Kumar's younger brother. The accounting system is simple, but effective, and entirely technology-free. The key to it all lies in a system of tattered, grubby exercise books. Without this support the Mona Lisa would grind to a halt and Mr Habib soon find himself sadly bankrupt. Each room has its own book and every meal (except breakfast which is included in the modest rate of US$30) is recorded—not for our eyes to check, of course, but the prices are so ridiculously low that most guests never insist. In a land of sweeping floods and devastating cyclones, it seems such a petty thing to do: to calculate whether you'd had one or two pots of tea on Monday, a grand difference of twenty cents.

'It all makes sense,' said Molly. And in a way she was right.

After a spell, life at the Mona Lisa always falls into place—
more or less; after a while it becomes less confusing and less
irrational, as does the world of Bangladesh outside its walls, and
most people eventually yield to both.

* * *

Scott, the bearded anthropologist from Australia, mutters into
his tea and even Erik and Jürgen the two German technicians
manage a smile.

Erik and Jürgen were an interesting pair of very rich men in
their mid-thirties. Once a year, instead of spending their holidays skiing in the Alps or drinking retsina on the island of
Corfu, they travelled to different African or South Asian countries to do voluntary work in partnership with local doctors.
They trained technicians in the latest methods of testing the
hearing impaired and to produce cheap, reliable hearing aids.
The two Germans were an affable pair, except for their on-going
feud with the Assistant Manager which so far Shamu was
winning by a mile.

Shamu had never heard of public relations and he clearly
considered the Mona Lisa's guests unworthy of his attention.
His moodiness upset Saleem who felt guests should be feted, not
ignored. Saleem tried to make up for Shamu's disdain by playing
the host. He would greet everyone each morning, asking politely
after our health and generally 'flying the flag'. I noticed that at
first Saleem excluded me from his morning rounds of convivi-
ality. He even managed to ignore me without being rude.

'You puzzle everyone,' explained Jahangir when I pointed this
out to him. I wasn't angry, just curious. 'You have Western ways,
but you don't look Western and you have a Muslim name.'

But in the end it only took a week or so for the Mona Lisa

men to worm my ancestral history out of me and to adapt themselves to my strangeness. At the beginning they found it difficult to understand that I was Australian—I didn't look like Scott, did I? There was no need to ask the question, their eyes gave them away. But eventually they accepted my story, that I was an Australian of Pakistani descent, here in Bangladesh to collect material for a book on Bangladeshi women. Everything else I kept to myself.

*　　*　　*

'Those Pakistanis next door are driving me crazy! How can I work with their bloody TV going all day!' Scott is having another bad day. Every morning the Pakistani businessman and his driver sally forth to conquer the world, leaving the wife behind. She apparently is in *purdah*, which keeps her secluded in her own quarters away from the eyes of everyone, idling her day away watching Bengali soapies. We imagine her lounging on her bed eating sweet, sticky *jelabis*, although no-one has ever glimpsed her and our image lacks decorum.

It is a ticklish situation. Her decency, melded to her husband's honour, must at all costs be protected from the gaze of strange men. Scott therefore can't simply knock on the door and ask her to turn down the volume. He expects Jahangir to do the dirty deed, but Jahangir, an orthodox Muslim whose own wife wears a long, concealing *burqa* when she leaves the house, rendering her 'invisible', knows better and has been fending Scott off for days, promising to speak to the husband when he comes home. By then of course Jahangir has disappeared for the day.

'What on earth does she do—where does she hide—when the beds need making and the floors have to be mopped?' we wonder aloud.

'I'm telling Jahangir that I'm leaving. No, I mean it! I'm not putting up with it.' Scott makes this threat at least once a week. We make faces at one another. Scott will stay, we all will— we've seen some of the horror guest houses around the corner. True, they might have telephones in every room, and rumour has it that the air conditioning doesn't sound like a constipated hippopotamus with the bends, but they are not the Mona Lisa and they don't have Saleem. Hotels are definitely out of our reach (except for the Germans who obviously enjoy slumming). We boast in a kind of inverted snobbery that residents at the Mona are not over-indulged consultants on US$150–$200 per diems, plus disgustingly fat expense accounts.

'Everyone knows where your guest house is,' said Farida Akhter, the first local woman I met. 'Staying at the Mona is ideologically sound.'

Still there were times when I would gladly have exchanged 'ideologically sound' for a telephone that worked ...

✳   ✳   ✳

Scott shouldn't have been eating with us, for he really belonged in the new wing of the guest house with its own small dining room and separate kitchen which kept Saleem on the move from one kitchen to the other. But Scott is a gregarious, young-at-heart, fifty year old who grows fidgety indoors and really longs to be away on his field work. Scott likes nothing better than sitting in an old leaky boat—inadvertently off-course and heading for the Bay of Bengal—with his local research assistant by his side scribbling frantically in a damp notebook, hoping a cyclone won't hit them, while Scott, with the rain pelting down, waves a microphone under the nose of local fishermen who think he's crazy! While the fishermen might want to throw him overboard they are too

polite. Scott feels restless when confined indoors, but the
unstable political situation means that demonstrations are
looming and so he has headed back to the Lisa where he
wanders around in a checked cotton *lungi*, or sarong, practising his Bangla aloud.

'He's going native,' said Molly Mac. She did not approve.

Her face belonged under a poke bonnet or whatever headgear
wild-west pioneer women used to wear while wrestling prairies,
runaway horses and stampeding cattle. With short blonde-grey
hair and an untidy fringe she was in her late fifties or early
sixties—it was hard to tell. She was knitting an orange sweater,
she told me, to add to her collection for any Bangladeshi babies
she might come across.

Driving a wagon westward with Molly would have been a
difficult business: she would have insisted on doing all the
driving and seizing the reins from her would have been about
as impossible as wresting the TV remote control from her iron
grip, as night after night we were forced to endure re-runs of
'The Flying Doctors' and 'I Love Lucy'. Molly had 'donated'
the VCR so we were also compelled to sit through Disney's
Pocahontas. She confessed to us that her girlhood hero had been
Jo from *Little Women*.

The night a member of the British royal family had been
performing yet another full frontal revelation (metaphorically
speaking), Molly crawled out of bed in her boxer shorts ('men's
underwear—far more comfortable,' she swore) at three in the
morning to sit in front of the little box, her eyes shining and a
box of tissues on her lap.

'I came to Bangladesh "cold", straight from my Caribbean
holiday. I flew Phoenix–LA–Seoul–Bangkok and then Zia
Airport where they picked me up and drove me straight to the
Mona Lisa. No, I didn't expect a hotel, I wouldn't have been

comfortable in one. I decided to stay because it relieved me from house hunting, having to furnish a place, having to look after a bunch of servants I didn't really want. I would've gone home after work and been alone in the evening; the Mona Lisa seemed a better deal for me. I made the right decision.

'You see, I didn't know *anything*,' she stressed, looking me straight in the eye, daring me to disbelieve. 'I had an open mind because I didn't bone up on Bangladesh; I didn't read a thing.'

Molly made it sound like a virtue but I still found it hard to swallow. 'You mean you read nothing at all?' I asked her, trying not to sound too challenging.

'Well, I started to read *The Lonely Planet Guide to Bangladesh*, but it sounded so awful,' she laughed, 'that I slammed it shut and decided not to finish reading it.'

Molly had a Bachelor of Science; a Library Degree; a Masters of Arts and a PhD in Environmental Studies. She worked in Dhaka as a computer programs systems analyst, and as a United Nations volunteer was part of the colony of foreign experts, but in her own mind she had failed.

'I'm really going home in disgrace, you know. My mission has not been successful. I know the CEO, when he writes up his report, will say that I have contributed nothing to the project. My own report will just be excuse after excuse: "I was not able to complete this or accomplish that because of this delay or this problem", and it is not going to look good.' By nature she was a fighter, but this debacle had proven too much and in trying to set up an E-mail system for the government bureau she'd been assigned to, she'd met her Waterloo.

'It's not as if I didn't try!' she exclaimed. She sounded as if she was on trial. 'I've given a good deal of money from my own personal funds to send three people to programming school. I bought two sets of screwdrivers, for heaven's sake! They didn't even have screwdrivers to work on the equipment—it makes me so damn mad! So when I was in Singapore last year on vacation and saw some on sale, I bought them.

'But everyone at the bureau is more interested in *me* helping *them* emigrate to America! I tell 'em straight out: "Get on the end of the queue like everybody else in Dhaka! I'm sorry, I can't help you".'

I could easily imagine Molly in a US border patrol uniform, arms folded and eyes hidden behind mirrored sunglasses.

'I know that two of them are going to the USA and I just hope they don't drop in on me. You know the custom here— they can drop in and you are expected to house them and feed them.'

Her constant use of 'they' and 'them' was starting to get on my nerves. Molly even managed to make the gesture of natural hospitality in South Asia and Islamic countries sound like a heinous crime! *Maybe 'they' were different in Arizona?*

'You can see where it comes from,' she went on. 'You know, when it was still desert—and what have you—and everybody dropped in.'

'There's no desert here, Molly! What are you talking about?' Even after two years, Molly's sense of regional geography was miserable.

'I keep thinking of this as a Middle East culture still.'

'It's not—it never was!' I worked hard at bringing my screech under control, reminding myself that my role was to listen and learn.

'The Muslim culture then ... a survival technique much needed at one time sure'—the woman was unflappable—'but it just doesn't fit in with the West's culture.'

Once Molly had decided on a position she was as difficult to shift as the desert sands which she insisted belonged to Bangladesh! There were times when she sounded like an amateur rather than a 'foreign expert'. I wondered if she was typical of the flock of international consultants who descend on Dhaka like migratory birds as part of the foreign aid landscape.

'What will you do if they—I mean, if your colleagues—get in touch with you?'

'Oh shoot, I don't know! I just hope that the fare from New York to Arizona is too much and they won't make it there.' Molly reached for a piece of star fruit and lazily dipped it into little mounds of chilli pepper, coconut and salt. Her favourite worker had brought her daily ration of vitamin C and she grinned at him. When Molly smiled her sweet smile, her face was unbelievably transformed—*she should try smiling more often.*

'Rusheek looks after me very well,' she said; he nodded back at her indulgently; his unruly infant had to be looked after. 'Last month he took me to a Hindu *puja* and then after the festival to Jahangir's house for afternoon tea.'

I hope the poor buggers never think of dropping into Arizona, I thought.

Rusheek is another of the Hindu workers at the Lisa—there are three in all. Hindu and Muslim work side by side with no apparent tensions. I find it strange that in this house full of men there is remarkably little noise, except for the everpresent, nausea-inducing sound of rattling phlegm. Occasionally some imagined slight might flare into an argument but the raised voices soon return to normal and the arguments are never based on religion.

Rusheek says little but notices everything. Now and then a flicker of silent disapproval might cross his face if he saw some infringement of what he believed to be proper behaviour. Kumar, for instance might do one of his regular disappearing acts, emerging an hour later with a cheeky grin on his face, having finished his snooze in one of the empty guest rooms. Rusheek's family lived in Mymensingh about 140 kilometres from Dhaka. He visited home twice a year for holidays and if a family problem needed his guidance his wife would come down to Dhaka.

Molly had been thrilled by the invitation to visit Jahangir's flat. 'It is a tiny, two-roomed place, very modest, and his wife has a little maid, about twelve years old I guess, to help in the kitchen. His wife is lovely but very shy. She made these delicious little samosa things and a creamy kind of sweet—nothing was too much trouble. One thing I've noticed here,' she said, 'everyone seems to have help; another colleague has a ten-year-old boy who seems to float around all the time. I don't know where they pick 'em up, how long they stay, how much they get—I don't imagine it's much.'

She asked Rusheek to switch on the fan and turned her thoughts away from Jahangir's domestic arrangements back to her doomed project.

Even her colleagues' repeated assurances did little to allay her sense of failure, she told me.

'If you hadn't been here jollying us along, we wouldn't have got anything done. And don't forget you got the Information Centre redecorated,' they'd said.

Drawing up plans to refurbish the Information Centre, however, wasn't why Molly had come here, she sternly reminded her co-workers. Molly refused to be comforted—even when people were being kind, her need was never to listen. 'They want foreign aid but not foreign volunteers,' she summed up.

The right of a sovereign nation to determine how its foreign aid should be handled escaped her. I wondered if Molly preferred to think of Bangladesh as a supplicant with hands outstretched. 'You know that Henry Kissinger called Bangladesh a basket case?' she told me for the second time that day, and for the second time that day, I winced as I began to understand why many Bangladeshis were fed up with 'foreign experts' like Molly.

There were times when it was easy to turn away from Molly. Her prejudice, her insensitivity ... And yet if you'd accused Molly of being a 'new colonialist' she would have been terribly hurt for she only meant to be kind, and I soon found out that the Mona Lisa men would do almost anything for Molly, who never forgot their children's birthdays and was always good for small loans which were never repaid. Right from the start the Mona Lisa men had coped with Molly by turning her into 'one of the boys'.

However, there came a night when an English guest suggested bluntly that she clear out of Bangladesh, if she didn't like what 'they' were doing.

'It was a night to remember, before your time,' said Scott. 'She went very quiet—you could've heard a pin drop. I felt sorry for her, but she had it coming.'

Looking back over her time in Bangladesh, Molly mulled over the personality politics that bedevilled her work situation, and one thing she was convinced of: she was certainly never treated with the respect that a foreign man with her qualifications would have received.

'They have never figured out how to treat me. Sometimes they treat me like a peon—you know, the office dogsbody, the lowly servant who fetches the tea and does messages. They treat me like a peon because I am paid like a peon,' she said matter-of-factly. 'The only money I get is my expense money. I don't get a salary and I live at a lower level like the old-time Peace Corps workers used to. I have no car and driver and use rickshaws and I don't live in Gulshan.' Molly wasn't complaining, she was just stating the facts. I realised then that Molly as a UN volunteer was certainly not receiving the high salary of other foreigners working in Dhaka.

17

Gulshan is the affluent diplomatic area where the expats hide behind their compound walls and never come out to play in the real world of Bangladesh. Molly didn't want to join in the expatriate games; she dressed very casually in skirts, T-shirts and sandals, owned a simple wristwatch, wore no make-up and refused to use her academic title. She was an enigma within the United Nations caste system. In all the time she had been there, never once had she been invited to the American Embassy or the American Club. Whether it was a deliberate snub or not who could tell, but she seemed hurt, and with good reason I thought. Her Bangladeshi co-workers were used to a very different kind of American; they had trouble reading Molly and had given up trying.

Molly was quite an expert on the subject of expats. 'They seem to stay in their own little world; go to their own clubs at night, keep to their own social scene. I don't know them that well, of course; I've not been invited to their homes,' she reminded me once again. 'Many set up their homes and their flats near their own social clubs.'

'Why do they hide away?' I asked her. It seemed ridiculous that foreigners would spend years trying to create replicas of the societies they'd left behind. After all they weren't immigrants permanently separated from their culture. Attitudes had moved on since the death of colonialism—or had they?

'It's just a fear of the unknown, I guess. Remember, all of the literature, everything you read tells you: "Don't drink the water! Don't breathe the air! Don't go out at night". All you hear are warnings, warnings—nothing but warnings. I'm not afraid,' said Molly. 'I walk the streets, look people straight in the eye; I smile and show them I'm not afraid. They stare because they're just curious and childlike; there's no harm in it you know.' *The spectre of Molly haunting the streets of downtown Dhaka, forcing eye contact and smiling remorselessly at passers-by, would make even a* mullah *tremble.*

❋   ❋   ❋

It was that time of day again and Kumar was about to strike. Every morning as we sat at breakfast feeling better for having let our frustrations rain down on his head, he would craftily turn the tables on us before we could escape for the day.

'Lunch? Dinner?' he would ask, sidling up.

Because there was no menu he felt free to bully us into eating what *he* thought we should eat, rather than what *we* really fancied. To make matters worse this must be done before anyone left the house in the morning, just when our imaginations were stunted by loaded stomachs toiling to digest a full breakfast. Molly insisted that she had once seen a proper, typed-out menu in a drawer about a year ago. When she mentioned it to Kumar, he pretended ignorance so she went in search of it only to find that it had disappeared. We found ourselves reordering the same old meals again and again, happy with the quality and the portions, but finding it rather monotonous.

'Let me see,' said Scott. 'I'll have rice and dhal for lunch, and rice, dhal and curried vegetables for dinner.' Scott was on an economy drive and had ordered the two cheapest meals available —in US currency seventy-five cents and a dollar respectively.

Molly lashed out on the 150 *taka* (US$3.50) special of soup and stir-fried chicken with almonds and I ordered Bangla salad and fried fish and vegetables. I yearned for curry and chappatis but found that Mr Hashmi was too generous with his ghee. The Assistant Cook believed that rich people's curries must swim in oil—how else could people know you were rich?

'Remember, you'll get three pieces of fish,' Molly warned me. She'd been battling for years to be served just one piece of fish—

she would pay the same price, she just wanted one piece of fish, not three. But no matter how often she explained to Kumar, three crowded portions of fish stared accusingly up at her from the plate. Recently however, she had managed to solve the problem.

'Oh, I've solved it all right,' she said. 'I've stopped ordering fish.'

Extorting lunch and dinner orders out of bloated guests amused Kumar. But because it was the key to Saleem's day, the cook kept a watchful eye on the proceedings, intervening if Kumar became too overbearing. Saleem made out the day's shopping list which he gave to Abdullah, the senior chowkhidar, a noisy man with a terrible cough, who would go to New Market with a pocketful of money and buy our daily needs.

✳   ✳   ✳

There is something strange about the Mona Lisa, but from the outside it passes muster. Any passer-by could easily mistake it for a private residence, instead of a guest house hiding behind tall green walls. Abdullah and Rashid laze around on chairs watching the passing parade, dutifully opening and closing the gate as we come and go. A caravan passes by: residents, school children, snake charmers, hawkers, blind beggars, rickshaw cycles and baby taxis—a never-ending pageant of bright colours, music and exotic, often strange smells. Urban life in Bangladesh: overcrowded and dynamic. Just a few streets away, in frantic Mirpur Road, the numbers and the chaos multiply into a nightmare. Thousands of rickshaws and scooter taxis struggle against trucks and throngs of people. A seething mass moving slowly along Mirpur and Elephant Roads; a hot dusty cavalcade lost in thick, choking traffic fumes—the noise is deafening and the flood of bodies and vehicles frightening. We are in Dhaka, a

20

city of ten million, not rural Bangladesh where villages are circled by fields and rivers, and planting and harvests and the sound of crickets mark the tempo of life—not honking horns. It is in rural Bangladesh that 85 per cent of the population live, of a total population of more than 120 million.

But for those of us living in Dhaka, the Mona Lisa remained a secret oasis and we were mostly grateful. The main bungalow, set on a large plot of land, is crowned with a flat cement roof that is used as a laundry. A garden separates it from a new two-storey wing housing more guests. The buildings are cement-rendered and well maintained, framed by cascades of deep pink, white and orange bougainvillea. The lush garden setting keeps Mr Haq the gardener watering, planting and weeding all day long. The house had once served as the Czech Consulate in the 1950s and '60s, I was told, before it fell into Mr Habib's hands.

The Mona Lisa is as discreet as a shadow on the wall. No telltale sign or house number reveals its presence—it is definitely the child of Mr Habib, the elusive owner. He might have been a phantom, for during my stay, never once did I catch sight of him, although I came close one day when someone yelled: 'There he goes!' and I looked up just in time to see a shadow disappearing around a corner. Molly swore that she had spoken to him once; Scott backed her up; the two Germans thought they knew who he was, but couldn't be sure and Jahangir, now and then, referred to him in a cavalier fashion. In my mind though he existed only through reputation—rather like the bogeyman naughty children are threatened with . . . Whoever he was, Mr Habib had worked out an ingenious formula for earning foreign currency. Officially we were all Mr Habib's personal guests, living comfortably in his private home, but in fact he lived a few streets away. He probably avoided paying tax by the simple, but illegal, means of remaining unregistered and keeping a few officials 'happy'—in Bangladesh this is not difficult to do.

The guest house lies in the heart of Dhaka in the area known as Dhanmondi, just one corner of this sprawling mega city. It had once seen better days, as the presence of the nearby Indian Embassy attests. India received the land in return for its assistance in the 1971 civil war against what was then West Pakistan. The embassy stands alone: these days embassies and consulates prefer the enclave of Gulshan, about as remote and sanitised from the real Bangladesh as one can get.

Open countryside until the 1950s, Dhanmondi still has a pastoral look at odds with the overcrowded slums and thronged streets, the by-ways and muddy lanes within a stone's throw. But everything is rapidly changing under the pressure of commercial and residential growth, which has brought multi-storeyed buildings to the area. The suburb fights back and still retains a rakish charm, in spite of the oppressive traffic pollution. Many residents still recall the Dhanmondi of the old days and some keep a few cows in their back gardens. Every morning cow herds lead one or two sluggish cows along the busy side roads to nearby parks, returning home with them at the end of a long day. They amble by under the canopy of cloth banners that garland the streets, advertising the merits of private colleges and universities like 'The Acropolis', 'The Madame Curie Lyceum' and 'The Oxford College' in a blaze of competitive colours and claims.

Dhanmondi became the first residential area to be developed outside the Old City of Dhaka in the years following the end of British rule.

Partition in 1947 divided the Indian subcontinent into India and Pakistan. The latter was made up of two ethnically, linguistically and culturally distinct wings, separated by two thousand kilometres of unfriendly Indian territory. At this point in history, what was later to become Bangladesh was known as East

Pakistan. Then in 1971, after bloody fighting, East Pakistan broke away, becoming the independent state of Bangladesh. Today memories of this civil war have not faded. For Bangladesh it remains the War of Liberation, a source of intense national pride that it threw off the domination of West Pakistan. But Pakistan finds the memories painful, bringing the very rationale for its existence into question.

But before politics and power-plays changed everything forever, large blocks of land were given to the Awami League politicians who were in power and other high ranking officials from 'good families' in East Pakistan. A 'good' family in those days didn't mean necessarily rich. Under the British, Dhaka had become a backwater, a rural outpost, very different from commercial, cultured Calcutta which was cosseted and watched over like a favourite child by the colonial rulers. Dhaka may have been the darling of the Mughal emperors, but that was centuries before; the old rulers had become the ruled and Dhaka was ignored like a distant country cousin.

Coming from a 'good family' in Dhaka signified an educated background, possibly from a clan with political ties, and included the slowly expanding class of lawyers, doctors, teachers and academics. At least two (today it is three) generations of educated people in one family meant that you 'had arrived'. These were important values in Dhaka in the 1950s and '60s. In many families education had a slow start, but today these people are the Establishment.

*　　*　　*

Saiful was far from Establishment and had only received four years schooling. He was a thin, nervous looking man and nothing was too much trouble for him. Despite an inauspicious beginning we had become friendly. One night as I passed the kitchen on my way down the corridor to my room, I walked into what looked like a bundle of rags under an ironing board that had been draped with mosquito netting. I had not expected to encounter a strange man sleeping under the ironing board; he had not expected to be trampled on. Next morning I learnt that Saiful was part of the house-gang, but had been away on holidays. For reasons I could not discover, he didn't like sleeping with the other men upstairs, preferring instead the colourful patterned cement floor outside the kitchen. Kumar always obligingly left the ironing board standing for Saiful to sleep under. Molly had supplied him with a specially made thin rubber mattress to be rolled away in the day time, but he only seemed to use it in winter. Jahangir permitted this unusual sleeping arrangement, believing that Saiful added to the Lisa's security arrangements.

The Mona Lisa soon became a kind of surrogate family. Like everyone else I was drawn in by its moods until its sense of 'otherness' gradually became familiar, as if I'd lived there for a long time. Admittedly there were moments when we turned a blind eye to things which should have been challenged, but when events became too much I could always retreat to my spacious, run-down-at-the-heels room and gaze up at the ceiling fan from under my huge mosquito net as it cranked away asthmatically through the hot air.

My room was hidden away down the long corridor where Kumar ironed shirts during the day and where Saiful bedded down for the night. Jahangir thought that a Muslim 'lady' travelling without her husband should be sequestered away from strange men—and why should I complain for I'd been given the largest room—more like an apartment—in the guest house.

Three large wooden doors controlled my life: a front door under which Rashid slid the morning papers; a bathroom door which if flung open quickly would lead to the death of at least two or three cockroaches (until one day they surrendered and decided to emigrate) and lastly, the most enigmatic of all ... a door which opened out into an enclosure, curtained off from the outside world by finely meshed fly-wire, with a further door leading into the garden. From this enclosure, I could see everything, overhear conversations—even look past the chowkhidars through the gate into the world beyond. Yet I remained invisible with nobody realising that I was free to listen and learn, to watch and record the comings and goings at the Mona Lisa at my leisure. It was like experiencing a world of 'partial purdah' and in an extravagant moment I likened it to a *zenana* or secluded women's area where male intruders were unwelcome and an intimate life of female visitors and entertainment took shape. With these fanciful notions one could slip comfortably into the role of *purdah nashin*: a woman shielded from the gaze of strangers, safe in her own private space, languidly observing rhythms and unwritten rules carved by others ... I stopped daydreaming just in time ... before I damned myself forever by slipping into my own brand of orientalism.

For the first few days I stayed inside, talking to one or two visitors; women who made their way past the chowkhidars and the gates to see me, to educate me and to drink tea. But I soon became restless and curiosity drew me away from the predictable confines of the zenana towards the confronting public domain outside the gates.

It seemed strange that, after coming to Bangladesh to write a book about women, I found myself living in a house of men. There were censors and guardians everywhere; there were walls within walls and secrets within secrets. Men dominated the Mona Lisa as surely as they commanded the world outside the gates.

I was not interested in a house of men. To begin my journey

I would have to leave my circle of protection and go in search of women.

Outside the gates there were many different female communities: women whose spirits chafed inside the confines of respectable society, women who through an accident of birth fell hopelessly outside the boundaries, and women who were branded as mavericks.

My need was to discover their world and learn for myself how they were breaking free from the restraints placed there by others, circling their lives and their dreams like the bangles they wore on their wrists.

Chapter 2

On the Trail of Taslima

* * *

There were a thousand stories circulating in Dhaka about Taslima Nasreen and most of them were scandalous. But by the time I arrived in Dhaka it was more than a year since her disappearance, and the frenzy over her banned book *Lajja*—or *Shame* as it is called in English—had died. The anti-Taslima campaign seemed to have run its course for the moment. Noisy street marches, with hordes of angry young men or stony-faced veterans, had ended as suddenly as they had begun; banners splashed with slogans advertising her name and her 'crime' had been rolled away out of sight for another day. The traditional form of protest called *hartal*—a way of life and a familiar show to anyone who has ever been to Bangladesh—had returned to the more familiar sport of either supporting or denouncing the government. Local papers no longer carried photos or wrote articles about her. While a court case was still pending, it would probably be conducted by a team of lawyers in her absence. Most

27

people I spoke to thought it a good idea that she remain in exile while secretly despising her for leaving.

Only the foreign media kept her name and face alive, against the odds and against the wishes of a society which wanted to put the Taslima Nasreen affair behind it like a bad dream—to pretend it had never happened. But that was impossible and perhaps the image of Bangladesh would never be quite the same again. A tolerant, middle-of-the-road nation, almost overnight Bangladesh became labelled by the West as a country of religious zealots with Taslima the doyenne of human rights and women's emancipation. The events which unfolded between 1992 and 1994 couldn't be changed. As with the aftermath of a cyclone, time was needed; time to repair the damage and rebuild again.

The 'Taslima Affair', as it became branded in my mind, was one of the reasons I had come to Bangladesh in 1995. For some time I had been observing the Taslima Nasreen case from a distance. Her story had captured my imagination and I found myself avidly searching the newspapers in Australia for more and more information. I felt tremendously sorry for this young woman facing death threats. She was a woman burdened with the pressure of being nonconformist in a traditional society, a place where women's lives were guided by principles defined and interpreted by father, husband and son. I felt guilty that I was able to write about Muslims and female discrimination—be as critical and searching as I chose—without running any risks, without running the gauntlet of censorship.

*   *   *

She looked like a schoolgirl—more like an eighteen year old than a woman in her mid-thirties who'd been married and divorced three times. These were my early impressions as I went through the newspapers in Australia, trying to piece together what was happening. She photographed well; a round, almost baby face with serious big brown eyes and short hair—unusual in Bangladesh, where even 'modern' women keep their hair long. There were no lines, no tell-tale smudges under the eyes; nothing that hinted of stress or pain. I wondered whether these were photographs from earlier, happier days when she was a budding celebrity climbing up the slippery heights of disapproval but not yet reviled as the most notorious woman in Bangladesh. My expectations were probably too romantic and I was disappointed, for I had expected some sign of intensity. Her poetry reeked of passion, but the face I saw was passive.

I grew used to hearing her voice on TV and radio and could recognise it instantly. Her words were soft; her manner, slightly hesitant and searching. She put her case with dignity.

Time passed and I continued to listen to her repeating the same phrases over and over, almost like a set piece: 'The fundamentalists hate me'; 'they want to kill me', 'everybody reads me', 'I am the only one who speaks out' . . . The words were beginning to sound clichéd and this began to bother me. Had Taslima nothing else to tell us? She was not comfortable speaking English, I reminded myself. Surely I could empathise. I could still recall the helplessness and humiliation of trying to discuss something complex in a foreign language, something which really mattered, only to end up sounding like a child—and not a very bright one at that. A long time ago I had spent eight years teaching English in West Germany. My German teaching colleagues thought me shy and introverted; they were kind but I could never reach out to them. Floundering in a language not your own perjures your identity. At the time their judgment had distressed me, but my German high school students knew better. Once I hit the classroom floor with English as my medium, I was 'home' again. This must be part of Taslima's dilemma. Obviously her arguments were more coherent and persuasive in Bengali, her mother tongue.

Nevertheless I began to sense an interesting inconsistency. How could this cherub-faced young woman be creating such havoc? Why were the right-wing religious groups issuing *fatwas*—in Bangladesh of all places! What was the government's real motive in banning her book? Slowly I began to wonder if there was another, more complex story buried beneath the newspaper accounts. Somehow I groped my way towards a faint outline of something I couldn't identify at this stage—certainly not from the other side of the Indian Ocean in Australia.

Something else began to bother me. Where were the voices of Bangladeshi women? If Taslima was the foremost feminist in her country as the media was telling us, why were other female activists so silent? I knew that Bangladesh had a seasoned women's movement which was alive and well. Yet the only female voices surfacing seemed to come from Western women inside Amnesty International and the Women's Committee of the internationally powerful PEN (Poets, Essayists and Novelists). Could it be jealousy? Or were Bangladeshi feminists being gagged, perhaps even threatened by the government? Surely Bangladeshi women were supporting Taslima? And where were the secularists and the intellectuals hiding? Why were their voices still? The forces behind the Liberation Movement were usually vigilant and uncompromising, ready for any advance by their opponents bent on creating an Islamic state. The silence grew . . .

I was just too far away from it all to understand what was really happening and this began to irritate me. I began to work out a possible solution, a way of trying to find answers to the Taslima puzzle while using her predicament to write about Muslim women in South Asia, something I'd wanted to do for a long time. Taslima's confrontation with the religious extremists could well be a microcosm of what was happening elsewhere in Islamic societies. I imagined a bizarre tango danced by feminists wanting to surge forward on the one hand, and fundamentalists wanting to step backward. Through the Taslima affair I thought I could glimpse the face of modern women struggling against age-old, customary laws and values created by men. Now it was time to stop agonising and find some answers for myself. This quest brought me to Dhaka where the Mona Lisa became my base of operations.

*　　*　　*

'Taslima and trouble have always gone hand in hand,' he said. 'It's no secret; she's very proud of it; in fact she enjoys telling anyone who will listen that, since she was a little girl, she has always questioned the way things are for women in our society.'

The first person I interviewed outside the Mona Lisa was a male journalist. I had been in Dhaka for nearly a week. My head had stopped reeling and I was beginning to find my feet. I had even overcome my initial fear of travelling through chaotic traffic in a fragile rickshaw. I soon discovered that women were reluctant to talk to a stranger about anything as sensitive as Taslima; they shied away from the topic. Men on the other hand were quite willing to open up and talk about her; they were blunt and wasted little time on niceties. There seemed little love lost between the male intelligentsia and Taslima.

If you see a pack of mad dogs
Run
Remember rabies
If you see a pack of men
Run
Remember syphilis.
　　　　—Taslima Nasreen

Eventually I would need to talk to women but it would take a few more days to organise personal introductions to local women's networks. Meanwhile, a friend had introduced me to Karim, a senior reporter and a very pleasant man, who specialised in political affairs and worked on a local English-language daily, located not far from the Mona Lisa Guest House.

He didn't bother to hide the fact that he disliked her intensely. I wasn't sure if this had always been the case or if he'd gradually distanced himself. Karim was a perfect example of the intellectual and liberal support, which had initially swung behind Taslima. Later large sections deserted her in what some people called her 'India phase'. I seemed to be bogged down sooner than I expected and while it was not the way I had planned to start, Karim's information, tucked away in files, archives and his phenomenal reporter's memory, would save me an awful lot of legwork. One thing I was already finding out and reluctantly learning to live with was that despite all my efforts to plan and maintain a schedule, time was a wilful, capricious creature here in Bangladesh—it had a mind of its own and no amount of prodding would change that. I waved goodbye to my penchant for structure, my weakness for colour coding and other amulets which I used to keep chaos at bay and let things happen ...

*　*　*

Trying to follow the trail of Taslima's early years, there is a sense of dark secrets and unhappy stories waiting to be discovered; they drift between the lines of her poetry and infiltrate the imagery she uses. I was starving for more biographical information but unfortunately had access to very little.

Taslima was brought up in Mymensingh, an isolated provincial town about 140 kilometres from Dhaka. It is in the northern part of the country, not far from the Indian border. During the British period the whole region was turned into one enormous jute plantation at the expense of other crops which fed people but were not as profitable for the Empire. Her father was the Assistant Professor in forensic medicine at the Mymensingh college and hospital and was the first in his poor family to have a university education. Through the custom of arranged marriage he married Taslima's mother when she was thirteen years old.

In an interview with the Indian magazine *Savvy* in November 1993, Taslima talked of her mother as a very religious person, very different from her father who was a believer, she said, but not a fanatic like her mother. Today she may regret these remarks, made well before the government ordered her arrest, for she and her family now act and speak as one. But in 1993 her comments were harsh and revealed a difficult childhood and adolescence.

'I hate dependent people like my mother and other women who are just like slaves and the earning member is like a master. My mother is a typical product of our system. She is a very religious person, I hate her activities and her utterings. She always tells me, "God will punish you—you don't believe in God. You're a *murtaad* [atheist]."'

As a child she loved her freedom and her happiest memories were playing on the banks of the Brahmaputra River where the local children would build sand castles . . . 'only to watch the water come and break my "house"! It's so much like life isn't it?'

But when little girls reach ten or so, society says they are little girls no longer. The older they grow, the more their movements become restricted and their childhood truncated. The rules of society do not allow them to run, to climb and to play physically active games any more. When she reached puberty at twelve, Taslima's parents told her she could no longer leave the house unless she was going to school or in the company of her elders. Life closed in even more after a strange boy threw a love letter into her rick-shaw. From that day forward, they hired a guard to accompany their fourteen-year-old daughter to school. While college was a place of learning, a place where the mind could grow, in another sense it extended Taslima's prison because a school guard stood at the gates and girls were forbidden to go outside. Boys' lives were very different—their movements were unrestricted.

Taslima did well at school. Her father in particular wanted his daughter to have a good education—in this way he was liberal. Her teachers were pleased with her. 'You are a brilliant girl,' they told her, 'but be careful and don't break the rules.' Voices older and wiser drummed in her ears the message that 'only bad girls break the rules'. They meant to instil a sense of duty and decency in the bright young girl. Being labelled 'a bad girl' meant you were not decent; it was a bleak moral judgment and young girls were surrounded by moral guardians ready to swoop on any signs of deviant behaviour. Social control hummed in the air like a wasp. But somehow or other Taslima eluded most of the stings. She drove everyone mad with her questions. Why were her brothers allowed to leave the house and she was not? Why couldn't she talk to boys? Why did she eat different food? Taslima questioned everything and she grew to hate the answers they gave her.

* * *

One morning while I was visiting Karim, his friend Ahmed walked into the office on the pretext of borrowing a book and decided to stay. Circles are fairly tight in Dhaka and word soon made the rounds that I was interested in discussing the Taslima case. Both Karim and Ahmed had been *Mukti Bahini*, or freedom fighters, in their teens; student leaders turned guerilla fighters against the West Pakistani army twenty-five years ago.

Now their hands were soft, but once they had gripped rifles and hurled grenades. Long ago they had crawled through dark wet fields and killed their enemies—it was hard to imagine that now. Both men made a point of telling me that they had known Taslima's first two husbands.

'She picked her husbands very carefully,' Ahmed said. He stood leaning up against the wall and kept an eye on the door, as if we were in the middle of a clandestine meeting. I found myself lowering my voice. He went on to insinuate that she married men who could further her literary ambitions.

'She's an excellent operator,' added Karim, 'she loves the lime-light. Her poetry may be anti-men, but watch her at parties. She snubs the women and heads straight for the men!' Obviously wherever she went all eyes were on Taslima—especially male eyes.

Many men seemed to desire Taslima; she was so different in her outlook, so non-conformist in the way she talked and behaved—she fascinated them and terrified them at the same time. There were many stories circulating about her beauty, her charm, her ruthlessness, and all of them were to do with men. In a place like Dhaka, men talked more about her morals than her writing. Dhaka is a conservative society in a conservative country: women do not live alone, do not have male friends, do not travel by themselves or smoke cigarettes publicly and most definitely they do not talk or write about sexual topics. In Dhaka these things matter and 'decent women' are supposed to play by the rules.

Most men did not like her poetry; I think it frightened them.

The other day in Ramna Park I saw a boy buying a girl.
I'd really like to buy a boy for five or ten taka,
a clean-shaven boy, with a fresh shirt, combed and parted
    hair,

a boy on the park bench, or standing on the main road
  in a curvaceous pose—

I'd like to grab the boy by his collar
  and pull him up into a rickshaw—
tickling his neck and belly, I'd make him giggle;
bringing him home, I'd give him a sound thrashing
with high-heeled shoes, and then throw him out—
  'Get lost, bastard!'

Sticking Band-Aids on their foreheads, the boys
  would doze on the sidewalks at dawn,
scratching at their scabies. Mangy dogs would lick at the
     yellow pus oozing out of the ulcers in their groins.
Seeing them, the girls would laugh with the tinkling sound
     of glass bangles breaking.

I really want to buy me a boy,
a fresh, nubile boy with a hairy chest—
I'll buy a boy and rough him up all over.
Kicking him hard in his shrivelled balls,
  I'll shout—'Get lost, bastard!'.

                       —'The Game in Reverse'

If Taslima had stayed a poet perhaps she would still be in Bangladesh today. But she flexed her literary talents, confident she
could expand, and began writing prose. She was savouring life
and she certainly enjoyed the attention. Free to express her
thoughts, her writing became an antidote to her well regulated
professional life in which she passed her days working as an
anaesthetist in government hospitals. Often in trouble with the
hospital hierarchy, she would find herself posted to remote
towns as a punishment. But sooner or later she always managed
to inveigle her way back to the capital where the literary, avant

garde circles attracted her and where she felt she belonged.

Taslima was fast becoming the talk of the town. Her erotic
poetry earned her a reputation for being deliberately provocative
and sensational. But once she started writing a regular newspaper
column, in 1989, her notoriety spiralled. She found a new audience; a younger audience shocked and titillated by the sexual
subject matter she chose to write about and the language she
used. Taslima talked about topics that were taboo—topics that
were never discussed publicly. In a country where there is no
Penthouse or other sex magazines; where there is no blue movie
industry, and expletives found in foreign TV shows are bleeped
over in a quaint form of censorship (with sometimes hilarious
results), young people—especially young men—found her
columns erotic. In Bangladeshi thinking, Taslima was nothing
but a writer of soft-core pornography! She advocated the
'freedom of the uterus' and suggested that women should rape
men in retaliation, startling many Bangladeshis who saw her as
a female guru for promiscuity and free sex. The tongues wagged
harder and the stories spread.

'Taslima talked a lot about rape. You just don't do that in
Bangladesh,' said an anonymous critic. 'She would describe in
physical detail, the act of rape ... it was the act itself and not
the victim she seemed concerned with.'

By daring to discuss sexual politics so openly, Taslima was far
ahead of her time, for even the most radical feminist groups
thought twice before raising sexuality in public.

If this was her way of promoting women's rights in Bangladesh, then many women activists were dismayed, fearing a backlash from right-wing elements and males nearer to home.
Husbands used this ammunition against them as husbands
always do. 'So you want to be another Taslima, do you? Is this
what your female equality means?'

Other women were less dismayed but more resentful. 'She was never one of us! She never joined any of our activities. Taslima was never part of the feminist movement.' I lost count of the number of times women leaders, young and old, repeated the same phrase, using it like a talisman to ward off 'the Taslima influence'. 'She was never part of the feminist movement here.' I believed them; nevertheless Taslima Nasreen had emerged as the most articulate champion of women's liberation in Bangladesh—in the eyes of the outside world.

Women were much kinder than men and left her private life alone. By now my new feminist networks were opening up wonderful doors of knowledge and experience and I found myself meeting strong energetic women, tremendously wrapped up in their work, but willing to talk to me once they found out that I had no preconceived ideas, only a lot of questions and a healthy scepticism.

❊   ❊   ❊

I arrived at Dhaka University by rickshaw and was taken aback by the noise and the crowds of students, the vendors selling snacks and the rickshaws jammed together waiting for student passengers. I found myself in the middle of a youth festival full of strident energy and colour. As I watched, a group of noisy young men carrying banners and shouting loudly marched by waving their fists, giving me my first glimpse of campus politics.

Reluctantly I tore myself away and asked for directions. Two extremely polite boys insisted on showing me the way and as we walked along the dim corridors of the old dilapidated English department, I passed groups of chattering female students dressed in the tunic and trousers called *shalwar kameez*—there was only the occasional figure of a girl clad in a dark concealing burqa.

Firdous Azim is a lecturer in English Literature and a member of Naripokkho [for women] a strong feminist organisation. Everyone who meets her for the first time is always fascinated by her deep velvety voice which diverts attention from what she is saying until one becomes used to it. I wondered if students managed to take notes during her lectures or were lulled to sleep by her voice. I blessed my tape recorder; her words were too important to miss.

'She has never been with us, but at the same time she has the right to say what she wishes; you shouldn't ban her books,' said Firdous, choosing her words with care. She reminded me that Naripokkho had officially protested the banning of Taslima's book, but I sensed some ambivalence. 'Personally I think her work is a mishmash of American feminist writing from the '60s and '70s—not that she does much reading herself. I had hoped that here in Bangladesh we could have learnt from the American experience and skipped over that confrontation style of women versus men.' She peered over her glasses and grinned at me from behind her large wooden desk littered with piles of papers and journals, the insignia of busy academics everywhere. Then suddenly she became serious again. 'When things were at their worst, in mid-1994, I was overseas in New York at a conference. I followed the story through *The New York Times*—it was a terrible experience—and do you know, I couldn't recognise my own country! The issue had been so manipulated. Bangladesh is not a fundamentalist country! It is not—I know it's not! At the time I was furious with Taslima, but today I feel sorry for her. She is in trouble; a woman lost in exile and now her patrons have dropped her.'

Firdous was alluding to India, which after initially supporting Taslima and making capital out of Bangladesh's international embarrassment, had only recently refused to grant her a visa, worried that her visit might stir up communal tensions between

Hindu and Muslim and provide the militant, right-wing Hindu party—the Bharatiya Janata Party (BJP) with ammunition.

Firdous was determined not to get caught up in the Taslima debacle. 'Last week some Swedish radio people asked me for an interview, I refused. The media seems to be changing its approach, but I don't want to play this Eastern woman versus Eastern woman game. There's been enough manipulation.' We stopped talking about Taslima and moved on to women writers like Jane Austen, whose novels were part of the English Literature course and great favourites with her students. There were many similarities between their own traditional society and 18th century England: strong family values buttressed by duties and obligations; dowries; arranged marriages (occasional elopements and undesirable liaisons); strong inheritance and property rights; rural elites and the less privileged—and the local clergy, anxious to keep everyone in their place. Firdous's students could understand all of this.

And then I met Samina, the union worker who'd learnt her American-English from videos. She lay back lazily in her cane chair as we chatted on my private verandah late one afternoon. Samina tried to organise women who worked in small food-processing factories. Their adversaries were not only the factory owners but also their male fellow unionists who still tried every dirty trick in the book to stop women from getting elected to union positions.

Samina admired Taslima. Eureka! At last I'd found a woman activist who appreciated Taslima! Later I discovered there were large numbers of women who read her columns and circulated copies of her books unbeknown to their husbands and brothers. But these were housewives and young students who didn't belong to organised groups; women with limited access to information and discussion.

In many ways, Samina would have loved to be as daring as

Taslima. But she was married with children and already her husband worried that she was doing too much, was too out-spoken—and what would people say? What would her mother-in-law say was the real problem. She promised me some insights on Bangladeshi mothers-in-law that would make my hair stand on end, if I ever returned.

'I have been working for years with women from the urban slums. I would love to have Taslima's courage,' Samina said. 'It's true that I speak out, but I modify what I say; I censor myself—and that's no good! In a society like ours you must have a thick skin, you have to work to get people's attention. She certainly gets your attention!' She shook her head admiringly. 'We needed this—we needed someone to speak out. Sometimes shocking people can be a good thing. Take my own work as an example. Now I've been talking about changing the Islamic inheritance laws for women for years, in the name of equal rights, but nobody listens to me! Taslima says it once and everyone sits up! They don't like it—their religious sentiments are hurt, but she gets the spotlight; she gets the debate going.' She paused, contemplating what she was about to say. 'I think it was time for us to have a Taslima in our lives,' she said slowly. 'I know I'm in the minority here and I don't talk about it very often; I get howled down. The quickest way to have an argument with my husband, or my in-laws, is to mention Taslima,' she laughed, but behind the laughter was the bitterness of a woman disappointed with herself for making too many compromises.

Matters came to a head in 1992 after Taslima received a major literary award from Ananda Bazaar Publishers in Calcutta for a compilation of her newspaper articles on female discrimination,

41

called *Nirbachito Column* (*Selected Columns*). She was the first non-Indian to receive this award. Apparently this had not gone down well in Bangladeshi literary circles where her prose writing was regarded by many as second rate—she was writing best sellers, but was it literature? Were they envious of her success? Her poetry was applauded by many senior poets, her collected columns were published in book form and whatever she wrote became a best seller. One could understand their suspicions, why they saw this award as a slap in the face. What were the Indian publishers trying to do? Many chose to believe the wild rumours that there were links between the Calcutta-based publishers and the BJP, which at the time was verging on the brink of an upset win at the forthcoming national elections. Why single out Taslima? There were other famous writers, well known and admired, whose literary qualities were exceptional. Rumours swept Dhaka that Taslima had been selected for this prestigious award only because she criticised Bangladesh society and Islam. Many saw it as an anti-Muslim piece of Hindu chauvinism. They were cynical—they were angry. Over the years Bangladesh had become far more anti-India, its one-time ally in the fight against Pakistan.

From the time Taslima received the award from India in 1992, there was no turning back. The events unfolded like a play—almost like a tragedy, except for the times when it degenerated scene by scene into the ignominy of a melodrama verging on farce! By then the stage was becoming so crowded it could hardly hold all the players. A collision was about to take place.

By about 1993 Taslima's writing had moved into another phase where she became increasingly outspoken against Islam and other organised religions but mainly attacked what she took to be Islamic principles. 'If the Qur'an says a man can have four wives, then women should be able to have four husbands,' she argued. The overseas media swooped on this but never questioned Taslima's religious credentials, accepting everything she said as 'gospel'. But if you read what she wrote about religion; if you listened carefully to her words, you soon realised that her religious learning was superficial. It rested on a literal acceptance of the Qur'an and misogynist aHadith interpretations that many Muslims do not themselves accept as authentic. Most Bangladeshi intellectuals started to believe that Taslima was telling the Western media and the Indian media what they wanted to hear. Even liberal Muslims were dismayed by what they saw as a lethal combination: a lack of knowledge and a loud mouth.

Before 1993 there were no orchestrated displays of outrage from the religiously militant groups. Their strongholds were in the rural areas and people in the villages didn't read Taslima—most of them couldn't read at all. Her audience was in Dhaka and so unimportant and basically irrelevant to fundamentalist interests, for the moment. And in Dhaka the powerful Jamaat-i-Islami, the religiously-based political party, was staying well away from the Taslima debate—biding their time? In 1990 people were preoccupied with protests against Prime Minister Ershad, in what became the anti-Ershad Pro-Democracy Movement. True, there had already been a few minor anti-Taslima demonstrations, but everyone told me they were of the 'rent-a-crowd' kind of demonstration not uncommon in Dhaka, when a number of unemployed, bored young men tramp around the streets with a loud-speaker denouncing someone or other in a desultory fashion, and when the money vanishes, so do they!

But there came a time when Taslima overreached herself and her luck petered out. Many of her early supporters—the women poets, the liberals, the intellectuals and older women activists—started to drift away. While they applauded her courage, her outspokenness and her determination, they abhorred her love of self-promotion and what they saw as a tendency to manipulate situations. They were hurt by the way she seemed to disparage other people's efforts—especially other women's efforts.

'She called us housewives. She said there was no woman's movement in Bangladesh!'

Taslima's folly rested in her ability to alienate many of her potential allies—but then again that was part of the Taslima attraction: a blend of charm, courage, egotism and vanity. Liberal-secular groups, the one successful element in the country which has always held the Islamic militants in check, were by now firmly disenchanted. There were some however, who remained devoted and her most loyal supporters continued to be a cadre of older male poets and intellectuals who had served her well when she needed mentors early on in her career.

A group of Dhaka University students calling themselves The Taslima Nasreen Suppression Committee seem to have appeared soon after she received the Calcutta award in 1992. In many of her later interviews, Taslima was to claim that at the Bangla Academy Book Fair in February 1993 a group of 500 fundamentalists (some accounts quoted her as saying 1000) attacked her, ransacked the book stall and burnt her books. An event similar to the one she described did indeed take place, although eyewitness accounts give different versions of the incident. Nevertheless it was a frightening affair meant to terrorise her and warn off local publishers.

In the numerous interviews Taslima gave to foreign media over this incident, the thugs were always described as 'fundamentalists'. There is evidence suggesting that on this occasion at least, the vandalism may have been organised by secular bigots, not religious bigots. And that the whole affair was the work of the short-lived Taslima Nasreen Suppression Committee, or in other words students from Dhaka University were to blame for the cowardly attack. However, very soon after, a religious extremist group followed suit by condemning her writing in no uncertain terms, putting a price on her head.

Why had the students attacked her? Three years earlier they might have been devoted fans. And why do some people believe the incident was distorted?

I was banging my head against a wall—too much had happened and I couldn't speak to the one person who might have helped me—Taslima herself. Shortly after the Book Fair attack, through the help of friends, she would begin contacting the foreign media. So perhaps it was important to keep the formula simple: everyone knew about Salman Rushdie; everyone knew about Muslim extremists; here stood Taslima Nasreen, a female Rushdie in the making.

A long-time Taslima observer is Tasmina Hossain, editor of *Anannya*, Bangladesh's premier women's magazine. (Tasmima Hossain has since been elected to Parliament as a member of the Jatiya Party.) An elegant woman dressed in a pale green silk sari, she visited me at the Mona Lisa one afternoon and we sat drinking tea served by an unusually solicitous Kumar, clearly impressed by the upper-class bearing of my visitor. I was moving up in the world and Kumar's eyes told me that he approved of my guest, who added to my kudos by leaving her luxury car and driver lingering outside the gates for all the men to gossip about during what turned out to be a rewarding three-hour visit.

Tasmima Hossain stood back from the whole affair and coolly appraised what she had seen and heard. Once upon a time she had been Taslima's boss, having hired her to write a column for *Anannya*. She knew Taslima; she knew her well. But even the poised Tasmima became ruffled when she considered the reaction from outside Bangladesh.

'Why did the West play with Taslima? I don't understand

this nonsense! I enjoy her poetry, but her books are poorly written and what she says is rubbish.' Tasmima Hossain couldn't for the life of her fathom the reasons behind Taslima's meteoric rise in the West. She looked at me as if I might have the answers, but I was still asking questions myself and as yet had no theory to put forward. 'All people know about Bangladesh is Taslima Nasreen and that is very humiliating—that is all they know.' Her words rang with pain and concern over a loss of national pride and personal dignity. How had it come to pass? She wasn't alone in wondering this.

The timing of the attack at the Book Fair was interesting because it happened at the same time as *Lajja* was first published—February 1993. People had been upset by her earlier writings but it was nothing like the disapproval that followed her latest offering which sold 60 000 copies in Dhaka within a short time. *Lajja* was just the story to inflame normally cool secular minds and incite the jingoism of the flocks of religious militants. The latter are too often lost under the ill-defined category of 'fundamentalists'—but that is another story.

The book's launch and the student attack were linked—one hastened the other. By writing what she did, the young hoods believed (or pretended to believe) that Taslima was attacking Bangladesh and indirectly themselves. The picture she painted of how Muslim Bangladeshis treated the Hindu minority (about 12 per cent of the population) was not a pretty one. The book was not only an indictment of Islamic extremism. There was an underlying message that religious intolerance was rampant and that the progressives had failed to keep the purveyors of religious hatred at bay—had even acted in partnership. The progressives were furious—and they had long memories.

Lajja was originally a seventy-six-page novel of dubious literary merit published in Bangladesh; a rushed piece of writing accomplished in just seven days! Later editions published in

India were revised and considerably expanded. Karim, and colleagues like his friend Ahmed, insisted that it was only possible because the publishing empire of Ananda, in Calcutta, had turned over their research to her. 'They badly wanted this book to be written. It is a book of lies.' Their eyes could see no further.

Shame (its English title, and one used by Salman Rushdie in an earlier work of his own) is a harrowing story which tells of the plight of Hindus in Bangladesh through the life of one family who lose everything and a community which sees its property seized, its temples destroyed and wives and daughters raped. There is not one instance in the book where a Bangladeshi Muslim of any persuasion is shown as liberal or secular or compassionate. No-one protects Hindu life or property. There are no simple acts of kindness; they all turn away.

The attacks on Hindu Bangladeshis which Taslima writes about were not imagined. They came in reaction to the destruction of the Babri Mosque in Ayodhya, North India, by Hindu extremists on 6 December 1992. Over 3000 Muslims were killed in the violence which broke out in parts of India. The story which Taslima chronicles takes place in Bangladesh thirteen days after the mosque in India is destroyed. The timing of Taslima's book—only a few months after the destruction of the Babri Mosque—was seen as a sinister move.

Millions of pirated copies were quickly sold in India in the streets and at railway stations and bus depots for a few rupees, by BJP extremists. Bangladeshis feared the book was being used by Hindu communalists as another excuse to attack Indian Muslims. Later a revised and expanded edition was translated into a number of Indian languages by Ananda Bazaar Publishers and widely promoted, and an English-language version was published by Penguin Books India (51 per cent owned by Ananda) in 1994.

Two years on, the book's message still upset Karim. 'We don't say that Hindus here are living in grand equality,' he said. 'Our society is undoubtedly Muslim dominated. And yes, there were instances of anti-Hindu criminal behaviour after the burning down of the Babri Mosque. I'm not pretending bad things didn't happen here, but it is nothing compared to the riots and murders in India against Muslims.' He tried hard to convince me and I wanted to be convinced, but I made a mental note to gather some research to learn for myself. 'In Bangladesh there were many instances where Muslims protected the life and property of their Hindu neighbours and friends. But does she write about that? Of course not!'

Karim's intensity showed that he and people like him remained deeply hurt. I kept reminding myself that I was not talking to religious extremists; I was not even talking to orthodox Muslims! My informants were mainly intellectuals, fervent believers in a secular, democratic Bangladesh. If they happened to describe their attachment to Islam at all, then they spoke of themselves as liberal Muslims, with a shrug of the shoulders and wry confessions of not following rituals like praying or fasting— of not really practising Islam, they said. They welcomed the chance to tell their side of the story—usually they were not asked. I would have to explore how widely the *Lajja* version of events was challenged. The two versions were incompatible, that much was clear.

❊   ❊   ❊

Finally in mid-1993, the Bangladesh Nationalist Party (BNP) Government made its move and banned *Lajja* on the grounds of its inflammatory tone which, it claimed, might cause mistrust and misunderstanding prejudicial to communal harmony. Strikes and protests were taking place on all sides. Some observers say the government acted because it was already under pressure from the religious factions. Others maintain the government wanted to break up the 'unofficial' alliance between the Awami League, the leading opposition party led by Sheikh Hasina, and Jamaat-i-Islami, the country's largest religiously-based political party. When in power in the 1970s the Awami League had pursued a secular policy and banned religious parties like Jamaat-i-Islami, but the three major opposition parties joined together in early 1994 to boycott parliament, a ten month boycott maintained by over 140 politicians.

In September 1993, an obscure group called the Soldiers of Islam put a price on her head, although their leader was to later deny this. Why would he deny it? When I asked Karim he suggested that perhaps the man was telling the truth. I wondered however if perhaps he now regretted turning Taslima into an international star. The luckless Soldiers of Islam were a group of rural religious fanatics; a body of rather unpleasant men from the north of the country. Nobody in the city had ever heard of them before! They seemed to emerge out of nowhere.

The anti-Taslima ranks continued to swell. By October 1993 Muslim intellectuals: liberal and secular Muslims and even pro-Chinese Communist politicians were staging their own small demonstrations against *Lajja*. Tension was building and the air humid with anti-Taslima aggression. It seems ironic that it was not her anti-religious writings which were the trigger, but a work of fiction. Although the book remained banned, debate continued, fuelled by the on-going media coverage and speculation over Taslima's fate. News soon reached Dhaka that another Bengali version was to be published in India. Believers of the conspiracy theory felt they were vindicated.

I had seen enough videos of the anti-Taslima demonstrations to know how frightening they must have been. Large crowds of chanting demonstrators denouncing her as 'Nasreen, the traitor!', 'Nasreen—puppet of the BJP! Puppet of the Hindu communalists!'. Voices of outrage; voices ringing with hate. And some of the religious extremists, I had little doubt, spurring their followers on by calling for dreadful punishments—shouting 'Hang her!'.

And yet my friends in Dhaka, people like gentle, scholarly Firdous—the Jane Austen fan—warned me, 'You need to understand that calling for somebody to be hanged is old hat in Dhaka. Demonstrators always call out *"Fashi!"* ("Kill her!"). It doesn't mean that they are really going to kill someone. If you know our political culture,' she went on, 'everything is not what it seems. There is another slogan called *"Murdabad"*—it means "Death to . . .". We are always yelling "Death to Nixon!", "Death to Bhutto!" (the father not the daughter). It's just a slogan; it doesn't mean anything much. So you see the Soldiers of Islam probably denied it because it wasn't really an official death sentence to them.'

It was beginning to sound like a scene from Monty Python! 'Yet people do get killed during demonstrations in Dhaka,' I remonstrated. Her argument sounded plausible and yes, my knowledge of local political culture was certainly hazy, but I needed more convincing . . .

'Yes, violence happens when one group clashes with an opposing political group or student wing,' she admitted. 'People get injured, now and then someone may be killed. But the Taslima thing is different.'

How different, I asked myself?

'I for one have never believed that her life was ever in danger.' She watched my face, wondering if she should keep going. After all, we had only just met. Could I be trusted not to twist her words? I was amazed! This turned everything I'd read on its head. Firdous was the first person to confide this—later others would hint at much the same though none were as candid. 'Our feelings are very complex and yes, we are a passionate people;

we give expression to our feelings in ways that outsiders may not understand. The anger against Taslima was genuine; it was very hostile but I don't think anyone would have killed her.'

I had to think this through. Bangladesh was certainly not Iran where the Iranian Government, through their Ayatollah, had placed the fatwa on Salman Rushdie's head. Taslima was no Rushdie—and the situations were different. Could I put my scepticism aside? Bangladeshis loved theatre, I knew, but my Western upbringing kept me prisoner, left me searching for some comparison I could relate to. Ridiculous pictures of football crowds calling 'Kill the umpire!' flashed through my head. Demonstrations were a passionate art form in Bangladesh and many other countries in the region. People expressed themselves differently—in fact they did more than merely express themselves; they re-enacted their feelings vigorously. Firdous had called it a different political culture. I needed to understand this, to stop fighting what was alien to my own experience.

But didn't they want to rid themselves of Taslima—one way or the other? Or were they really only trying to frighten her, to silence her? She was a disobedient woman, an affront to ideas of decency and a traitor, or so everyone thought.

I felt confused. Was this something that the intellectuals needed to believe: that the death threats were not real? Why should Taslima and her family not take these warnings seriously?

Later I realised that these were the questions I should have asked when I'd had the chance. Separating play-acting from real intent—on this first visit I did not have the expertise or enough knowledge to tell the difference for myself.

✳   ✳   ✳

By late '93 Taslima had many enemies and not too many friends in Bangladesh. The sympathy that she needed—the attention

that she now craved—lay overseas. Demonstrations continued
... Later there would be many different estimates of the size of
the crowds and the number of the protests—some observers
insisting they were insignificant in spite of evidence to the contrary. Taslima remained inside her comfortable apartment with
members of her family by her side and a police guard downstairs.
She gave numerous interviews to foreign media, either in person
or on the phone, although she stopped going out. The Taslima
Affair was starting to attract attention outside Bangladesh and
India and in early October Amnesty International and PEN
appeared onstage.

In her dealings with the powerful overseas lobby groups,
Taslima and her go-betweens pleaded that she feared for her life,
but in a November interview she told a journalist: 'I am not
scared at all'. This defiance was probably bravado—so many
things were not what they seemed at this time.

Banned or not, *Lajja* was a runaway best seller, both at home
and across the border in West Bengal, India.

Invitations from overseas to speak at various human rights
conferences began to arrive and Taslima found herself in
demand. After pressure from Amnesty International, the government reluctantly returned her passport which had been confis-
cated earlier and the author had her first taste of the
international celebrity circuit in May 1994. It proved intoxi-
cating and once outside Bangladesh, Taslima's statements found
a new, receptive audience. And every interview she gave, every
criticism she made, appeared in Bangladeshi newspapers or was
shown on satellite TV.

On her way home she stopped over in Calcutta and gave an
interview to the *Statesman* on 4 May 1994. This became her
undoing: her words would in a few months lead to her exile.
She must have forgotten who her audience was; perhaps she

imagined she was still in Paris with enthusiastic supporters hanging on her every word.

'Hanging on her every word.' The phrase sounds ominous now, but Indian journalist, Sujata Sen, swears she neither misquoted nor misunderstood Taslima. 'The Qur'an should be revised thoroughly'—this was the intemperate (to some Bangladeshis blasphemous) remark she insisted came straight from Taslima's mouth. The writer went 'into hiding' once more, remaining inside her apartment under police guard. Her cries, her letters to the press claiming that she had been misquoted, fell on deaf ears. The non-Muslim reporter didn't understand, said the author—unfortunately the interview was not taped. She had been talking about making changes to the *Shariah*, or Personal Laws, to improve women's lives, not the Holy Qur'an. No-one believed Taslima any more and the Indian journalist stood by her article. Perhaps only Taslima's lawyers believed the statement she sent to the Bangladesh Parliament, where she took pains to emphasise that not a single word of the Qur'an could be changed, insisting to the end that she had been misquoted.

Nobody gave credence to what she now said because like a naughty schoolgirl, Taslima had been caught out. A BBC TV interview beamed pictures into every household of a smiling Taslima holding centre-stage, smoking a cigarette while she handled the Qur'an and openly criticised it. Another interview with *Der Spiegel* quoted her again calling for a revision of the Qur'an. Back home people thought she was taunting them. Once again the demonstrations started and in a matter of months the proud writer was brought down.

But what lay behind the demonstrations? Were certain forces trying to use the Taslima Affair to create the impression that there was an increasing public demand for a blasphemy law?

Was it a political stunt from the religious right wing Jamaat-i-Islami, which had first tabled a Draft Blasphemy Bill in Parliament in mid-1992?

On 4 June the government, under enormous pressure from religious extremist groups, issued a no-bail warrant for her arrest. She had broken the law, the government said, under section 295A of the Bangladesh Penal Code of 1860 (an obscure British-era statute) which makes it an offence punishable by imprisonment or by fine, or both, to deliberately and maliciously outrage the religious feelings of any class of citizens of Bangladesh.

The powerful Jamaat-i-Islami, a member of the coalition of parties opposing the government, had played a clever game. To the surprise of many it at first appeared to stay out of the debacle. With the foreign media and international human rights agencies rallying behind Taslima the party knew its image would be severely damaged. So it stayed in the background as long as it could without losing face.

Within a few hours of the warrant for her arrest, Taslima vanished from her apartment and this time she really did go into hiding. She was plainly terrified and believed her life was in danger.

The final act took place on 3 August 1994. A small woman wearing a *dupatta* (scarf) over her head and surrounded by an army of lawyers entered the court. Her appearance had changed; the smiles were gone and she looked tense and drawn. She had the look of a woman who was not sleeping well—a woman who seemed at last to realise that the demons she'd unleashed were out of control. In a small voice she apologised to the judges for the dissension she'd caused and was granted bail. Accompanied by police she returned home to be reunited with her family and was driven away under police guard to an undisclosed place of hiding.

Six days later, on 9 August, Taslima Nasreen appeared in

Sweden. She had been smuggled out of the country with the aid of Amnesty International, PEN, sympathetic Western governments and the connivance of a quietly relieved Bangladeshi Government.

While I was in Dhaka I spoke to a close friend of Taslima, a man who'd stayed by her side, counselling her, helping her deal with the media attention. I asked him to tell me where it had all gone wrong. To my surprise he ignored the Calcutta interview. Instead he blamed the government for issuing the warrant of arrest—done, he maintained, to appease the religious political groups. 'This action,' he said, 'was more important than the death threats from the mullahs.'

✳   ✳   ✳

Sigma Huda is a famous human rights activist with a long and, some would say dangerous, record of involvement in social justice matters. She is a lawyer who speaks her mind, and it is damnably frustrating and exhausting trying to keep up with her flow of words! You are kept on the edge of your chair trying to catch sentences hurled with the fury and speed of a hand grenade. During one of the hartals which usually keep everyone close to home, I was able to visit her on foot one afternoon. I lost my way—I even lost the address, but everyone in Dhaka knew where Sigma Huda and her husband, a high ranking member of government, lived.

Like many in her field she believed that Taslima had the freedom to write as she wished. But also that if she hurt the religious sentiments of others then she should be taken to court by her opponents in accordance with the law. 'Don't these people have a right to their religious beliefs?' To me it seemed a no-win situation, although I understood the principles she put forward. 'But Taslima is no prisoner of conscience,' she argued, 'as Amnesty International tried to make out. She is a woman who used shock tactics and sensationalism, but these simply do not introduce lasting change in patriarchal societies like ours— they only alienate. Smoking a cigarette on TV while you are reading the Qur'an only alienates people. You are not helping the cause. You are definitely not with the movement. Through Taslima's activities she rendered everyone else's work invisible. We lost a lot of ground.'

Begum Sufia Kamal is another Bangladeshi poet, but unlike Taslima she is unknown outside her own country. She is a tiny, bird-like woman of enormous moral stature. Men and women speak of her with an affection and reverence that is touching. The only enemies this devout, eighty-seven year old has, are the religious militants who hate her.

As a teenage bride she began working with village women and destitute women from the slums. During the Liberation War she nursed soldiers in the underground movement. There are hundreds of stories about this modest woman—her compassion and her bravery are legendary. Sufia Kamal has received numerous death threats over the seven decades she has spent working as an activist and she is not alone. Like most of the intellectuals and other women radicals I met, she ignores the death threats and carries on with her work. Her organisation is the Mahila Parishad with a membership of over 30 000 women. It is a well-respected organisation, with a proud record of fighting to end female discrimination and oppression. They understand the forces ranged against them and work hard to transform women's lives. Of late, many similar organisations have faced increasing opposition from conservative forces. Because they were mainly urban they were either tolerated or ignored by village mullahs in the past, for they were not critical of Islam. Things are different now—because of Taslima, they say. Perhaps they are exaggerating the adverse impact on their activities—time will tell.

In her ill-fated Calcutta interview, Taslima described tough women activists like Begum Sufia Kamal in these words: 'Most are afraid of fundamentalists. They play limited roles. Following the Shariah is all they believe in. They are happy to live as housewives.' Now I understood why Bangladeshi feminists had not taken to the streets in support of Taslima.

'Who is the woman you most admire?'

I asked every Bangladeshi woman I met the same question and they all answered back without hesitation, 'Sufia Kamal and Begum Rokeya Hossain'. (Rokeya Hossain was the Bengali author of the first feminist Utopian book, *Sultana's Dream*, 1905.) Not the woman Prime Minister, not the woman Leader of the Opposition and definitely not Taslima Nasreen.

In the collision of forces which took place in Bangladesh in 1994 there were no victors, although initially it looked as though the extremists had won. Taslima Nasreen became a writer in exile, a cause célèbre on the international speakers' circuit; the extremist Islamic forces received the kind of international media attention which money can't buy, but in the end failed to win any extra votes; women activists anticipated a backlash which they claimed would set them back years; human rights activists and the secularists prepared to resist another call for blasphemy laws, and the image of Bangladesh projected to the outside world was badly damaged.

With the passage of time the *enfant terrible* of the Bengali literary scene has almost become the forgotten woman in her own country. From outside, the debacle resembles a theatre of the absurd—except the issues at the time were life and death; censorship or free speech; religious vilification or communal harmony.

Many Bangladeshis however, like to believe there was a master puppeteer manipulating events and they point a finger at the Indian publishing giant, Ananda Bazaar Publishers. I found that the story I originally looked for changed shape before my eyes. Many questions remain unanswered—there is more to the Taslima Affair than I at first realised, and of course the drama is not yet ended.

Wounds need to heal, and I think that one day they will. It will take time. Only after speaking to many people did I come to understand the impact of that Calcutta interview and why at present very few Muslims have a good word to say about Taslima. In the eyes of the world they would appear unsympathetic and even jealous of her success.

In 1996 Taslima was once again refused a visa by the Indian Government. In a newspaper report she said she was bitterly disappointed. 'They have used me and now they turn their back on me.' I wonder what she makes of her new exciting literary life as she flits from one speaking engagement to the other— between Berlin, New York and London . . . She must be lonely: cut off from her Bengali language, the beautiful tongue she thinks and writes in. Far away from Bengali-speaking cities like Dhaka and Calcutta and like-minded friends, her exile now seems poignant rather than self-seeking.

Edward Said has described exile as 'the unhealable rift between a human being and a native place, between the self and its true home: its essential sadness can never be surmounted'.

There is no word on Taslima's trial in Bangladesh, which is still pending.

CHAPTER 3

The Season of Hartals

* * *

I'm not sure when I began to turn away from Taslima. At first
it seemed more a shift in focus rather than a deliberate decision.
Her name closed doors rather than opened them, making it
impossible for me to pass through, at least on this journey. More
time needed to elapse before the enigma of Taslima Nasreen
could be unravelled, I warned myself. She was not your typical
Bangladeshi woman. I had been mistaken; the exiled writer was
cast in a different mould—that much was clear. But at first only
the sound of Taslima's name registered and I was deaf to anything else. When people offered up a new name I was inatten-
tive—until one day I began asking the questions I should have
asked all along, and started down a new path which would eventually lead me outside Dhaka.

* * *

Reading about poverty, illiteracy and malnutrition from academic texts never prepares anyone. You sit watching television documentaries from comfortable armchairs—Chardonnay in one hand, pizza in the other, and you delude yourself. Everything is at arm's length and poverty, disease and death become sanitised. You know nothing—you realise that later. Nothing prepares you—how can it? Your cocoon is shed soon after you arrive and the distance between you and a world crowded with pain is instantly reduced. You develop a protective veneer just to get through the day and you hate yourself for doing this.

According to rough estimates, half the people in Dhaka (five million) live below the poverty line and about three million are identified as slum dwellers or in the language of research reports, 'hard core poor'. An estimated 30 to 46 per cent of the people are ill at any given time. About 55 per cent of Dhaka's poor have no access to sanitary latrines.

There is no dignity in poverty and most of the people of Bangladesh have been poor for a very long time. More than half the population of 120 million simply do not get enough to eat and struggle for survival. River erosion and tidal floods turn peasants into rickshaw drivers and create a daily flow of people from remote villages into the urban shanty slums of Dhaka and other cities where they are often worse off in terms of shelter, sanitation and drinking water.

Sometimes women come to the city with their men and sometimes they stay behind. But no matter where they are physically located there is one place uniquely theirs: the bottom rung of a very crowded ladder. Women make sacrifices for their families which eat into their own chances of survival, but they keep fighting.

For hours on end a long chain of tiny malnourished women sit on their haunches amid building rubble, breaking bricks with the crudest of implements in their small rough hands. In all that dust and heat and with their children running and playing in the mounds of broken bricks, they sing and joke and laughingly urge each other on. They feed their babies without downing tools, for their pay depends on their output. And if they are very lucky they will get to work another day.

Deprivation and death are never far away. Like understudies they wait smugly in the wings knowing that if they are patient, their moment will come—and they don't have long to wait, with the average life expectancy for women 53.4 years and for men, 54.2.

There is no dignity in poverty, but there is courage in the way ordinary people live their lives and in their great resilience: how they plan for the future, no matter how small their hopes seem to an outsider—some poultry, a cow so they can sell the milk, a rickshaw. And there is immense dignity in the way women negotiate a bearable existence for themselves and their families. Women all over the world learn to manipulate the space they are handed down, but in Bangladesh it can mean life or death. As I listened to their stories, the real Bangladeshi woman began to take shape, far removed from the towns and cities.

Paradoxically, the gatekeepers who could give me access to women in rural towns and villages, were middle-class women linked to non-government organisations—the NGOs as they are called—with their main offices in Dhaka.

NGOs are a strange species and Bangladesh attracts them like moths to a flame. There are nearly 1000 agencies supported by the United Nations and foreign donor countries. Out of this vast number there are probably about 200 which are really significant with a development, rather than welfare, orientation. They form a subterranean world of thousands of programs and projects, where seminars and model schemes produce hundreds of reports and conference-going is a way of life for NGO subadars and foot soldiers. Local agencies have become part of the landscape, but their international 'backers' have forged a chain of dependency that threatens to choke Bangladesh—everything comes at a price. An over-reliance on NGOs produces ad hoc solutions, allowing the government of the day to 'pass the buck'. With such munificence of foreign aid (approximately two billion dollars in development assistance) the government, as some critics say, abdicates its responsibility in many areas, especially education, women's programs and local government. In fact some of the NGOs have grown into giants simply because there is no effective local government in Bangladesh.

The question of the country losing control of its own development is also a concern. A climate exists where the larger NGOs—those with the track records and the funds (about 80 per cent of foreign aid)—are expected to solve immense problems which even the state machinery can't resolve, almost like an alternative government. Critics describe development aid as a form of evasion where basic reforms in sanitation, education, and employment lose out to short-term, Band-Aid solutions. It is an on-going debate throughout South Asia. 'People are tired of development; they just want to live,' said a veteran field-officer.

Because NGOs manage practically all women's programs, this helps the government avoid confrontations when strategies to improve women's lives clash with the values of a deeply patriarchal society. And that is the dilemma: without foreign aid, women's programs such as literacy courses, family planning, income-generation schemes, health and legal education would collapse like empty promises. So in spite of the transitory nature of NGOs and the welfare orientation of many of the smaller agencies; in spite of the mishandling of funds and lack of accountability which everyone was quick to tell me about, the larger NGOs have become a powerful force for change and symbol of hope in the lives of many women, which explains why they are usually detested by their archenemies, the fundamentalist religious factions. The NGO discussion tends to be a minefield throughout the region. To be truly effective, NGOs must work hard to avoid being controlled by the World Bank or the overseas agency funding them on the one hand, and by their own government on the other—they are the music squeezed out of the accordion. But they become quite adept at accepting international funds while continuing to do work they really want to do. Unlike the donor agencies and their handsomely paid foreign experts who float by from time to time, do the rounds in four-wheel-drives and whiz out again, local workers know the kinds of projects which can effect change, and those likely to fail. They are not easily impressed by the latest buzz word to come out of the UN or someone's head in New York or Zurich.

Like small jungle animals, the hundreds of ineffectual agencies that often have self-serving, dishonest administrators, are fair game for local commentators. There is always ammunition to hand and critical shots are fired from many quarters including activists seeking alternative forms of development and the militant 'greybeards' of religion, who watch NGO women's programs with a seething anger which sometimes spills over into confrontation.

Journalists watch cynically from the sidelines and from time to time they cannot resist poking a stick at internationally funded agencies.

NGO: Non Government Organisation—Password for doing whatever you like wherever you like and whenever you like in Bangladesh. Of course 90 per cent have HQs [headquarters] in Dhaka, and guess who rides 90 per cent of the Pajeros and Nissan Patrols? It's great business this NGO thing. Concoct a catchy program, slap on a signboard about helping the downtrodden, then help yourself to the dollars that roll

in. All in the name of aid to the poor. Thank God for the
poor in whose name we can get rich.

—'The Dhaka Dictionary', *Daily Star*

*   *   *

Stepping down from my rickshaw I tripped and my bag fell into
a gutter over-flowing with foul water. I had hoped to make a
more dignified entry into the Feminist Bookshop in down-town
Dhaka, but I didn't think it would bother the woman I was
coming to meet. Farida Akhter is the Executive Director of
UBINIG (in English, Policy Research for Alternative Development), a private research organisation. It is fiercely independent—just like Farida.

'No-one can call me an elite woman sitting behind a desk in
Dhaka,' she said. (Take care, I thought, this woman is a mind-
reader!) 'They can say anything else they like about me, but they
can never say that I don't know my rural Bangladesh.'

She sounded like a woman used to criticism but she looked
like someone out of a fashion magazine. In a land of small
women Farida walked like a queen and the saris she wore were
hand woven and dyed in the most discriminating, understated
colours. She wore her long dark hair in a sleek plait with every
strand in place; her movements were graceful and her manners
charming—she was all pride and elegance and she made me feel
like a clumsy peasant. Only later did I notice the shrewd eyes
of the experienced campaigner and realise that she was as tough
as old boots! Answering her questions was like walking a tight-
rope. I had better watch my step—this woman would know if
I put a foot wrong.

Just as Farida and I had stopped circling one another and
were getting past the typical first encounter rituals—Who was
I? What was I doing in Dhaka? How did I get her name?—a

young woman bounded into the room clutching an armful of papers.

Natasha (named after the heroine in *War and Peace*) seemed different from other young women in Dhaka. She had the fresh, cheeky air of a girl half her age although she was really twenty-eight. Her long hair streamed untidily down her back and over her shoulders and I was glad to see that she had as much trouble stopping her dupatta from slipping off her shoulders as I did. She leant over the desk to talk to Farida and spoke quickly in Bangla. I thought I heard the name Yasmeen mentioned, but that was all I could make out.

Her face bore an uncanny likeness to a younger, darker Sophia Loren—the doe eyes, the wide mouth and the cheek-bones were identical. I had to work hard to censor these irrelevant associations; I knew that I was 'auditioning' and that Farida was closely watching my every move.

The tunic and trousers of the shalwar kameez seemed better suited to Natasha somehow, much more than the sophisticated urban woman's sari. Traditional dress for girls is all the rage at the moment and women rarely wear Western clothes. Middle-class men who like to see their women romanticised and immo-bilised in traditional clothes and long flowing hair are non-traditional when it comes to their own clothes. Not for them the poor man's lungi—at least never in public! Male status is increased if daughters and wives wear expensive saris or shalwar, but not if they themselves don the traditional Bengali male attire, a humble piece of cloth wrapped around their middle worn with a knee-length shirt.

At this first meeting I was very sensitive to any signals passing between Farida and Natasha. But they seemed to silently agree that I could be trusted and might even prove useful. They answered questions about Taslima politely but without any enthusiasm; their answers were perfunctory and designed to keep me from probing too deeply. They were simply tired of talking about Taslima Nasreen and tired of explaining what had gone wrong; they were focused on the work at hand.

'Have you heard about Yasmeen?' asked Natasha, changing the subject after a quick look at Farida. I didn't resist because I could always find alternative routes to the information I needed. So I answered no, I didn't believe I'd heard of Yasmeen.

'Yes,' said Farida. 'You might be interested in her story . . . It has reached out to a lot of people. Why don't you ask around about Yasmeen and then come back to us later.'

They were showing me the direction but leaving me to find my own way and I thought it strange. Once started however, the difference was remarkable. Doors which began to close when Taslima's name was raised would swing wide open at the mention of Yasmeen.

❉   ❉   ❉

Comfortable middle-class women, gliding by in their saris . . . By comparison, they lead lives of comfort and privilege, although male control and traditions infiltrate their dreams and life choices in ways that some are aware of and others close their eyes to. Silken threads of elitism link their lives to families of their own class—although some fight hard to hold this at bay and through their activism and commitment to social justice and human rights, cross over and work night and day to offset, what Farida believed was, after all, just an accident of birth. Again and again women told me, 'Poverty and lack of education are the natural enemies of women in Bangladesh—not religion.'

'I'm not an elite woman!' Natasha yelled at me a week later. We were in the back of a cramped baby taxi, zigzagging and bouncing along the pot-holed main roads, shouting at one another above the din of traffic and muffling our mouths against the stomach-churning traffic fumes. The baby taxi or auto cycle was a hellish way of travelling, but faster than the cycle rickshaw.

Provoking Natasha helped pass the time and she found it difficult to keep her guard up, especially in the back of a baby taxi where the main concern was protecting a bruised backbone and watching out for trucks. Cool, collected Farida would have seen through my ruse and responded differently, going on the attack immediately and not allowing me to get a word in.

'Look, I'm not saying that you lead a life of idle luxury. Elite women certainly don't travel this way!' I yelled back, closing my eyes and cowering as we narrowly avoided colliding with two rickshaws. No wonder Muslims always use the Arabic phrase '*Insha'Allah*' to one another when we talk about meeting again! Travelling this way gave new meaning to the phrase 'if God wills it'!

'You'd probably have your own car, with driver and air conditioner.' (It might not be ideologically sound, but at the moment it had a lot going for it.) 'But in comparison to most women, you come from "a good family"; you've had access to higher education, overseas travel and a good job. And of course you have servants. I'm just describing your background, not your ideology.'

'Everyone has "house-helpers", you know.' Natasha would go to any lengths to avoid using the words servant or maid or cook. Later I found that some progressive people were starting to discard the word servant. Its equivalent in Bangla—*chakor*—was seen as degrading and insulting, while on the other hand, the English word 'servant' reminded people of colonial times. Natasha put an end to our conversation by reminding me that the word 'elite' was used differently in Bangladesh, didn't apply to the middle classes and had nothing to do with having 'house-helpers'!

Middle-class women like Farida, Natasha and their friends

join the fight and work hard at avoiding compromise; others lead lives inured against the daily pain of their surroundings; and there are also women with families joining long queues outside foreign consulates seeking a passport to a new life. And then middle-class women like myself, come to observe, to comment, to steal information—fragments of people's lives, like shards of broken glass—and then retire to the side-lines once more. But we are never the same again because we come close to a vortex of pain which marks us for life.

We choose our paths, or so I used to think—somewhere, at some stage in our lives, we choose. But the longer I spent in Bangladesh, the emptier this homily seemed: a self-indulgent idea that ignored most of the world's female population. There are many places in the world where women have little say about the passage of their lives: the culture of poverty and male domination give them little choice. The barriers squat like mountains; immense and seemingly impassable—change inches ahead slowly. Women accept pain and self-sacrifice as part of their identities as wives and mothers; they are wedding bangles given to them by their in-laws on the day they pass from the protection and control of one man, to the protection and control of their new guardian—their husband.

More than twenty years ago Farida Akhter had chosen her path and had never looked back. One lazy afternoon she dropped into the Mona Lisa to lend me some books and as we sat drinking tea, it seemed the perfect opportunity to explore her own background—if she would open up and talk about herself for once. Farida began her activist work as a field researcher, but the more she went into villages to talk to women, the more frustrated she grew and the more she questioned what she was doing.

'My eyes were opened,' she said. 'The women think you will solve all their problems. I found I could do so little—not even help them get clean water—and then I started to feel guilty about wasting their time and raising their hopes. I questioned my motives because I was just after the information I needed.' (My own conscience began to prick.) 'I asked myself what was I giving in return,' she went on. 'I had nothing to give and no way of giving it!'

She leaned towards me as she spoke and her words tumbled out with an intensity that could have been disconcerting, if I hadn't caught a glimpse of myself in her. People are not ashamed to show their feelings in Bangladesh. Men and women speak with passion and spirit and poetry-reading sessions attract the kind of audiences that rock concerts do in the West. 'A land of poverty and poetry sessions—that is the enigma of this country,' confessed one journalist with a mixture of shame and pride in his voice. Civilised moderation and intellectual balance are the virtues prized in the so-called 'developed world'; and perhaps we have lost the capacity to feel intensely.

Farida's intensity struck a chord with me, something that I remembered and now missed in modern feminist debate. Feeling passionately about politics and people in many Western countries (unless they're sporting heroes) almost smacks of bad taste nowadays. We have moved on to feeling passionate about the environment and the sanctity of gun licences; this is still permitted. I had thought that the kind of fervour Farida showed belonged to one's youth; now I wasn't so sure.

Farida and like-minded friends began wondering what was happening to the research they were producing and eventually they started their own research organisation, UBINIG. Their activities have expanded but commissioned research is how they basically survive. They also form part of a strong international network focusing on the politics of population control programs and reproductive rights. They are opposed to coercive population control methods they believe masquerade as family planning programs, imposed by foreign governments and multinational drug companies. It has been discovered that some companies have been dumping chemical contraceptives in Bangladesh, and testing implant devices, while they were still being trialled in the USA. In some instances drugs were used which were not approved for American use. Years ago, UBINIG made the deliberate decision to be independent of the government and donor organisations but it came at a price, said Farida. They were not as well off as others but they survived and undertook projects which they believed made a difference.

'Our long colonial history has helped us feel inferior,' said Farida. 'We think that swallowing Western education will change us. We have become drunk without tasting the good wine from the West!' she cried. 'When you become educated here,' she said, 'the first thing you do is try to forget your own background. You are ashamed of your parents because they are not literate enough. If you can say, "My father is a government worker, or my father has a salaried position", this seems an honour to you. You feel no honour if your father is a farmer.' There was never any dissembling with Farida; even if it made her unpopular, she spoke her mind.

Becoming Westernised to Farida meant becoming alienated from your own culture. In Bangladesh there was an intense rivalry between Bangla-medium schools and English-medium schools which often spilled into the newspapers. It was widely believed that the latter, through their English instruction, provided better educational outcomes for students and prepared them for university, while alienating them from their own language and culture. Students from these schools were also said to look down on students from Bangla-medium schools. *Madrassahs*, or religious schools, were usually the choice for parents who were either very pious or could not afford higher school fees, but their educational standards and fairly rigid syllabi were found wanting and they provided no academic competition. Many Bangladeshis who supported a secular state were angry that the BNP Government was providing funding for the religious schools which they saw as recruiting grounds for student fundamentalists.

'I have had the opportunity for higher education, but it would be wrong, for me, to sit by idly or work in a foreign embassy for 50 000 taka.' Farida never pulled any punches. 'I have done nothing to deserve that! Your duty is to go back to other women,' she said firmly 'and return what you have received. Some women feel they got their education because they worked hard at their studies and so they deserve it—almost as if it is their right! I don't think so! It is really an accident of birth that has given them this privilege.

'When middle-class activist types like me go to the villages to talk to the women,' she said, 'we think they don't understand broader issues of what is happening in the world outside their own village, let alone what is happening outside the country. We think they can only understand their own particular problems and that their vision is narrow; in a way we are insulting them. Just because they are illiterate doesn't mean they are stupid! They always have clear reasons why they support somebody or don't like somebody else. During the Gulf Crisis, for example, I asked the women in the villages I went to if they knew about the war and what did they think. I found they were so well informed!

' "Oh yes," they said. "The Kerosene War!" That is what they called it because they use small kerosene stoves for cooking in the villages. We might think of it as the "Oil War", but they related it back to their own experience. They were pro-Saddam and anti-President Bush. Some women told me they would not listen to the BBC anymore because they said the BBC was against Saddam. During this time,' she laughed, 'hundreds and hundreds of newborn baby boys in the villages were called Saddam.

'They always have clear reasons as to why they support somebody, or something, and it may seem silly to us, but they know their own minds and I have been educating myself with all of their wisdom. At one village I asked the women, "Did you vote for Khaleda Zia or Sheikh Hasina?" (Farida was asking them if they voted for the Prime Minister and leader of the BNP, or the Leader of the Opposition and the Awami League. Khaleda Zia of the BNP and Sheikh Hasina of the Awami League were both women and both at war with each other.)

' "Oh *apa*!" they said. "We voted for Khaleda of course! Poor Khaleda, losing her husband like that. Life is hard for a widow".

' "But Hasina has lost her father", I reminded them. "He was murdered as well and she is very sad. Don't you feel sorry for her too?"

' "Yes," they answered, "but she has a husband to look after her. He is still alive and she is not alone in the world".'

Bangladesh often seems like a land of widows, especially in the villages. Husbands die or disappear; it is a common enough fate for women to lose what little security they have pieced together. They may count themselves lucky if a father or brother or uncle can afford to take them and their children back once more into their natal household; doubly fortunate if their in-laws keep them. The women Farida spoke with knew what might lie ahead. A woman without male protection was a woman in desperate straits: destitute and consigned to the fringes of her husband's village, maybe forced into the life of an itinerant beggar wandering from village to village or the hard life of servitude in a rich man's household.

Widows and daughters, vulnerable to the misfortunes of their families ...

Once upon a time, in the Land of Hartal, the people elected the Widow Khaleda as their Wazir. She promised her people that she would banish hunger and shield them from the calamities that stalked the land. 'Dhal and bhat' were the twin promises she made throughout the kingdom: dhal and rice for their empty stomachs and hope for their hearts.

The people believed her as they had believed her husband before her, the kind wise General who ruled the land for the good of the people, but who was struck down by his enemies in the darkness of night. In his memory, his followers chose his wife, the Widow Khaleda, to take his place. They were cunning and wanted to retain their power and authority which they prized above everything else. They knew that the good people of Hartal would grieve with the Widow and elect her to take her husband's place, even though she was but a mere woman. Only the mullahs would take this for an unforgivable blasphemy and speak against it in mosques across the land—for they believed that Allah had forbidden women to ever rule over men. But in the end the will of the people defeated the Greybeards who wailed loudly but had no choice except to return muttering to their prayer mats and bide their time.

It was not an easy task for the Widow for she had no knowledge of palace politics and intrigues and had always been a dutiful wife to her husband, and a loving mother to their children. But her husband's advisers—and there were many who surrounded her in the forty long days of mourning—whispered in her ear and urged her to take control and put on the magic gold collar of office carved with the letters BNP. And the Widow listened and was persuaded to take their counsel, for did they not have the good of the people in their hearts?

And so she took up the reigns of government, and tried her hardest, but not everyone in the land was happy with the way the Widow ruled the kingdom. Her foes muttered that she was an usurper and must make way for another, brighter star.

A younger woman, sharp of face and with a long burning memory, believed that she was destined to rule the land, not the Widow

Khaleda. Many years ago her father had founded the kingdom and as the wisest and most beloved of all caliphs had won many battles for his people—this was long before the rule of the General–Wazir. But her father, the Caliph, had also been struck down by his enemies: by soldiers unhappy with his alliances to the north and aggrieved by his new laws; they began to harbour thoughts which could not be spoken aloud. One terrible dark night they had surrounded his palace and murdered his entire family, except for his daughter Hasina and her sister, who had been sent across the Black Waters by their father to gain more knowledge. Hasina had inherited her father's powerful aura and had grown up surrounded by the allure of politics and so her father's cohorts found it easy to entice her when they came with tears in their eyes to pay allegiance to her. With honeyed voices they begged her to lead them in their fight against the Widow. They pressed into her hands a magic silver box with the letters AL set in pearls—her own private talisman to keep the sorcery of the Widow Wazir away. Quietly in the dead of night they hastened to the houses of their former enemies the Greybeards and the Warrior Clan. In a hundred dark corners they sought to carve alliances in their fight against the Widow.

Years passed and the Widow and the Daughter wove a golden net of silence between them and kept well apart. In spite of the urging of the common people of the land, they refused to write to each other; they even refused to talk. Instead they would glide past one another in the People's Palace, their veils trembling in anger, and stare through one another icily from opposite sides in the Court of Shouting, their chins high in the air, their manner haughty. Reasonable men—and there were a handful on both sides—found themselves shouted down by their greedy brothers until they grew silent.

Because of the private armies both women had recruited to protect their power, the people could not protest. They could only hide in their houses when the two rival armies passed by shouting their war cries, shaking their spears and robbing the people while marching under false banners which promised the dawn of a new day.

Over time the women's hatred for each other knew no bounds and was fuelled by the malicious voices of their courtiers who grew powerful like the mighty zamindars of old. They mocked all those who protested, who dared wonder aloud what had happened to the Paradise of Progress and Democracy they had been promised, in the days when they were wooed for their magical pieces of coloured paper covered in spells which had given them the power to choose their leaders.

And so it came to pass that on the Festival of Farces these two proud women commenced a battle unto death. Their followers devised ingenious war plans to bring each other down and the air was thick with plots and counterplots. Only the Djinns of Anarchy and Bedlam looked down and laughed at what had transpired without them even lifting a finger. There was much confusion and the people of Hartal suffered grievously—but there was nobody left to care.

✳   ✳   ✳

Many observers find it puzzling that countries like Bangladesh or Sri Lanka or Pakistan—even India once upon a time—may have women as their heads of state and yet have what could be called a culture of contempt for women, with appalling records of women's oppression. Women leaders are certainly anomalies in countries where patriarchal values are deeply entrenched. But they serve a unifying purpose—they are politically useful (in lieu of male heirs) for they hold their husbands' or fathers' political parties together. So they become honorary males, and are transformed into politicians almost overnight.

Both Sheikh Hasina and Khaleda Zia still possess the aura surrounding legends—in this instance powerful, charismatic, masculine figures which hearken back to a golden time. Throughout South Asia you find this focus on leaders, rather than parliament and other democratic institutions. Thousands of kilometres away in Pakistan, Benazir Bhutto—even though she has fallen from power—is still touched (some might even say trapped) by the legend of a father who, many believe, died before his time. She too is a member of the widows and daughters club.

*　　*　　*

They say that winter is the season of hartals, the season of weddings and the season of visiting consultants. There were no wedding invitations but that winter we were all uninvited guests at the hartals which lay siege to Bangladesh. The dawn-to-dusk curfews and the constant strikes and demonstrations halted our activities and we bowed our heads submissively enough at first, but later resentment took hold and we became a mutinous lot.

'You know if it weren't for the sound of those baby bombs exploding,' Molly said, 'and the army helicopters buzzing so low overhead and then the truckloads of demonstrators shouting slogans as they pass by—it might almost be a holiday,' she concluded laconically.

Hartals are a fascinating ritual usually organised by opposition parties. They are giant political disturbances combining the characteristics of a general strike and a boycott; the whole process tied together with political marches, demonstrations and curfews. No-one went to work or to school; bus, rail and air services were cancelled; trucks and taxis disappeared from sight, factories and shops were closed and the city was barricaded so that transport could not enter or leave. It seemed like an act of national defiance which everyone was forced to participate in— whether they agreed with it or not! The aim was to show the government the might of the opposition and to force its hand. They happened simultaneously everywhere in Bangladesh on days announced well in advance—so that people could go on holidays, back to their villages or to a foreign country for a few days.

We woke up to hartals and went to sleep with hartals—hartals became the order of the day. They were brought about by a political impasse between the Government (led by the Widow) and the Opposition parties (led by the Daughter) which had lasted for twenty months. Ironically, the concept of hartal was honed in British India by Mahatma Gandhi and people had fasted and prayed. There certainly wasn't much fasting or praying going on at the moment!

Under the Mahatma, hartals were the highest form of protest and had a strong moral and ethical base. They were only to be called against the government when all other avenues had been explored and failed. Non-co-operation and non-violence were the ethical principles in the early days of the nationalist movement in India. Now Bangladesh was suffering badly from an epidemic of hartals: at least 144 hartals, ranging from six to ninety-six hours at a time, were held over a ten-month period that year.

The Bangladesh economy was hurting badly and foreign investors sidled nervously away. Seventy million dollars were being lost per day, was one estimate. A journalist worked out that fifty-two days a year were lost to normal weekly holidays, fifty-six days because of hartals and twenty days for other religious holidays.

So there we were at the Mona Lisa lazing in the winter sun like beached whales, unable to move until the curfew was raised at sunset and the streets once more came alive. The first hartal lasted for nine days and I wondered how long it would take for cabin fever to set in. I had been forced to cancel two trips, one by ferry along the long waterways of the country to the south at Barisal, another to the north. We lounged in deck chairs out in the garden and discussed the ethics of modern-day hartals.

77

'They are supposed to happen spontaneously through the will of the people,' Scott told us in lecture mode. He was fretting and becoming argumentative because he'd been forced to return to Dhaka, leaving his fishermen friends behind. In Dhaka, he complained, the hartals were being enforced rigidly by party stalwarts and their hired goons.

'They say some people are hiding in ambulances and getting a lift to work that way,' said Erik. Ambulances were usually allowed to career through the streets and sometimes a press car might be allowed through—and then again it might be overturned and burnt!

'They'll need an ambulance all right, if the pickets find them,' joked Scott.

The aim of the hartal was to force the BNP Government to step down and appoint a neutral caretaker government to oversee the national elections. No-one trusted the Widow's party to supervise anything as fragile as an election—there were claims that an earlier by-election had been rigged. The surreal quality of politics in Bangladesh and its turbulent political culture were impossible to fathom—even Bangladeshis shook their heads. There seemed to be a thin line between reality and fantasy. One day saw the launch of the national hartal against the government; the next day witnessed a counter-hartal organised by the government itself so it could protest against the holding of protests! And so it dragged on ... Even the business community held a fifteen-minute symbolic hartal against the national hartal!

'When the shop-keepers close their doors for fifteen minutes in Bangladesh, you know things are getting desperate.' wrote a journalist.

Owners of export garment factories found a way out, however, and were allowed to stay open—if they paid large sums of money to local muscle men so they could make their deliveries on time. Law and order was becoming a flexible commodity in Bangladesh. And the common man and woman seemed like pawns: there to embellish the politicians' rhetoric, but outside the scope of the real game, for the main players and constituencies all came from the privileged classes. Towering above everyone stood the charismatic politicians, promising the usual rice and dhal and a land free of vice and corruption.

'Bangladesh is a con-man's paradise and politics are like a bad Hindi movie with no end in sight,' another local writer complained. 'It's all sound and fury, signifying nothing! This country is a writer's paradise—chaos and disorder are just what great literature requires. It must be terrible to be a writer in Switzerland—all those clocks and everything working.'

Molly enjoyed the hartals; she stayed at home, knitting in the sun and waylaying anyone who came within her reach. The Mona Lisa maintained a skeleton staff and most of the men disappeared in a hartal holiday mood back to their villages for a week, an unexpected windfall that united them with their families. We all enjoyed the peace and quiet of the deserted roads and a sky bewildered by the lack of pollution. Even Saleem had forsaken the kitchen and wandered away, back home to his village in Syhlet to observe the anniversary of his mother's death, leaving us in the hands of Kumar Gupta and Mr Hashmi.

'Very religious people in Syhlet,' I said to Saleem gravely, the day before he left. He smiled back at me obviously delighted that I knew something about his home province in the north. Even with his conspicuous piety, I imagined that Saleem must find Syhlet difficult and how did Syhlet find Saleem, I wondered. Syhlet was often in the headlines because it was a religiously conservative area where many fundamentalist groups thrived and where from time to time notorious anti-women fatwas were pronounced when the mood struck the brotherhood of moral guardians. The first organised rallies against Taslima had been initiated by the Soldiers of Islam, an unknown group from a locale auspiciously named the Maulvi's Bazaar, in Syhlet.

'I wonder how they feel about homosexuality in Syhlet?' I remarked to Scott. He was sitting out in the garden with the two Germans and another guest, a PhD student from America called Maxwell.

'What do you mean?' said Scott.

'Well, Syhlet is a fundamentalist stronghold and Islam is anti-homosexual and I was just wondering how Saleem manages it all.'

'Come off it! Are you saying that Saleem's gay?' Scott snapped back; cracks were starting to appear in the usual Mona Lisa bonhomie.

'Yes, of course he is!'

'Bullshit!'

I was faced by a stubborn wall of male supremacy. None of the four men believed me and there were even hints that I was homophobic. How blind they were! Saleem was the only man in the house over twenty who went around clean-shaven in hirsute Bangladesh; his array of rings—four on each hand; his fondness for peach-coloured nail polish and a few other signs, including the way he looked at Scott and more recently Maxwell, seemed fairly transparent.

A week after Saleem returned however, three sheepish men sought me out one by one.

Erik and Jürgen had come across Saleem in the company of some of his friends one night and were now convinced that he was indeed gay (not that it really mattered, they assured me). With Maxwell a closer encounter had been building up for some time. Maxwell was an intelligent red-faced young man in his late twenties, friendly to a fault, who couldn't help looking like a cross between Bashful and Dopey from the Seven Dwarfs when he smiled. Maxwell the nutrition expert, who ate with his hands and was not to be trusted, I thought, when first I met him. Watching uninitiated Westerners eat with their hands was always a grisly sight—they always seemed to be up to their elbows in curry. Maxwell had developed the habit of sauntering into the kitchen three or four times a day to lean on the counter and talk to Saleem and the kitchen workers; it was just his friendly American way of showing how egalitarian he was as well as a chance to practise his kitchen Bangla. Unfortunately Saleem had misinterpreted this as a flirtatious overture and was delighted with his foreign conquest.

'I know you come to see me,' he said in a soft seductive whisper, his eyes lowered modestly.

'No, no!' protested Maxwell, 'I'm married.'

Saleem merely smiled, wise to the ways of the world and men separated from their wives for long periods. After that little episode Maxwell stayed out of the kitchen and practised his Bangla on Mr Haq the gardener—out in the open air—and avoided the steamy kitchen and its bubbling pots.

✳   ✳   ✳

'Have you met Khushi Kabir?' people asked. 'She's Sigma Huda's sister, you know, the famous lawyer. You really should meet Khushi.'

Bangladeshis are great storytellers and like all good tellers of tales they loved to leave you guessing. So while everyone hinted at Khushi's fame and insisted that I meet her, no-one would tell me why. Finally one afternoon at Farida's Feminist Bookshop— there she was larger than life—the famous Khushi Kabir. We arranged to meet later that night.

Perhaps what triggered my imagination was her light coloured sari which looked like a toga, or was it the wide bangle she wore on her upper arm? But in another time and place I swear that Khushi could have passed for a Roman matron: neatly carved classical features, an interesting forehead and a dignified cast to her face; she was a woman sure of her antecedents and her skills, with just a hint of a patrician background in the way she carried herself and made eye contact. But fortunately she never took herself too seriously. I liked her.

Although it was always difficult to tell people's ages in Bangladesh, my guess wasn't too wide of the mark. She was in her forties; solidly built with a smooth round face, delicate feathery black eyebrows and hair, sprinkled with grey strands, swept off her face with just a few unruly tendrils spilling over her neck. Everything about her seemed in harmony—except for one bizarre feature which took me by surprise. In the middle of her forehead she wore a large vermilion coloured *bindi*—like a married Hindu woman. But she couldn't be Hindu, she was from a highly respected, well-known Muslim family, so what was Khushi doing wearing a Hindu symbol?

Her modest, sparsely furnished flat was on the third floor of a dilapidated building in what seemed to be a poor section of Dhanmondi. Outside, a noisy concert of rickshaw bells and motor horns played non-stop. Her children were doing their homework in another room and her husband had not yet returned from work.

Twenty-five years ago Khushi had changed the course of her life when she insisted on an NGO posting to a remote village. The director thought she would be totally useless and cause nothing but trouble.

'Where are you going to sleep?' he asked.

'I'll stay where everyone else stays,' Khushi answered.

'But they are all men!'

'Well then, I'll have a room to myself.'

'We have no room for you,' he said.

'Okay,' retaliated Khushi, 'I'll share with the men. It's their problem if they get embarrassed. I'm not going to get embarrassed. By the way, do you have a room to yourself? You do? Good! Then I'll have your room and you share with the boys.'

Khushi stayed there for seven years; even today there are hardly any female NGO women working in the area.

The journey, which she made two or three times a year, took two and a half days. The crowded night train from Dhaka left at ten and arrived in Srimangar at six the next morning. An hour later she would board a bus crammed with passengers to Shaypoor where she would wait patiently for the launch to take her to the village. Often the boat was running late and she would camp by the roadside, waiting for hours without even a shed for shelter. She had plenty of time to observe the countryside, the heart of Bangladesh, and best of all she learnt how to observe people—especially women. After the six-hour launch trip Khushi was nearly at her destination: only a sixteen-kilometre walk remained, and then her journey was complete.

For the first time in her life, Khushi appreciated the natural beauty of Bangladesh: the strong wilful rivers, the flooded padi fields, the wildlife, the exquisite colours marking dawn and sunset—everything was colour, light and flowing water. And all these wonders were juxtaposed with the ugliness of class and communal relations, for she was staying in a Hindu majority area within a Muslim majority country. Even today she is still remembered as the woman who went alone to the marshy hinterlands of a remote rural area and learnt first hand about village life and village women.

Khushi's background made her different from other women. 'There are a many things that rich women do that other women can only dream of,' I said to her. 'Other women have much stricter, well-patrolled boundaries.'

She agreed that she came from a privileged background. 'My

83

father worked in government and while we were not rich, we were comfortable,' she said. 'Nothing nasty ever happened to me,' she added. 'I grew up in a liberal household with no separate roles or rules for boys and girls, or any kind of segregation. Doors were always open to me and then I went to Art College which was also a liberal institution.

'In the village what I saw changed my whole life. For the first time my eyes were open and I saw how the rules of law are not meant for the poor. I saw for myself how few resources reached such remote places and how the administration and the police behaved like local rajahs. I saw how police behaved with Hindu women and with the minority Hindu community,' Khushi explained. 'With poor people from any community—Muslim or Hindu—the further you got away from the city, the worse their behaviour.

'They would come and say, today we will eat here at your house, and the family would have to run around and get chickens and cook pilau—food they could never afford for themselves, and the men would use vulgar and sexual language with women even in front of their husbands.'

Khushi loved to shock men—any men—it didn't matter if they were mullahs or bus conductors or her own colleagues. 'I thought it was important then—and I still do—that village women see other ways of behaving; that they could see with their own eyes that customs could be broken or at least challenged.

'I travelled on my own and refused to sit in the women's cabin of the boat which was always crammed because the women were packed in with their children and the chickens, and the kids would be crying and being sick. The mullahs would get angry: "Why aren't you sitting with the rest of the women? Why are you sitting with us? This is the men's area!"

' "Because the women's cabin is overcrowded and I don't have problems sitting with men," I would answer. "But we have problems," they would say. "Well then you go and stand outside on the deck!"

'The men would try to stop me by stretching out their legs and saying "No room!". "Put your legs together and there will be space for me," I'd say, and they never knew how to handle that.

'It was the same on the buses. You see here the men always pay the fares and the women sit separately in the back section of the bus.

'The bus conductors always yell out "Whose woman is this?" when they reach the seats for women. Well I always insisted on paying for my colleagues and when the conductor reached my seat and yelled "Whose woman is this?", I would answer "This is nobody's woman, but those men are mine!"'

✳   ✳   ✳

The village people accepted Khushi, at first with curiosity, but later with affection. It was unheard of—an unmarried Bengali woman from the city, far away from the protection of father and brothers! She was twenty but looked younger. She wore plain cotton saris and left her jewellery at home, but she never covered her head, and she did unconventional things like walking with the men and carrying her own bags. Generally she found herself accepted by men who, it turned out, had not really expected her to obey the same rules as their own women.

'Almost a *bhai*, not really an apa,' they were fond of saying with grudging respect. Almost 'one of the boys', they meant—not really a woman or sister.

We talked about women's boundaries. Women whose families owned no land had to move around (never alone, of course) from village to village, looking for work in order to survive. But

85

middle-class women in purdah belonged to families with land and didn't seek work outside the home; they would look after the cattle, the seeds, the vegetable garden. They had their own space: their kitchens, their own rooms and family compounds, but when a strange man entered the family space—the *bari* or cluster of clan homes, they retreated inside, to a space that could not be invaded or 'defiled'. Muslim or Hindu women—it was all the same, she found. Purdah values were deeply entrenched—and still are in remote rural areas amongst orthodox religious families or those trying to boost their family status through notions of female honour which come down hard on their women.

Khushi told me that middle-class rural women in the village, were intensely curious about her own personal freedom. She must have seemed a freak to them.

Twenty years have passed, but some things remain unchanged.

'Women who are more creative: women who like to sing, or to write, feel their lack of freedom most of all, I think. Sometimes a woman even becomes "possessed" by a djinn; it's a kind of coping mechanism I guess,' said Khushi. 'If it goes on for too long then another woman calls in the traditional healer who makes his living from banishing bad djinns.'

'Does he do it by inflicting pain?' I asked Khushi. Years ago through the books of my favourite author, Lebanese novelist Hanan-Al-Shaykh, I had developed an interest in women's neurotic behaviour, especially their hysteria, depression and the remedies practised by folk Islam. Many of traditional remedies, I found, were similar throughout Muslim societies, especially where there was a Sufi, mystical influence.

'Yes. He pricks or pinches the little finger of the left hand to give her a sensation of feeling, just a small pain really. And she snaps out of it.'

But before he comes, I thought, she is free to behave as

spontaneously as she wants. Nobody can censor or control her—
she can keep her family, the community—everything—at bay.
When the pressures become too unbearable she can remove
herself from frustration and unhappiness, turn her back on
responsibilities—have a holiday. The 'sick' woman returns to a
kind of childhood with no inhibitions at all; she can swear,
clamber up trees, laugh loudly, sing songs and run around shouting crazily.

Women are so inventive about stealing more space for themselves or guarding what they have.

Khushi told me many stories about women using new ways
to combat old tyrannies. 'You must have heard,' she began, 'that
after harvest the wandering *pirs*, the sufi mystics, come to the
villages for their all night *waz* sessions: prayers and talks and
sermons and the like. And everyone in the village or the town
must contribute to this great occasion which the mullah often
organises.'

All the men look forward to these religious meetings, I gathered, which are always entertaining as well as uplifting—rather
like the evangelical 'Hallelujah Brother!' travelling circuses of the
Deep South in the USA, I imagined.

'The villagers donate money or chickens or goats—whatever
they can afford,' continued Khushi. 'Now this was a very conservative area in the south where the men are often away for
months at a time fishing. And one of the local mullahs kept
pressing this poor woman for her contribution and she told him,
"I haven't got much, I'll give what I can, but please stop trying
to force me".'

'Well even though she gave him a chicken he still kept coming
back and finally she got fed up. She told her women's group
about this greedy man and they laid a trap. The mullah
descended again and this time the woman started yelling for help
and all the women came running. The woman covered her face

with mud and she said to her friends, "This man has bad intentions, for I've already sent money and a chicken; he knows my husband is not here and still he keeps coming to my house!" So the women took out a procession, as the custom is, and walked around in public through the village shouting slogans. "You men start looking after your mullah," they yelled, "or we'll take action!"

'The women relish telling these stories you know, but I've always noticed that the men sit there looking uncomfortable with all the joking, with this "disgraceful" challenging of religious traditions and lack of respect towards the mullah.'

We had settled into an easy camaraderie and it seemed like a good moment to ask Khushi why she wore a Hindu dot on her forehead. She didn't mind my curiosity at all. I suspect she was waiting to be asked.

'I wear this spot on my forehead for many reasons,' she answered, and I could tell she'd often been asked the same question. 'Firstly because it means being Bengali to me; secondly because I strongly disagree with—no, dislike is a better word—these rules that are being set up that tell us that "this is Muslim dress and that is Hindu dress" or that this is "the Muslim way" and that is "the Hindu way". For me religion is something personal and it isn't to do with the way you eat or dress—those are cultural things; culture merged with history and class and a lot else. Bengal is a place where there has been a lot of mergers; so I wear this as a sign of no cultural division between Muslim or Hindu. I certainly don't wear it as a beauty spot!' I had my answer—Khushi, from a Muslim background, insisted on wearing the red dot of a traditional Hindu woman, as a political statement.

'Well, the red mark has caused me a few problems I can tell you,' said Khushi. She was in good form now, we'd finished dinner and were once again sitting together on cushions on the

88

floor. Her children were watching television and the only interruption came when the telephone rang. No matter who I talked
to in Dhaka, the tyranny of the telephone was never far away.
It is a phone-mad society, partly because of the difficulty in
getting around in the wet months and partly because people like
Khushi and Farida are the rallying point for their organisations,
constantly being called on to make decisions—I never saw much
delegation.

'There are times when, if I'm going to a religiously conservative village, I won't wear such a large bindi; no point in being
overly provocative,' she grinned. 'One of the women, her name
was Halima, said to me, "You know, apa, the mullah says if you
wear that kind of spot, it means that when you die, that part of
you will not go to heaven".

' "Does that mean I'll go to heaven with a hole in my head?"
I asked Halima.

'The women couldn't stop laughing. As I've said, the women
love these jokes—it's only the men who look at one another
uncomfortably!'

The following night we went together to the launch of a
unique documentary which went on to show to packed houses.
Mukthir Gaan (Song of Freedom) is the first ever full length
feature film on Bangladesh's 1971 liberation war against Pakistan. It is based on film maker Lear Levin's work which lay in
a Brooklyn basement for twenty years because he couldn't find
a commercial buyer. A US-based Bangladeshi couple, the
Masuds, stumbled across this footage and pieced together this
historical work. The film was taken from the back of a 'freedom
truck' which travelled through the war zone and remote village
areas performing folk plays (with political messages) for the local
people, telling them the latest news and keeping their spirits
high. It was an artists' odyssey: ten young students—men and
women, Hindu and Muslim—were on board and it was

dangerous work. One girl with a long thick plait down her back had drawn my eye as she clambered on and off trucks or sat rehearsing on a hastily constructed bamboo stage—perhaps it was her sad, homesick eyes or her high sweet voice singing patriotic songs. She turned out to be a good friend of Khushi's. When the war ended, she married (one of the young men from the truck) and retired from public life; until she heard of the Yasmeen tragedy.

'She came to me and said, "Khushi, please. We must do something. We can't just stand by and silently watch". So after all these years she has "come back", if you like to think of it that way. Because of Yasmeen, she has dropped her respectable housewifely duties and rejoined us. She travels to all the districts talking and urging men and women to protest.'

By now I knew that Yasmeen was dead. She had died alone by the side of a road. Many women stalked by violence die and the nature of their deaths goes unheeded. But Yasmeen's death had not been allowed to melt into anonymity. Why was the Yasmeen case so different?

CHAPTER 4

Fatwas

*　*　*

'It smells of Taslima, but we'll go ahead anyway,' the television producer said to his colleagues.

What transpired at this private meeting was later related to me by Shireen, actor/writer/social activist—and the woman who was giving them all a headache. Shireen had spies planted everywhere and nothing went on at the studios without her finding out.

For more than two hours management had wrestled with the Shireen problem and the producer's words summed up the frustration they all felt as the meeting limped to a desultory conclusion. After the chairman and his entourage left the room, the two remaining executives glanced at each other uneasily. Here they were, stuck with the task of mopping up. Shireen Kabir's new TV drama had been scheduled for the very same day a minor hartal against Taslima Nasreen was planned. They both knew what needed to be done. The station's policy remained unequivocal and the orders were clear: 'Avoid any confrontation with the *fatwabaaz*'. Fatwabaaz was the derisive term used by progressive Bangladeshis to label religious extremists—especially those with a penchant for flinging fatwas at vulnerable women.

'They summoned me into the room,' said Shireen, 'asked me to sit down, and broke the news. Some sections of my script must be edited—with certain lines omitted altogether—or else my play wouldn't be televised. A great pity, they told me, but unavoidable if they wanted to prevent the government censor from imposing a total ban.'

'Give me back my script!' she said.

'Now Shireen, be reasonable,' pleaded her producer, recognising he had a fight on his hands. 'You've gone too far this time! You know you can't get away with these kind of statements: you can't say that our political parties don't support women's liberation; you can't say they won't amend the laws because they're afraid of losing men's votes! You're sitting on a time bomb if you do!' He clutched his head, wondering again why he had ever gone into this crazy business and how soon he could escape to the sanctity of his home where a more tractable woman sat waiting.

The station manager rallied and made a show of supporting his colleague. 'And that section where one of your female characters—what's her name, Lily Begum?—looks into the mirror and says she is being tortured and hates being dependent on men, but must learn to hide this: learn to deceive everyone and find other ways of happiness, etcetera, etcetera. All that must go, my dear!' He wagged a finger playfully in her direction, but he was watching her closely and he began to fiddle nervously with a pen on the desk in front of him as he waited for her reply.

Shireen was not a happy writer. She'd started writing because the television plays she'd acted in, and all the Hindi and Bengali films she saw, always showed women compromising.

'What you want is the ideal Bengali woman,' she fired at them. Both men shifted uneasily in their chairs; they'd had similar discussions before and knew by now what to expect from Shireen Kabir once she was riled. 'The good housewife and the perfect daughter-in-law,' she went on sarcastically, 'all suffering and self-sacrifice and in the end you get the love of your husband and the respect of your son!' She stood up and started pacing the floor.

'Oh, yes, I know, I know,' she said as they tried half-heartedly to interrupt her, 'you think it's changed; the image is more progressive now—she may go out to work, but basically it's the same old recipe. No, I won't change a word!' she ended defiantly.

The two men looked at each other. Damn it! This was a messy affair. They sighed and tried again; after all, they were experts at massaging actors' egos. But it was just as well that everyone liked Shireen and she was such a good actress, because there were times . . . Still it was a great script: plenty of drama, plenty of tears and enough controversy in the main story without forcing the hand of the government censor.

❋　　❋　　❋

'What happened?' I asked Shireen two years later. 'How did it all turn out in the end?' The confrontation had all the melo-drama of a 'soapie within a soapie'.

'Well, they went ahead and censored it without my permission,' she replied, and had the grace to look embarrassed. Hunching her shoulders, she raised her hands as if pleading with some invisible referee—amusement, annoyance, a suggestion of helplessness—she used her face and body superbly.

Obviously she was not telling me everything but I decided not to force the issue. I changed track. 'Tell me more about the plot,' I requested instead.

She then proceeded to outline a tale of betrayal, murder and chicanery that was so Byzantine—(read Bengali!) that I became lost in a maze of crises and counter-crises. The protagonist, a female lawyer, finds herself divorced for defying her husband by defending her dead girlfriend's reputation and honour in court—or was it the dead girl's *lover's* reputation and honour? The female lawyer continues her battle and they all—husband, media and society—turn away. In the end, of course, she wins THE CASE and everyone flocks to her in admiration, even the political parties. Congratulations pour down; they all want to enlist her for a myriad of causes—but now the tables are turned and she meets them with ice-cold dignity:

'I don't need you now.' The camera zooms in for a close-up as she holds herself tall and proud, tossing withering glances right and left. The camera moves away to the crowd of well-wishing sycophants; their arms laden with garlands to place around her neck. They fall silent as she begins to speak.

'At the start, when I was all alone, when I really needed your support, no-one came to my assistance. Now that I have won, I can go on alone.' She turns her back and walks away. She climbs onto a motor bike and rides into the distance (she is not wearing a sari). The camera follows her until she is out of sight.

THE END: FADE TO BLACK

Stunned, I sat back in my chair and looked at Shireen who was worn out after her re-enactment. Shireen's face boasted the kind of cheekbones that cameras love. Her seductive voice cast a spell over her listener—an attractive woman, you would say, by any standards. But once she started 'acting', she became transformed into a different creature, into a beautiful, Scheherazade-like spinner of magic tales.

The teleplay 'Let Me Walk Alone' went on to win a top TV

award. Many of her fans were over the moon and sent flowers and cards. Television is a powerful influence in Bangladesh and even the orthodox religious factions have learnt to harness its technology.

'My fans said they wanted to behave like the heroine, but they couldn't. They were frightened of gossip; they were frightened of their families.'

Shireen loves her career. 'Acting is central to everything I do,' she admitted freely. When she goes into the slums to talk to people about their rights, hundreds come running at the sound of her name, and crowds follow her wherever she goes, hanging on her every word. She exploits her popularity and is used to being in the limelight. From the age of five she began acting at school and then two years later starred in soapies where she usually found herself playing the heroine's winsome daughter.

She mentioned carefully that she came from a very good upper-class family which was 'culturally enriched', as she put it—a *zamindari* or landed family. 'While our mothers might encourage us to act, our mothers-in-law urge us to give up the profession,' she confessed. 'I am very conscientious about the kind of parts I take and where I go, with whom I'm seen and make sure I stay out of the gossip columns. Most actresses don't continue acting after they're married.'

I guessed that the less she appeared on television, the better her in-laws liked it. I could smell a few skirmishes from the past, sensed compromises she must have negotiated at some time or other in her married life, but if she was bearing any scars they were well hidden.

'My husband would be the happiest man in Bangladesh if I gave up acting,' she laughed. 'He doesn't like his wife to be on display. In our society, you'll find that a brother is ready to give his sister and mother rights that he is unwilling to give to his own wife! On marriage a woman may even enter her husband's household to find that his sisters have more freedom than his wife does!' She rolled her eyes to show what she thought of that! 'But apart from this aversion to me acting, he's a wonderful husband and father, so I've learnt that if you want a good marriage you have to make some compromises.

'The TV authorities have refused another of my plays, you know,' confided Shireen, leaning towards me from behind her office desk. I found myself responding and edged my chair forward; she was very good at making you feel her accomplice. 'It is about a woman who throws a *maulvi*'s dead body into the jungle,' she said, without blinking an eye.

I couldn't stop from laughing aloud, for she had taken me by surprise, although I knew that maulvis, or religious scholars, were nothing to laugh about and neither was the subject of mullahs versus women.

'I based it on a true story, but they say they can't show it because it criticises the fundamentalists. It's all about a village maulvi, or mullah, who pronounces a fatwa on a sick elderly widow, accusing her of once being a prostitute and decreeing that no-one in the village is to give her food, or give her a decent burial when she dies, nor read the *janaza* at her grave. Well, when she dies her daughter is powerless to stop them treating her mother's body in this scandalous way. In fact they throw her body into the jungle. Of course these men are using religion as a shield; the headman wants the widow's land and the mullah is after the young daughter.'

She paused for breath while I carefully put down my cup of tea and applied the kind of concentration Shireen's stories demanded. 'Well as you can imagine the daughter takes a terrible revenge on the mullah when he dies and the play finishes with her crying out "Anybody who dares to call us nasty—is nasty! nasty! nasty!".' She raised her chin defiantly and used her hands forcefully in memory of her village heroine.

But wait—something sounded wrong. The word 'nasty' rang with a quaintness that suggested some kind of coy euphemism at work. Shireen admitted that in the script she had used the Bangla equivalent for 'bastard' which I knew was pretty hot stuff even in urban Dhaka. I sat back and gently applauded although I wasn't sure if I was applauding the actor or the writer.

Shireen is truly disappointed that her most recent effort has never got to air. But she has moved on. Her latest plan is to stage a hunger strike to get the custody laws, which are based on Muslim Personal Law, changed—that is, if she's able to convince her husband and family that going on a hunger strike won't damage her health or the family's precious reputation.

'It would have tremendous impact,' she enthused. 'I can just see the headlines! "HUNGER STRIKE OF FAMOUS ACTRESS!"; it would be in every paper and magazine, I can tell you.'

'What does your husband think?' I asked, although to tell the truth I already had a fair idea.

'He says if I go down this road, everyone will think I have a very unhappy married life. He says they will think we are divorcing and that I am trying to get custody of our son.'

'Why don't you tell him you'll issue a media statement announcing that you couldn't do this without the support of your wonderful husband, who incidentally is going to join you in your hunger strike.'

We looked at one another and burst out laughing.

I hoped that Shireen Kabir would continue to write her impudent plays, continue to push the boundaries of free expression. Her writing reveals the arguments used to silence women, drawing them out from the wings onto centre stage. She questions the status quo through female characters who often disobey husbands, defy 'tyrannical' mullahs and challenge the fatwas brought down on their heads as punishment by a worried male establishment.

❋　　❋　　❋

There is nothing funny in real life about the fatwa industry in Bangladesh, especially those fatwas which reek of anti-women sentiments. The meaning of the word has been completely distorted from its scholarly origins. Traditionally, a fatwa is an opinion given by a jurist, learned in Islamic law, in response to a question involving a point of religious law. The word 'fatwa' ricocheted into the English language in 1989 in the wake of Salman Rushdie's *Satanic Verses* and the Iranian Government's perverse reaction to the book.

In Bangladesh today, fatwas are being applied illegally by groups commonly described as 'fundamentalists' by Western commentators, although the term 'religiously-based political parties' or 'religious extremists' is probably a more accurate description. But today most Muslim academics seem to have given up the battle of semantics and use the more popular term 'fundamentalist'—more out of expediency than conviction. They're not happy with it; they feel it's a loaded term, at best a contested concept used exclusively to describe Muslims—and it's a valid point. But outside academic circles, perhaps it's irrelevant what they're called, because the goal of these groups is clear.

The fundamentalist parties clearly crave political control of the country and have reorganised themselves—they are now part of the process of modernisation, not something from the past. It's not so much the rule of Islam they hanker after, but their own authoritarian rule as self-declared 'religious experts'. To this end they use religion as a tool to control and coerce people in the religiously conservative parts of Bangladesh, pretending that Islam is under attack.

Bangladeshi fundamentalists and their allies delight in using fatwas which now contain messages with dark, vitriolic verdicts against individual women and against all womankind. They are determined to prevent the break up of the old economic order that gives them the power to keep women sequestered and less well-off families under control.

＊　　＊　　＊

'You've asked me some difficult questions,' said Khushi Kabir. We sat together on my verandah at the Mona Lisa. The usual background noise of the traffic was drowned out as the air— it seemed the whole sky—resonated with a dozen or more voices in different registers and rhythms all calling out the *azan* for the sunset prayer, the rise and fall of voices descending like heavy drops of rain. Any minute now Saleem the cook would disappear through the gates on his way to the Pearl Mosque and return within an hour or so a ritually cleansed and happier man, ready to prepare our dinners.

Why, I wanted to know, have some parts of Bangladesh moved towards a climate of moral coercion, away from the popular Islam of rural Bangladesh, which represents the softer, more syncretic culture of Bengal. This local tradition is based on a blend of Sufism, yogism and different animist and Hindu cults: a world of spirits, of trees, snakes and birds, of dreams and visions going back centuries. Buddhist, Hindu and Sufi influences all merged, and then came together with the more legalistic Sunni Islam of the nineteenth century.

Khushi explained patiently that even within this earlier

tradition, a misogynist strain was alive in Bangladesh. So this has provided fertile soil for the latest ultra-orthodox views more often associated with Pakistan and parts of the Middle East.

But there was still another question bothering me: were fatwas increasing or were they only more visible because local press were now alert? Khushi had spent twenty-three years observing and interacting with village life—what had she seen?

'No, I don't think fatwas have increased; they've always been with us,' she answered. 'The women's movement has certainly sensitised the press to human rights violations and now there's more reporting in both Bangla and English-medium papers.' Khushi paused, her forehead wrinkled in concentration and her red bindi moved up and down. 'But,' she said, 'what I *have* noticed is a change in the kind of punishments meted out. There's a savagery to these physical punishments inflicted by the village *salish*, or council, that wasn't there before.'

At first I wasn't sure what she meant. Physical punishment in a Western context covers a range of practices including parents smacking their children, corporal punishment handed out at some schools, men beating their wives—in the minds of many these are harsh practices, and in certain countries they are criminal acts. Caning of children and prisoners is considered a savage punishment in some societies and banned; many people throughout the world consider capital punishment savage—others do not. Yet the parallels I searched for prevented me at first from understanding Khushi. There are times when it's wiser to stop searching for cross-cultural parallels and just listen—and this seemed to be one of those times.

'It's certainly not as simple as it seems,' she went on. She cautioned me against becoming 'mullah-phobic' and I knew she was giving me good advice. 'I must say that our society is not riddled with mad mullahs handing down fatwas arbitrarily—I need to make that clear,' she stressed. 'In most parts of the country you don't find anti-women fatwas.

'Again, as you know, it would be a mistake to think that all orthodox Muslims are fundamentalists.' Khushi sounded like the old Khushi now, confident and clear. 'When I am talking to someone who is Caucasian—male or female—I let them know that when we are talking about religious fundamentalism, the picture of Islam as a monolithic, backward and violent religion is something I object to strongly. I let them know I object to this because within each religion you have fascist and fundamentalist trends. The Ku Klux Klan are Christians—are all Christians racists? Again closer to home in India, not all Hindus are communalists at heart.'

Like most of the Bangladeshi intelligentsia, Khushi looked at religious extremism as a political movement rather than a religious or spiritual one. She was not opposed to the village mullah or imam going about his normal business. From birth to death the maulvi plays a significant role in important life-cycle rituals: birth, marriage and death as well as major religious festivals like Eid-ul-Fitre at the end of Ramazan, the month of fasting, and Eid-ul-Adha, the feast of sacrifices that celebrates Abraham's readiness to sacrifice his son to God.

We were not talking about religious faith in all its different shades of expression; nor were we talking about orthodox Islam and the average practising Muslim. What we both feared lay locked inside the organised political movement carried out in the name of Islam, with its proponents claiming that they were defending Islam—'Islam in danger' was their favourite catch-cry. Religiously-based political parties were unscrupulous in using religion and violence to reach their goals. Their willingness to go outside the law, to let loose their violent student wings made it hard to counteract their influence—at least without imitating them and meeting violence with violence.

But so far they'd been held in check, though not by the government—in fact the ruling BNP Government, in the case of Taslima Nasreen, appeared to acquiesce with groups like Jamaat-i-Islami, the strongest religious party. What held them in check were the protests of, and alliances amongst, Bangladeshi secularists: the human rights activists, the judiciary, the feminists, the writers and academics, the students and journalists and many others. This grouping was diverse: supporters of different political parties; people who might have many different attachments to Islam—practising and non-practising Muslims, the devout and the nominal; the atheist and the agnostic; Hindus, Christians and Buddhists. They all fervently believed in the original secular principles and freedom of religious worship as pledged in the Constitution of 1972. This however was amended, against great opposition, in 1988 by Ershad's government, establishing Islam as the state religion although still guaranteeing freedom of worship. The Pro-Democracy Movement of 1991 toppled Ershad, but the changes to the Constitution remained and the role of religion in the state continues to be hotly debated.

But the fundamentalists boasted enormous street power. 'We will never leave the streets,' they threatened, 'until Shariah Law [Religious Personal law] is in place!' They controlled many madrassahs, or religious schools, and could drum up a mob in the twinkling of an eye, ready to take to the streets after Friday prayers, worshippers who'd just been 'pepped up' by a persuasive, imagery-laden sermon calling on the believers to chastise the *kafirs* (unbelievers) and other anti-God elements in the land.

There was no institution or group strong enough to counter their religious stranglehold. The country lacked properly trained theologians with their own scholarly tradition, which made it susceptible to foreign Islamist movements.

'Years ago,' Khushi continued, 'I would see rules and sanctions imposed on women and I would see the same women

ostracised and when their own families supported them and disagreed with the kind of submissiveness required, then they too
would be dealt with. Families,' she said, 'would often have to
leave the village, because they would be denied access to the
village pond, or the road or even refused work. And I don't
trivialise any of these punishments,' she emphasised. 'But what
I never found—what I never heard anecdotes about—was the
kind of barbarity that has been used over the last few years: the
lashings, the stoning, the burying.'

❊   ❊   ❊

I was starting to worry about being trapped in Dhaka for the
duration of my stay with little chance of getting to the rural
heart of Bangladesh. The situation seemed ludicrous—here I was
trying to write about Bangladeshi women, 80 per cent of whom
lived outside Dhaka, and I hadn't yet stepped foot outside the
capital! The hartals were ruining everything. It was all very well
theorising, talking about the 'real face of Bangladeshi women'
but I certainly wasn't going to meet her at the Mona Lisa ...
And then one day I found a new guide.

'People thought I was crazy returning to Bangladesh.' Selina was
a whip-smart young woman who'd gone to the London School
of Economics and graduated with a double degree. Life would
have been easy with UK qualifications in her pocket. The high
level of affluence needed to support overseas study showed too
in the beautiful sitting room where we sat talking one late
November afternoon, drinking tea and eating savouries delivered
by a small thin woman I took to be the maid. The cool dark
chamber was a small museum full of exquisite sculptures,
antiques, paintings and hangings. The contrast between the
grubby cramped office where we'd first met and the elegance of

her family sitting room took me by surprise. Selina's sophistication made it hard to imagine her bumping along country roads in a four-wheel drive, fording streams to reach remote places, and eating and living simply as she moved from village to village. But when she left her desk and travelled south-west to visit her agency's projects, she left her city ways behind.

Selina insisted—hartal or no hartal—that we should visit a group of villages she knew of so I could meet the 'New Bangladeshi Woman', as she called her. Fortunately the strikes had been suspended for a few days because the West Indian Under-21 Cricket Team was visiting Bangladesh and as the opposition parties said, they didn't want to 'penalise the youth [young men] of the country', and so with their collective and very pragmatic noses sniffing the wind they had suspended the hartal. At the Mona Lisa we all came alive: Scott went fishing, Molly went back to the office, Maxwell trotted off to the American Club for another game of tennis and I went to catch a plane.

There were times when working one's way around the hartal became a child's board game. You avoided landing on certain bases and tried to reach home safely before dragons and sorcerers menaced you! Once caught outside Dhaka at the commencement of an hartal, you were trapped until it was lifted—this could take days.

During the short flight, Selina talked about her student years in London. Buried beneath her memories of London's exotic charm and all the different opportunities opening up for her, were the racist comments many student friends made without even being aware of what they were saying. This made it worse in her eyes.

'Everyone expected me to stay in the UK. "Good God!" they said. "What on earth can you do over there?" Selina's accent was pure Oxbridge, her delivery sharp, her words almost flung at you. I couldn't imagine Selina holding her tongue if she felt strongly about anything, but apparently, as a student, there were times when she turned her back and walked away rather than confront the ignorance surrounding her. Gradually the young foreign student hardened: maturity, an enhanced sense of identity and self-esteem weathered her into a formidable opponent. Polite subterfuge had vanished years ago, I guessed.

'Whenever news came about the latest cyclone, someone was bound to tell me "Selina, you should be so grateful that you're here with us". I mixed mostly with other foreign students. I remember once when a German friend became very upset because an American girl asked her whether Germany had electricity or not—that's pretty bad even by American standards,' she laughed. 'But then the German girl went on to say to me, "After all it's not as if it's Bangladesh where people live in trees". I told her she was ignorant and walked away quickly before I did something dreadful to her!

'I knew I was very lucky that I came from a privileged family. Now I want to plough something back,' she said, her round eyes were serious. 'And so here I am back home, instead of forming part of the expatriate colony in the UK.'

We landed at our destination, a small airport, and were met by half a dozen excited people, whose names I couldn't remember, who were going to escort us to one of the villages about an hour's drive away. As we drove past recently harvested green fields, Selina reminded me that it was winter; three months earlier the roads would have been flooded and boats needed to reach villages stranded on high ground surrounded by flooded fields. No matter how often people told me this I could never quite imagine the earth I was walking on would disappear when the rains came.

At the first village, the women's *samaj*, or association, had been running along for ten years and now there were groups mushrooming everywhere in the district. There were hundreds of different programs, most of them set up by NGOs.

Everyone wanted to hug Selina and exchange news all at once. As none of the women spoke any English, Selina interpreted as we went along and the stories I'd come so far to hear slowly emerged. One excited woman, Aruna, pushed herself to the front. The other women gathered to listen in a semi-circle on the ground just as they sat for their regular meetings; they never grew tired of hearing the same stories, Selina said. They survived through working together and the stories gave them a feeling of relief. Perhaps it was a mixture of traditional storytelling and group therapy, a Bengali version of daytime television talk shows.

'My name is Aruna and I have three daughters. Their names I will tell you, apa. They are called Diamond, Pearl and Adieu,' she said proudly and everyone laughed at the old joke I was about to hear. I looked at this woman called Aruna, dressed in an orange and green sari, tied in the simple no-nonsense way village women tied their saris. Because my visit made it a formal occasion everyone wore the ends of their saris over their heads. Aruna was an ordinary-looking woman with bad teeth who couldn't sit still. She twisted her two red glass bangles and looked down at her feet; she was wearing her best sandals for the occasion. I noticed a small gold nose-ring glittering as her bright eyes watched me to make sure I followed her story as Selina interpreted for us both.

I entered the game. 'Aruna, why did you call your baby Adieu?'

She clapped her hands and the laughter started again. 'Apa, I called her Adieu because I was saying goodbye to childbearing. "It is enough!" I said. "Three children is enough and I don't care if they're all girls!"' She simulated her defiance but we all knew that in spite of her jokes, her stand must have been tremendously difficult. Son-preference was traditional through-out South Asia. I made a mental note to ask Selina what kind of contraception Aruna was using. More and more women in Bangladesh were learning to control their own reproduction, but they wanted to be treated as people, not faceless targets in a population control program.

'Aruna is one of our great success stories,' said Selina with a flourish; she reminded me of a magician pulling a rabbit from a hat. 'She's been through all our courses and her husband runs some of our literacy classes. By the way, let me tell you something about her husband.' She paused for a moment to ask Aruna's permission before continuing. I liked the way Selina interacted with everyone; she took care to explain to the women why I was there and why I was interested in their stories—there was no talking down, no high-handedness.

'When I first met her husband, I was thoroughly charmed. What a lovely man, I thought. "If only the other husbands were like him!" I said to the field worker I was walking with, and she started laughing like mad because, just a few years earlier, when Aruna first joined our program, her husband was bitterly opposed. Other men, you see, made fun of him. "Why is your wife working?"; "What kind of things are they teaching her?"; "She will turn into a disobedient woman and shame you." And so he took out his frustration on Aruna and there were beatings and that kind of abuse. But she was determined she was going to get an education and so crept out of the house and found ways of learning. On one occasion he even tore up all her books and this upset her terribly and she begged the staff to give her another set.'

I looked across the circle at Aruna knowing that she understood I was hearing the details of her one-woman revolt: of the dark days when she would sneak out of the house in order to steal pieces of her education; taking care to hide her books before creeping back inside her house to wash the rice and pound her spices and prepare a meal for a tired husband.

Selina went on, 'Gradually, very gradually I would say, a change came over her husband. He seemed to slowly comprehend why she was desperate to get some learning and why and what she was doing. As you can see she is now one of our leaders and travels for miles around the district, by herself I might add, organising other groups.

'I think he changed because he saw the benefits for the family: the income that was coming into the house and the different kind of status that her education brought to their house and indirectly to him. He's a good man and one of the few I've ever met who admits he behaved like a complete shit. "I was awful," he freely admits, "and it shames me now that I beat her and behaved so badly—but they all laughed at me. It struck at my manhood and I retaliated by clamping down on her."

'I think they have a great relationship,' said Selina. 'His earnings support the family and her earnings go into a bank account—the account is in her name and is controlled by her. I asked him why because this is most unusual. He said, "Well, it is my job to look after the family and what she earns is her money. I know if the family really needed it she would help and until we do the money should remain completely hers. I saw how she slaved to become educated and she deserves it."'

When Aruna's husband finally saw for himself the positive benefits from his wife's education, it made him strong enough to stand up to the social coercion in the guise of teasing from his male friends. After I returned to Dhaka, I learnt that middle-class men are now more likely to be derided for *not* providing for a daughter's education. Friends will say, 'Are you a fundamentalist, what's wrong with you?' But Dhaka is not Bangladesh and other ways must be found in the villages.

Women become very adept at stealing—they make ideal thieves: pilfering fragments of time and a little space and sanity for themselves, negotiating a bearable life, stealing across and around the barriers meant to imprison them. There are numerous ways of doing this, some modern and some steeped in custom and religious tradition. Women (more often than men) visit local pirs and attend their shrines in times of distress, looking for the solace and miraculous escapes which the holy mystics seem to offer—escape from oppressive circumstances. But Aruna had looked for different solutions, stealing an education, stubbornly putting the pieces together. No doubt there were some who saw her as a dangerous woman, an affront to the strict, male-imposed boundaries encircling 'decent women'. Her friends however wanted to imitate her because they saw how education had changed the quality of her family's life.

Selina's women, as I came to call them, were different from other women. None of them wore burqas when they stepped outside; obviously none of them were sequestered within their houses—they were working women and did not observe purdah. Purdah-observing women might well have been watching me from inside their houses, but I could not see them. We were sitting out in the open and a few curious men stopped to see what was going on, but that was all. The women ignored the men pointedly and they soon disappeared. Selina's women couldn't afford to stay at home; restrictions of dress and movement fall mainly on middle-class women in the rural towns and villages. But the might of the fatwa bears down on poorer women; it threatens those who dare to move out of the system, who cannot afford to stay at home like their better-off sisters. Desperate women may break with custom and become economically independent or refuse to obey some edict; show signs of social disobedience or dissent by flouting traditional mores. They and their families try to move beyond the control of the powerful elites such as those of the village salish. But the elites can punish these 'disobedient women' in ugly and dreadful ways.

The women continued to chat, enjoying the social event.

Some nursed babies, but I noticed there were no other small children around. Selina told me that because this was an 'official visit' they were being looked after at the schoolhouse.

Bangladeshi women are as slight as the wind: their average weight is 40.90 kilograms, which is less than the mean weight of women in most Third World countries. To say that life is hard for these women is a puerile understatement. They marry early, as young as fourteen. Their small, often still undeveloped bodies and small pelvic sizes cause all kinds of complications at birth, and traditions and customs mean that pregnant women eat even less food than normal. Pregnant women hoping for smaller babies and thus an easier childbirth often eat less, in the belief that the baby will grow less. Others may eat more, thinking that this will crowd the baby and keep it small. Such beliefs are hard to shift; they have been passed down by women over the centuries to try to protect themselves from the dangers of childbirth. Even if a woman's attitude changes through contact with health workers and doctors, there is always her mother-in-law who lives in the same house. 'Are you crazy?' she says. 'If you take these food supplements, you'll have a large baby!' And after all, the mother-in-law is the one who has the authority and the husband will always side with his mother. Selina's agency also promoted prenatal education clinics and was at pains to try to include the mother-in-law as well as the wife—the husband too if they could persuade him. So far their income generation projects had been more successful than their prenatal classes, but they weren't giving up.

Suddenly an older woman addressed me in Bangla. She refused to believe that I couldn't speak her language although Selina explained that I came from across the seas. 'She doesn't believe you are a foreigner,' Selina laughed. 'She says your skin is brown and thinks you're trying to trick everyone. Anyway she wants to tell you about her papaya orchard. She has ten trees and she calls it her orchard. She's telling you that she has papaya coming out of her teeth, as we say. She also organises the child-care arrangements for the co-operative. They have a fantastic system of division of labour and husbands are also included in the childcare arrangements. This is necessary if a woman has to go to the market. Usually there are twenty to thirty women in each group. Fifteen are nominated to work in the fields; others go on with their normal activities. The farming women are paid a wage and care is taken to ensure that they get paid the same daily wage as a male farm labourer—they are very sensitive about that. The surplus profit from the crops is paid to everyone else in the group.

'This area is conservative, although not a Jumaat stronghold, but there are still champions of the status quo here. Just how conservative, Aruna can tell you. Don't think it's all smooth sailing,' Selina concluded. 'I'm showing you the end result of what has taken years to achieve.'

'Well,' said Aruna taking up the story, 'one morning I heard that the mullah was saying bad things about me; gossiping about me to people in the village. He said I should be wearing burqa and I shouldn't be walking around. Why wasn't I inside the house, like any decent woman; the usual things that mullahs say about women like me. So the next time I saw him I said "Why did you say those bad things about me? All right, then you pay me 300 taka a month and I'll stay home! Why don't you pay all thirty of us in the group 300 taka each and we'll all stay in our houses, 'cause it's no fun working all day in the fields you know." '

'Yes,' Selina confirmed. 'She was walking past him in the lane near the mosque after *jumma*, the Friday prayer and he muttered something out of the side of his mouth, "You slut", or some-thing like that,' she laughed, 'and Aruna confronted him and announced in a loud voice to the rest of the men standing

111

around, "And that includes all you worthy gentlemen here as well!"'. Aruna doesn't go looking for trouble,' said Selina, 'but don't give her any bullshit or she'll give you a hard time. Now this incident was three years ago and today the same imam tells anyone who'll listen that it is very important for both parents to be working for the sake of the children's future. Even mullahs can be converted, you see!'

But not all mullahs are as yielding as the one in Aruna's story. At the village level where most people are illiterate (literacy rates are extremely low—23 per cent for women and 30 per cent for men), the mullah's influence is strong and visible, and the secularists far away in Dhaka and other towns have a negligible effect. Nevertheless in this district a quiet revolution was happening.

'I went to the mosque with some food to give the imam because it was a special festival,' said Minu, a tired-looking woman. Minu's eyes protruded slightly, one of the signs of goitre which is widespread among town and village women because of the lack of iodine in their diets. 'His face grew dark with anger and he shouted at me, "You women are all hussies! Your group comes from the devil and I don't want your kind or your food near the mosque. You pollute everything!"'

'She marched down the lane,' said Selina. 'She rounded up ten *tokai* as we call them—there are always plenty of these homeless kids around—and she lined them up in front of the mosque and served the food to them right in front of the mullah, who couldn't believe his eyes. You have never seen a man so flummoxed in your life!'

'I told him,' said Minu, ' "See these children whose hearts are as pure as flowers with no evil thoughts to contaminate them? With men you can never tell what they are thinking and even mullahs are men so I am never going to feed mullahs again. I will feed these children. And as to your comments that you are never going to buy our food, everything in the market is produced by us: you eat our eggs, drink our milk, eat our chickens, our rice. Let's see how long you last without eating anything produced by us!"'

'It is just unprecedented for a village woman to stand up to a mullah that way,' explained Selina.

Women acquire great self-confidence once they have a chance and if they can stand together. Selina seemed to need these stories as much as the other women. When times were hard they kept everyone's spirits going.

Selina's women: indefatigable Aruna, defiant Minu and all the others, are multiplying throughout Bangladesh. Daring women, I thought, and also very lucky women. They came from a part of the country where NGO income generation programs offered an alternative form of patronage to the money poured into rural areas by fundamentalist groups who defended Islamic values and built a powerful rural base through a combination of welfare activities and proselytising.

Bangladesh is a society undergoing rapid social change and NGO activities are at the forefront of development aid—many of the activities focus on empowering women. This often puts them on a collision course with local, traditional interests. In more remote parts of the country, village salish could easily have pronounced fatwas against Selina's women—women who are literally more visible and disturbingly independent.

The salish is a traditional form of mediation used for the arbitration of disputes. Those who preside are usually members of the local elite (village elders, the madrassah principal or schoolmaster, the imam, the money lender, landowners and rich peasants). Their decisions are not, however, legally binding and in the past they were never enforced. These councils are also called by the village elders on their own initiative on matters of customary law, when individuals are accused of misbehaviour and a variety of sentences illegally meted out. Who is there to stop them? They have now become newly reconstructed as networks of power and patronage by local elites drawn to pro-Islamic, often anti-Western messages. They set themselves up as arbiters of morality and justice. In the process these so-called 'Islamic courts' are illegally supplanting judicial authority.

A placard at a woman's rally expressed it all: 'Judges and magistrates stay home while the mullah now metes out justice'. The unstable political situation, which has resulted in a weak state structure, has created conditions favouring increased Islamist activities. The government's deafening silence on the fatwas pronounced against women implicitly endorses their actions.

The rural elites, including the men of religion, are facing rapid social and economic changes which threatens their status and livelihoods. Their small world is changing. Money lenders are losing business to income generation projects and credit institutions like the Grameen Bank which lends money to women with no collateral. Imams, usually the least educated and the worst paid in the hierarchy of Islamic 'scholars' (most women don't want to marry them) are often dependent for their meagre living on local rich men. Sometimes the village imams and mullahs become their tools.

Mullahs are no longer the sole custodians of wisdom and knowledge; the NGOs now rival them and the existence of thousands and thousands of co-operatives and literacy groups makes it clear that many parents are no longer sending their children to the madrassahs for education. They prefer the secular education at NGO schools. Why should they go to the mullah for holy water or Qur'anic verses scribbled down on a scrap of paper and worn around their necks? The health clinics run by NGOs and the government offer modern services. The poor old mullah is missing out, for there is less money to be donated to the mosque and indirectly into his pocket. They are losing income and becoming more and more dependent on those village elders and richer men who can give them additional income, security or favours. In return they may offer so-called religious injunctions—fatwas—for any of their patrons who want to divorce their wives; they can apply pressure on families to agree to a marriage, and of course they are very useful when brothers want to deprive their sisters of their inheritance rights under Islamic law. *So many patriarchal interests to serve . . . so little time!*

The Arunas and the Minas of the world defy the status quo and are an 'affront' to the ideal of Muslim womanhood reflected in the simple phrase 'Heaven lies under the feet of your husband'—as nasty a piece of Hadith perjury as ever there was, for the original lines say that 'Heaven lies under the feet of the Mother'. But illiterate people have little hope of finding out the truth. Who would dream that a mullah could be wrong?

Selina's kind of women challenge and sometimes appear so threatening that fatwas are pronounced against them to bring them to heel. But I badly needed to hear the good news stories at the other end of the spectrum which never reached beyond the magazines and annual reports of international aid agencies. I needed them badly to counter the depression I felt mounting when I read the lists of women punished by fatwas and watched documentary videos. *Eclipse* is one such very moving documentary. It was produced by the human rights centre Ain O Salish Kendra (ASK) in Dhaka.

✳ ✳ ✳

Three years have passed since his daughter Noorjehan committed suicide; three years ago in the District of Maulvibazaar in Syhlet she took poison. Her father talks directly into the camera, sensing that beyond the lens he can reach thousands of people who care enough about his daughter's death to protest and demand the justice which he as a poor man has no chance of finding by himself.

Till the end of his days, he will be Noorjehan's father—this is now his identity. There is both bitterness and sadness in this. While she lived, Noorjehan's own identity lay submerged, locked away from discovery. She was the daughter of her father; she was someone's wife—the men in her life who controlled her and protected her, gave her a place in society. Now the father's identity is embraced by *her* death; they are inseparable because he belongs to his dead daughter now, for he is Noorjehan's father ...

He is a thin man with a long white beard flowing down to his chest and he wears the white round cap of a religious man who says his prayers and submits to the will of Allah. He keeps himself warm inside the folds of a bright blue shawl. The colourful shawl distracts from an emaciated face which, in spite of his efforts, crumbles into a dreadful sorrow; it is painful to witness and the observer welcomes the chance to bury her eyes in the blueness of his cloak.

'When I buried her, I buried my grief.' I can't believe his words; has someone made a mistake in translating the video subtitles I am reading? For his grief is palpable: you hear it as his voice breaks when he repeats his seventeen-year-old daughter's plea for help. His anguish is there as he describes how he couldn't intervene, couldn't stop them from carrying out the sentence handed down by the local imam and seven other men from the village. Noorjehan had moved beyond his protection and was now under the control of men interested only in censure, chastisement and the public humiliation of a young woman.

Who can remember her crime? The salish, representing the influential men of the village, handed down a fatwa against

Noorjehan, indicting her for a second marriage. The punishment was simple enough: bury her to her waist in a ditch and throw 101 pebbles at her. Her father makes no mention of the fact that he and his wife are sentenced to fifty lashes for aiding and abetting the supposedly illegal second marriage of their daughter.

She called to him for help: 'Father, please speak to them! Why are they condemning me?'

'But they wouldn't listen to me; they kept repeating, "The law is in our hands". Maulana Mannan and the others ordered her to stand in the pit. She begged them for permission to speak to me, but they refused. Then I told her, "My child, do what they say ..." They dragged her to the pit and pushed her in,' he said, walking away from the camera and pointing to a place on the ground; there is no longer a hole and all one can see are a few banana trees. The site selected for torturing a woman looks so commonplace—the sentence carried out in bright sunshine as if they had nothing to be ashamed of ... A few small boys stood around with serious faces; they understood the enormity of what had taken place, for there is nothing private in a villager's life. Even death is a village event.

'She covered her face with her shawl and they threw pebbles at her. One of the elders kept saying "Shame on you, whore! Why don't you take poison and die!" '

The face of Noorjehan's sister fills the screen as she takes over the role of chronicler. 'Later that day she took poison and began to feel ill. When I asked her why she took it she said, "I have been so humiliated. How can I live?" '

Following protests by women's and human rights organisations, a case was filed against Maulana Mannan and seven others; they all received seven years 'rigorous imprisonment' and heavy fines on 22 February 1994. They have since appealed to the High Court. This is not an isolated story.

Three months after the death of her name-sake, another Noor-jehan from Faridpur District is tied to a stake, kerosene is poured over her and she is burnt to death. Her murder follows the verdict of the village salish called by an influential family accusing her of adultery. There is no information available about their motives. A year later the case against the powerful villagers is dismissed due to lack of evidence. The Mahila Parishad, a strong woman's organisation, refuses to give up and submits a petition to the High Court which orders fresh investigations.

Rokeya's head is shaven and she is forced to parade through the village street with shoes strung around her neck––the ultimate symbol of humiliation—then tied to a tree for eight hours. Later that night she is raped by four men. Rokeya was pregnant and the village chairman and members had pronounced a fatwa against her on the grounds of a premarital relationship. The police were able to rescue Rokeya and although a case was filed no progress has been reported, in spite of women's organised protests, because the main family is so influential.

I read down the list compiled between January 1993 and August 1995. I read through the twenty-three cases listed, compiled by Ain O Salish Kendra (ASK) from newspaper reports and through its own investigations.

I learn that in many instances the force of the punishment lies in its psychological impact: in the degradation and humiliation that women feel. A mother weeps as she recalls that 'no-one would help me save my daughter!'.

On the ASK video a psychiatrist discusses how women are humiliated to the point of suicide. 'When a woman is degraded and humiliated by the fatwa, there is nothing left for her, so she rejects society by killing herself.' The psychiatrist goes on to talk about the psychology of those who regard themselves as the

118

custodians of Islam. It is an interesting comment on abnormal psychology and how punishment and discipline become a way of life.

7,9,11'From childhood they are taught absolute obedience in religious schools, the madrassahs. They are punished severely for breaking any rules and that is when they begin to learn to punish others. If they can't punish, they feel they have failed—they are forever projecting their feelings. Instead of recognising their own faults they must prove they are good—and that others are bad and should be punished. Women are easy targets for them.'

*   *   *

Listening to the recorded speeches of hard-line religious leaders on cassette is a popular past-time in Bangladesh. Their loud insistent voices can be heard at bus terminals, at bazaars and tea stalls, wherever men congregate—sometimes outside mosques. The cassettes are cheap and one can feel virtuous while being entertained. Their influence is pernicious.

The voice delivering the speech is persuasive and charming; there is no fanatical shouting, nothing to repel—only the words are insane, but from the reaction of the large audience, a good time is had by all.

Every woman must cover herself. Her head, her neck, her breasts must be hidden from public view. This doesn't mean that women should be locked in their homes. When they go out they should be covered with a veil. Burqas have doors, windows, ventilators. You'll be more attractive to men. Your value will increase and your chastity will be protected. If women are easily available, they lose their value. So don't listen to those 'progressives', they will lead you to disaster.

Later friends tell me that I have been listening to a mild—one might even say friendly—kind of message. There are other speeches which go much further . . .

Sometimes as a visitor it becomes hard to see anything else but the bleak pictures of a repressive version of Islam. One must spend more time in Bangladesh to counter the images promoting the idea that it is a country where religious fundamentalism runs riot. For this is not the case—there is more to Bangladesh than fatwas, although the fight to keep the extremist elements at bay is on-going.

The fundamentalists' strongholds are confined to certain areas and while on some occasions they roam the streets giving the impression of having enormous support this is not so. They use the religious card to enter the political arena because they have failed to make significant headway through the democratic process. Elections are the true indicators of their power. And the people of Bangladesh have continually denied them political power, refused them a meaningful political role.

ASK and other human rights groups continue to monitor violations of every kind. 'A fatwa is an opinion given by a jurist, learned in Islamic law, in response to a question involving a point of law.' They keep repeating this so that people won't forget. 'The fatwa is now being used to bolster the authority of the village elite. It is being pronounced by people who have no authority or scholarship and it is used not to clarify an ambiguous legal situation but to weigh up evidence, which is not the function of a fatwa-giver. So fatwas are being given by the wrong person, in the wrong circumstances and for the wrong purposes.'

I know the words by heart. They are like the small prayer beads, *tasbih*, which devout Muslims hold in their hands. By repeating the words I can almost blot out the images of the Noorjehans, and the young Rokeyas, and the desolate faces of their parents.

CHAPTER 5

The Maid's Daughter

*   *   *

One morning Molly Mac introduced me to her protégé, Mrs Nargis, who came once a week to the Mona Lisa to give Molly a massage. Gupta made it his business to supervise the comings and goings of Mrs N and the old fox always ensured that a few taka notes slipped into his hands before he allowed her past the gates. She was a woman who struggled to make a living by giving facials and massages to private clients. Molly was a regular and paid Mrs Nargis five US dollars to be pounded and pinched and oiled, every Wednesday afternoon, to her heart's content.

Mrs N wasted no time. 'Madam likes massage?' she asked, clutching a small bottle of Johnson's Baby Oil. 'No, thank you,' madam replied, but before her face dropped, I explained that I would much rather have a story than a massage and so we came to a business arrangement. Instead of stealing a story, this time I would pay for one.

Mrs Nargis had the face of a discontented woman who refused to disguise her feelings with smiles and other tokens of good humour. But because her moods couldn't be permitted to rule her pocket, she soon discovered that a little friendliness oiled the wheels of her business transactions. While she hoarded her smiles like a miser hoards his gold, her voice played the part of a woman dependent on favours. A high voice whined from narrow lips which failed to conceal small protruding teeth. Her words wheedled and fawned and stroked the listener, just like her hands patted and fondled the bodies she massaged day after day—if she was lucky and work came rolling in. She was a woman who envied other women. Fate had been unkind and she lived out her life waiting and serving, needing and wanting, while other women had servants and cars and ate meat every day.

She was born in a village in Dhaka District and lived for twelve years with her three sisters and four brothers in the house of a wealthy, land-owning family—she called it a 'landlord's house'. Her father worked now and then as a cook, but it was her mother's drudgery which kept them alive. They held no land and life was not easy because her father loved gambling and village liquor more than anything else.

'My mother worked as a maid for this family, from six in the morning till late at night. She worked for twelve years looking after the children, doing the shopping, the cooking and cleaning—all the household work, and in return they gave her food and shelter for us all. The rich woman would tell my mother, "Your husband comes here every night to sleep, you have everything you need—don't complain; what do you want money for?".'

Working as a maid or domestic servant is about the lowest occupation for a 'respectable' woman. Today city women complain about the shortage of maids because uneducated women from the villages would rather work in garment factories where wages and conditions are better. By Western standards,

Bangladeshi factory conditions are poor, and at first it is hard to understand that for village or slum women, working in such a factory is regarded as a choice job. Among their numbers are former maids who have turned their backs on their employers. Garment workers have more self-confidence than maids: you see them everywhere in Dhaka walking in twos or threes, on their way to work, or shopping at the bazaars, buying a lipstick or a ribbon. They exhibit an easy camaraderie which maids watch enviously, especially those servants kept isolated by employers, who dread the gossip which keeps choice pieces of information going round like meat on a rotisserie.

Later I met Mrs Nargis' mother, a plump elderly lady with a sweet beaming smile who walked with difficulty, slowly hobbling down the corridors of the Mona Lisa to my room. We drank tea and Seven-Up served by a confused Kumar Gupta, who had trouble understanding how Mrs N and her mother had been transformed into guests overnight. He disapproved, and his sur-liness made us all uncomfortable, but I refused to capitulate—I thought it was good for Gupta's soul, even though I could read his mind. 'What was Kumar Gupta doing,' he was thinking, 'serving these women who normally asked his permission to enter the gates!'

'Conditions got better over the years,' said Mrs N. 'There were presents now and then, a sari for Eid or a visit to the cinema. The rich woman would say to my mother, "You are like my sister. Come! We will go to the cinema together".'

'The woman called me her daughter. You see I played with her children and we all slept together in one bed; we ate the same food, so I thought they were my brothers and sisters. I called the rich woman "Mother".'

'And what did you call your real mother?' I asked her.

'Oh I called her Aunty, like everyone else. I didn't think of her as my mother, you see.' She looked down at the hand-

kerchief held tightly in her hand. 'She was only a servant; all
the children called her "Aunty", it is the custom,' she said. 'Even
today I still call her "Aunty"; I don't use the word "mother". I
know it hurts her. She sometimes complains, "Why do you
never call me Mother?".'

Occasionally maids' daughters are brought up as members of
the family, a kind of unofficial adoption accepted by the maid
who wants her daughter to grow up to be a 'lady'. Girls call
their real mother 'Aunty', sometimes not knowing the truth
until it comes time to get married. When they learn they have
been duped (for the best of reasons), they often develop psychological problems. But despite Mrs N's claims, I had my
doubts. The pattern of her childhood was different from the
clinical case studies I'd read about; her predicament had a will
of its own, just like Mrs N.

Mrs Nargis wanted to hurt her real mother. Until she turned
twelve, she lived in this house—treated like one of the children,
she claimed, but there were small discrepancies in her story and
I believed that as the years passed, the young girl came to realise
her inferior status, to understand that the woman who worked
night and day for no money and who was so lowly placed in
the household was really her mother.

When the rich woman's children went to school and she
remained at home—she must have begun to wonder. How did
she feel when she found herself looking after her real brothers
and sisters while her own mother looked after the children of
the house who always came first? When had she started to reject
this woman who looked after other babies? There had to be some
reason why she kept on punishing her mother by always calling
her 'Aunty'?

Young girls learn very early about their place in society, they
observe where they stand as females and grow aware of their
families ranking—they inhale these lessons as part of growing

up. They begin to internalise what they see around them, accepting subordination and discrimination because they are girls, as natural and just; they believe restrictions are there to protect them. As a child Mrs N hid her feelings, but unlike other girls of her age, she never learnt to swallow the discrimination, to see it as something natural in her life, a second skin which she couldn't shed. But by the time our paths crossed, the early sparks of rebellion had died into a muted hostility towards life in general.

When Mrs N was twelve her family moved to Dhaka and life improved. Her mother found someone willing to train her in massage which led to work at a leading hotel where many foreigners stayed and where the modest salary could be supplemented by tips. Later strings were pulled and she found work in the same hotel for her daughter, and that was how Mrs N became a masseur and finally 'went private'.

Her married life has been better than most, she told me, although the start was inauspicious. 'My mother asked me if I wanted to get married when I was fourteen and so I said okay Ma. It was my mother's idea,' she explained, 'because my father wasn't working again and there was not enough food for us all. After the ceremony my mother said now go and sleep with your husband. "What do you mean?" I said. "I always sleep with you; why should I sleep with him?" I cried and cried, but they made me. I didn't want him to touch my body, but he was very patient and he told me that he loved me.' She was proud of this, she lifted her chin. 'He was also my cousin, you see. I used to wonder why he came to visit us so often. He told me that he'd loved me for a long time.'

She was fifteen when her first baby was born and she still didn't understand her body.

She had trouble with her mother-in-law. 'You see she wanted dowry and I had no dowry—my husband said it didn't matter, but she was jealous and living with her was terrible. I said, "Momma, please give me a sari." I had only one sari, you see. We were very poor. On the day we were married she gave me a sari, but the next day when I came to live with her she took it back. She didn't hit me, but she was so mean to me. I would do everything: I would massage her feet and do all of the work, but still she hated me.' A small smile lit her oval face for a second or two. 'Today I have twenty-five saris.' She patted her coconut-oiled hair, checking to see that no hair had escaped from her bun at the nape of her neck, and for the moment her voice sounded satisfied, but the smile never quite reached her eyes, for she counted her saris like the king counted out his money bags, more from habit than from any pleasure it gave him.

'I have a good husband, he gives all his money to me, but I can't say that I'm happy or unhappy ...' By now she was so used to disciplining herself, so practised at slipping into a kind of indifference that had become second nature, that she withheld her feelings from everyone around her. No, her husband didn't gamble like many working men and he didn't throw away his money on 'hootch' as it was called in Bengali English ('Binglish'). An image grew of a man forever trying to please a wife whose resentment could never be assuaged for long.

I watched Mrs N carefully. I tried to picture her as a mother singing songs and playing with her small children—but she was always so solemn. Even her manner towards her mother and younger sister, a shy pretty woman who allowed herself to be bullied, lacked warmth and affection. But I admired Mrs N: she fought back in her own way. Her daughters would be the first women in her family to read and write in their own language.

It was nearly time for Mrs N to leave and she took out her small diary to work out a time for our next storytelling session.

I asked her where she had learnt to speak English. 'At the

127

hotel,' she said. 'But I cannot read or write in my own language for I only had one year at school.'

'But what are you writing in your diary then, Mrs Nargis?' I asked.

'I write down the numbers only. I can read and write numbers in Bangla—the names I keep in my head. When I first went private I went knocking from door to door at the rich houses in Gulshan. "Do you want a massage, madam?" I asked. I met an English lady in this way. She said, "Yes, you can come back next Tuesday". I didn't know what is called Tuesday so I kept repeating "Tuesday, Tuesday," and I asked a man what Tuesday is and he laughed and told me in Bangla. Mrs Elliot, the English lady, gave me a lot of customers.'

'Does your mother still do massages?'

'Only for one woman, Mrs Khan in Gulshan; she likes my mother very much and calls her apa—elder sister. But I don't like her. She is very rich and I am very poor. I do not like to go inside the houses of rich women; I don't feel good. My mother is old-fashioned and she doesn't mind, but I feel sad. Why do I have nothing and they have everything?'

I sensed that Mrs Nargis didn't like me either although she hid it quite well. Barriers had been put in place a long time ago, before we even met, and there was nothing I could do about it without seeming patronising and blind to the inequality between us. I tried to ignore it at first, tried to ease my guilt by denial. After all I came from a servantless society. In Australia our lives weren't eased through having others do the laundry, the cooking, the driving, cleaning, child-care, shopping, gardening; with people to serve tea and fold clothes, to pick up and put away; to answer the door and massage tired limbs—we had machines instead. I engineered all of these rebuttals in my daydreams, reducing the class barriers separating us, and fed myself all sorts of excuses. But although I might claim that my personal freedom and lifestyle was independent of the labour of an under-class of women and men, Mrs N knew something about the world I came from. In her place I would have felt the same. Envy and need would have overpowered the chance for a fleeting friendship—even one based on mutual expediency. The friendship, had it been nurtured, would have made me feel better, but I doubt that it would have done much for Mrs N. Empathy and shared gender could not bridge our differences.

By the time she was fourteen Mrs N knew only too well what prematurely awaits a girl from her class: dowry demands, marriage, childbirth, child rearing, scraping together a living; all against a swirl of poverty that threatens to suck you down. While I could empathise with her hard life, while we could travel by rickshaw together and go shopping at the markets even drink tea together—at the end of the day I would return to the Mona Lisa while she returned to a neighbourhood bursting at the seams, with families living in one or two rooms, where people struggled to retain a semblance of respectability as the nearby slums moved closer. A certain vagueness descended on our conversations whenever she talked about her home. I could only remember one small domestic detail: she had great trouble keeping her saris fresh and clean.

She hoarded her saris, even gave massages in her sari petticoat and *chola* blouse to protect them. Her pretty cotton saris were a shield keeping poverty at arm's length, boosting her self-esteem; Mrs N said she owned twenty-five, her mother told me her daughter possessed forty, but her younger sister whispered in an aside that her sister really owned ten. Still, I knew that a woman with ten cotton saris to her name was not destitute—poor perhaps, but not penniless.

For most of her life, Yasmeen's mother owned two cotton saris.

CHAPTER 6

Yasmeen of Dinajpur

＊　　＊　　＊

There were too many unanswered questions. And as I tried to piece together the narrative, all the discrepancies and the gaps in reporting began to trouble me. There were too many missing voices in a story filled with shouting and protests and songs of anger and grief.

I wondered what she looked like. I would never know—there were no photographs to tell me. The only one that ever came to light showed Yasmeen's body lying uncovered on top of a rickshaw cart and the death mask she wore bore little resemblance to her, I was told later, much later. I could never bring myself to ask her mother what she looked like, whether she resembled her or not; if her voice sounded like the chattering of a young happy girl, or the light whisper of a shy girl-woman.

Yasmeen is a popular name with Muslim families the world over, a name given to princesses and maids alike. It comes from the beautiful white, deeply scented jasmine flower. But when they found her lying face down, a small figure by the side of the dusty road, bloodied and broken, no-one knew her name.

The police removed her body. They left behind a few fragments of glass—all that remained of her broken bangles. The
image of those small pieces of coloured glass glinting in the dust
stayed with me a long time.

*　　*　　*

Two weeks have passed. The journalists in Dhaka are becoming
impatient. The rain is coming down and they worry that the
large crowd will disperse. They need their photos and they have
deadlines to meet; so they ask the organisers to start the
demonstration ahead of schedule.

The leaders refuse. 'No one will leave. The rain won't drive
anyone away,' they insist. And of course they are right—there
are no defections and everyone remains.

Later that day, 1200 women march through the streets of
Dhaka. *Lathis* (batons) wielded by women police fail to deter
them. The following month a crowd of nearly 15 000 protest;
this time the women are joined by thousands of men.

Days later, in twelve districts across Bangladesh, simultaneous
protests are organised by feminists and human rights groups and
crowds of two to three thousand rally in sympathy. Their anger
is sharp and focused. In rural towns throughout the country,
crowds are shouting slogans and waving banners for a young girl
no one had ever heard of before.

'Remember Yasmeen!' voices call out. The banners are equally
insistent: 'Yasmeen is our daughter!' they read. 'Yasmeen is our
sister!'; 'Yasmeen is Bangladesh!'

*　　*　　*

Yasmeen Akhter died on 24 August 1995. Three months later I went to Dinajpur where it all happened.

For weeks I had been puzzling over the death of Yasmeen, poring over newspaper accounts and talking to people. Gradually I came to understand why Farida and Natasha, at our very first meeting, had gently pushed me in the dead girl's direction, silently hoping that I would follow her story. Much later I learnt that Farida represented her agency, UBINIG, on the Sammilito Nari Samaj. This coalition of twenty women's organisations had, in a great show of strength, proved that Bangladeshi women could stand united on a common platform, putting aside for once their ideological differences and their competitive sense of priorities. Farida, characteristically, had left me alone to discover Yasmeen's place as an icon in the women's movement before revealing her own commitment. Anyone claiming that she had pushed me towards the story for her own reasons would find themselves on shaky ground. In hindsight it was an astute move on her part and the gamble (if that's what it was) had paid off. I respected her reasoning although, by the time I returned from Dinajpur, it didn't seem to matter any more. I had my own agenda by then: I *wanted* to be used and I also wanted to discover why Yasmeen had run away and why the story was never reported by the foreign media, except for a brief mention on the Voice of America.

Shima became my shadow in Dinajpur. Farida, silently and efficiently, made the arrangements. She decided that Shima, her senior research officer at UBINIG, would be the ideal guide and interpreter because Dinajpur was her home town, the place where her widowed mother and extended family lived. Our visit would be short because we were taking advantage of another break in the ongoing strikes and protests, permitting us to hurry off to Dinajpur in the north for a few days, and returning just before the hartal curtain descended once more.

So the two of us flew off to the northern town and it was only when she handed me her card during the flight, that I read for the first time, her full name—Shima Das Shimu—and realised that she was Hindu. I should have realised by her first name, but telling the difference between a Hindu or a Muslim Bangladeshi just by looking was beyond me. The language is identical, the patriotic yearning is the same, the customs and values are similar and there has been a shared history. Only Muslim or Hindu communalists would claim that religious differences cut off one human being from another. To everyone who worked with her and knew her, Shima was just another of Farida's hard working officers who, as luck would have it, came from Yasmeen's home town.

Three smiling matrons in their forties greeted us after we landed at Saidpur, an hour's drive away from our destination. Razia and her two friends were solid, unpretentious women of the town and leaders of the local women's organisation who'd played an important role in the Yasmeen story, alerting women activists in Dhaka about the drama in Dinajpur as soon as it unfolded.

Dinajpur lies in the northern part of the country, close to the Indian border. Famous for its different varieties of rice, for its jute, sugar cane, cotton seedlings and mangoes, it is also famous for its smuggling activities, although at the time of my visit this was not revealed to me. Many of the peasants lease their holdings from richer farmers. However, because of the Zamindari Act of 1952, the vast feudal holdings of these relics from the past have vanished. But feudal attitudes still pepper the countryside and are shown in the way many still defer to those who are wealthier or better educated, or who have powerful relations—whether local or in far away Dhaka.

The sky was overcast and the winter sunshine which I'd grown used to in Dhaka seemed to have disappeared. We drove along the dusty narrow road, bouncing from one pot-hole to the next. From time to time we passed rickshaws swaying along and demon buses sped by us, keeping other vehicles at bay with their ear-shattering horn blasts. The buses are the terrorists of the highways, urged along by their dare-devil young ticket sellers who lean dangerously outside the speeding bus from an open door, hanging on like grim death with one hand, while the other bangs the side of the bus in a secret code to tell the driver when to accelerate and overtake. Often they misjudge and wrecked buses, injured passengers and dead bodies litter the road. Each week scores of accidents are reported in the papers. Vehicle maintenance hardly matters and skilled drivers, prepared to follow such traffic rules as might exist, are in short supply.

A newspaper editorial I'd come across fulminated on the dangers of undertaking a journey in Bangladesh. The editorial, however, neglected to mention that any female passenger, forced to travel alone, found the hazards increased a hundredfold when she stepped down from the bus and became exposed, like a small animal leaving its hole. And the pity of it all was that Yasmeen was so near to home: so close to her mother, Sharifa Begum, only sixteen kilometres away asleep and dreaming of a daughter she thought safe in her bed in Dhaka.

My guides suggested that we follow Yasmeen's footsteps after she stepped down from the bus at Dosh-mile. Dosh-mile Crossing is the dusty, isolated bus junction where Yasmeen arrived at about 3.30 am on that August morning, exhausted after an all-night trip from Dhaka. Half a dozen or so stalls catered to the passing trade. Constructed from bamboo, with rusty pieces of corrugated iron providing some form of roof, they were otherwise open to the elements. Javed Ali sat cross-legged on a small wooden platform inside his *paan* shop, his quick fingers rolling betel nut and cardamom into paan leaves.

'Speak to Javed Ali,' urged my new friends. 'He is an honest man—he will tell you what he saw.' Javed Ali's tiny stall contained packets of cigarettes, opened and ready to be sold one or two at a time, matches, biscuits and a few bottles of coconut oil, all neatly stacked on a few narrow shelves made from packing cases. Two cardboard signs promoted one of his lines as the cigarettes of 'royal taste and satisfaction'. The stall was as immaculate and as ordered as Javed Ali himself, who sat cross-legged, his bare feet tucked under his body, quietly waiting for his visitors from the city to approach. The blue-and-white striped shirt and checked lungi he wore looked clean, no mean feat considering the buses and other vehicles which were constantly arriving in a whirl of dust only to depart ten minutes later in another whirl of dust. By nature he was a neat man, oily hair slicked back, moustache trimmed; the picture of a hard working vendor who put in long hours but seemed quite prepared to stop and talk. People took their time in the country, only the buses rushed by, and even they were usually late.

Careful and deliberate, he impressed me as an eyewitness. 'My name is Javed Ali,' he began. Slowly a small crowd of young men and boys gathered, eager to listen and stare at the strangers—we were the only females in sight. 'My shop stays open twenty-four hours a day and I have two helpers who work on a shift basis. I am married and I have two children. Yes, you can use my information if you wish. I have no objection to that.'

And so he began the story of what happened that night. 'The bus from Dhaka arrived before dawn, on its way to Thakurgaon. The bus supervisor stepped down off the bus with this very young girl and said to me and my friend, the owner of the tea stall over there,' he paused to point out a young-looking man in a singlet and lungi, busily pouring tea from a large tin kettle into glasses for his customers, 'he said to us, "We have brought this girl with us from Dhaka and she wants to go to Dinajpur. Please look after her and make sure she gets on to the right bus in the morning—even if it costs some money". "All right, bhai," we answered, "even if it costs something we'll make sure she gets on the right bus." '

Simple men of the road extended these courtesies to one another. And if you helped a traveller in need, then the day would surely come when your own wife or daughter, your mother or son would also be helped by a stranger.

Javed Ali and his friend Hafizur told the tired girl to sit down. Just before the bus went on its way, a boy got off and told the supervisor that he too was going to Dinajpur. 'Well, bhai,' said the supervisor, 'if you are going there too, please take the girl with you and look after her.'

'Thirty minutes later,' said Javed, 'the police van arrived on its way to Dinajpur. They stopped here and called out to Hafizur, the tea stall owner, "Bhai, get us a glass of water". Then they noticed the two young people sitting in front of the tea stall chatting and called them over separately to question them.'

It was hard to understand from Javed's explanation why the police had noticed the young girl, although he seemed to suggest that some men around the tea stall and the modest 'hotel', an open area where drivers rested on string beds, started to ask questions—wanting to know what a young girl and boy were doing together at this hour of the morning; the police had interrupted, asking, 'What is going on here? What is all this fuss about?'. When they heard the story, they offered to give Yasmeen a lift to Dinajpur where they were headed anyway.

Javed Ali, relieved that the three policemen were offering to give the girl a lift to her destination, believed that Yasmeen was safe under police protection. Looking back, he now recalled that the thirteen-year-old girl had seemed reluctant to go with the policemen. 'Three times they told her to get in the back of the van and she stayed still. They kept insisting and only then did she obey.'

Onlookers who witnessed Yasmeen leaving quietly with the police, and other passers-by, on their way to the mosque to offer their dawn prayers (who saw the van stop twice, eight kilometres or so further down the road) would, in the days to come, play a vital role in telling what really happened, exposing the official lies.

At the crossroads the local people have erected a modest memorial to Yasmeen Akhter; it stands just where she stepped down from the bus. A group of barefoot nine- or ten-year-old boys, who earn money by selling bananas and nuts to the bus passengers, cluster around hoping their photos will be taken. They shoo away the goats nibbling grass at the base of the grey stone memorial and noisily point out everything they think I should know, in words I cannot understand.

Our small caravan moves on its way down the road towards Dinajpur, stopping eight kilometres away where her body was found later that morning. Trees and bushes line the narrow road and further away I can see the school run by the local NGO.

Within a short time of leaving Dosh-mile, Yasmeen died—allegedly raped and murdered by the three policeman who then dumped her body by the roadside. Watching eyes saw the police van make two stops that morning; eyewitnesses swore they saw the police dragging the body of a girl into their van only three kilometres away from Dosh-mile. Curious to see what was going on, they found a sandal, a handkerchief, some broken bangles and blood on the ground—but nothing else. Another group discovered her body about five kilometres further along the way, and noticed that her clothes were torn ... 'Realising they had killed her, the cowards just dumped the body and fled,' said an old man returning from the mosque.

For as long as anyone could remember, the police had been despised and feared in Dinajpur. In a land where corruption is endemic, the local police often behave like bandits; 'They are no better than *dacoits*,' people sneer behind their backs. Corruption is a way of life to them and rich and poor alike feel the police boot on their necks, the only difference being that those with money can buy their way out of trouble.

When the British ruled the subcontinent they fine-tuned their local police force into a tool of colonial repression, and for well over a hundred years this was the way. Since independence nothing much has changed and the police remain alienated from the people, an armed military-style force, housed in barracks.

Corruption is a way of life from the top police down. Everyone knows—even the magistrates know—that if a police officer wanted a transfer to another police station in the district, he would have to pay a sizeable sum of money to someone higher up—not a bribe; simply a 'charge'. How do poorly paid policemen raise this money? By passing the 'charge' on to ordinary citizens, of course. Back in Dhaka, cynical journalist friends would shrug their shoulders when I told them about the Dinajpur complaints. It happens everywhere, they said; this was how transfers and promotions happened. But I remained convinced that matters were much worse in the border town of Dinajpur, for the further away you were from Dhaka, the more you came to realise that law and order could disappear in a puff of wind at any time, leaving the custodians of law and order roaming at large almost like a private army.

'Even to lodge a simple complaint at the station, we all know a fixed rate will be charged,' said the head of a group of local human rights activists. They described incident after incident—

a culture of corruption flourished in Dinajpur and justice came at a stiff price.

The police handled the Yasmeen case badly. Their clumsy, insensitive manoeuvres misfired and ignited the troubled town of Dinajpur. As usual the local administration and the police joined forces to mount a cover-up and rumours spread like wildfire through the town. And still her mother knew nothing. No one had bothered to telephone from Dhaka to tell Sharifa Begum that her daughter was missing.

How did Yasmeen come to be in Dhaka in the first place? Why was she trying to reach Dinajpur by herself that night? There must have been compelling reasons which drove Yasmeen to attempt something which every nerve, every instinct, everything she'd ever learnt as a young girl, told her was wrong and dangerous. I doubted that I would ever learn the whole story for a part of it lay buried somewhere in Dhaka. For a long time these questions preoccupied me: even after I'd left Bangladesh and returned to Australia I wanted to dig deeper. But these were not the significant issues for the local people of Dinajpur, nor for the human rights activists in Dhaka. I had to respect that but the missing pieces bothered me.

For activists, the immediate issues were systemic police violence and the state system which condoned it. And in the months to come Yasmeen would become the rallying point for a national movement, a symbol focusing attention on violence towards women and the ruling government's reluctance to move beyond political rhetoric and uphold the law.

I felt the real Yasmeen slipping away as if she was being buried yet again by the sheer weight of events which transpired after her death. But I kept my concerns to myself—I did not own the Yasmeen story.

✳   ✳   ✳

At around 6.30 am on 24 August the policemen who'd picked up Yasmeen reported that an unknown prostitute had jumped to her death from their van. Meanwhile a village guard arrived at the *thana* (police station) to report the incident quite independently. By now people up and down the road were talking about what they'd seen and the Dosh-mile people had recognised the body as the girl who'd left with the police a few hours earlier.

Three on-duty policemen, who'd taken down the guard's report, went to the scene to fetch the body, accompanied by their senior officer, a Sub-Inspector they'd met along the way. By now it was 10.00 am. Sub-Inspector Shapan conducted an inquest by the side of the road by removing the young girl's shalwar and checking the sexual organs with the aid of a stick. He did this in front of the many onlookers who by now had gathered. The body was lifted on top of a rickshaw cart and left uncovered. The two constables followed it through the town to the Sadar Medical College for what turned out to be a highly irregular autopsy.

In Dinajpur, autopsies are always done exactly according to police specifications. Given their control of the town, it is hardly surprising. 'What has been happening for many years now,' said a forensic pathologist 'is that whenever the police tell us to do an autopsy, they specify the nature of the death for us. They tell us it's rape or suicide or murder and that is what we look for. In Yasmeen's case, we just did the autopsy of an unnatural death according to the police specifications—no more and no less.'

According to the policemen, she had of course jumped out of the moving van. Medical sources confirmed later that the autopsy was conducted with 'surprising speed' by the pathologist in charge. The report found that she'd died of severe head injuries; she also had multiple injuries to her body. No semen test was ever done. As an unknown person her body was handed to a local religious welfare organisation for burial.

✻   ✻   ✻

No-one seemed to know why Yasmeen ran away from her employer's home in Dhaka that day, without saying a word to anyone and leaving all her belongings behind. The well-to-do family who'd employed her told the police they couldn't understand her actions. Neighbours remembered the girl because she had good manners and looked so innocent and cute. 'We took her for a member of the family,' they said, 'because she was always dressed so well.' Newspaper accounts were at pains to stress that she was not ill-treated. Her employers, they said, did not belong to the class of persons who mistreated their maids or saw them as silent robots at their beck and call. Reporters were told, 'We were quite pleased with her. We liked her as someone of the family, so we had her well-dressed.'

But run away she did. After dropping off her employer's nine-year-old son at school in the morning, she returned as usual by rickshaw, and then left four hours later in the early afternoon to pick him up once more. She had been working for the family for a year and the master of the house said that after she failed to return home, he filed a report later that day with the police, reporting that she had gone missing.

Her steps were traced to one of Dhaka's many inter-district bus terminals. More than 800 buses leave each day from the Gabtoli bus terminal, where Yasmeen went to that day and this is just one of nine or more inter-district terminals. City bus terminals are like Dante's inferno; passengers of both sexes often find themselves harassed by transport workers ready to cheat or even assault them. The depots have become havens for criminals of all kinds. Toll extortion by *mastaans* has turned into a fine art. These muscle men collect illegal tolls from private bus companies on behalf of 'influential people', under the banner of various groups of transport owners and workers' associations— gun battles are not uncommon between rival groups. Passengers arriving without tickets may find themselves in the middle of a tug of war by rival caller boys, shoving and pushing the poor passengers to their bus counters so that the caller boy can win his TK 20 commission for long haul passengers. Noise, anarchy, bus fumes and dust are everywhere.

Yasmeen must have wanted to reach home very badly to have braved this bedlam. She arrived at the Gabtoli bus terminal on 23 August with no money. She stayed by the counter too petrified to move anywhere else and entreated anyone within earshot to help her travel to Dinajpur to join her mother and her twelve-year-old brother.

Milan, the counter ticketseller, told reporters: 'She hung around our counter all day asking for a free bus ride. In the evening one of the Thakurgaon-bound bus supervisors took her in, but only on condition that she get off at Dosh-mile, about sixteen kilometres from her home. Every day,' he continued, 'destitute girls come to us and ask for the same favour—they have no money, but they want to go home.'

✳   ✳   ✳

These housewives are decent women. They talk to me quite frankly about their servant problems. They are progressive women, but I sense that somewhere along the way they have become desensitised to the people who work for them.

Preparing for my visit to Dinajpur I am trying to learn as much as I can about the army of workers who toil in the better-off homes of Dhaka.

Lost in the private world of servant and employer, the women talk about a domestic world beyond my ken. The two *Bibi Shaheb* (ladies of the house) sit draped in their beautiful afternoon saris of chiffon, in an immaculately kept garden and talk about the problems of keeping and training good help. Momentarily I have a flash of guilt thinking how Farida would disapprove of the language being used. Farida, Natasha and others reject the word 'servant' as demeaning, a leftover from the colonial era; they prefer 'domestic worker' or 'home help' in their attempts to change attitudes and improve working conditions. Perhaps Farida is right and this change in language is the first step toward ensuring some minimal conditions for people who are without protection, but I remain cynical. Changing the social structure, voluntarily ensuring minimal hours and wages, hardly seems in the interests of the upper- or middle-classes.

Hamida and Roksana chat on about social values and a subclass in society to which they are attached like a lifeline: uncomfortable in many respects but something they couldn't live without. Middle-class Bangladeshi feminists are tormented by similar concerns. They are well aware (well, many of them seem to be) that their own freedom is ballasted by men and women belonging to a sub-class of 'domestic helpers'.

Amazingly, Hamida and Roksana aim their barbs at the so-called affluence of Gulshan and Banani. A world of servants, they said—blind to their own gracious surroundings in New Bailey Road.

'Drivers, ayahs, chowkhidars—the houses out there are flooded with servants,' they told me. 'Each house,' insists Hamida, 'must have about ten or twelve servants and they sit like idlers staring at people who pass by.'

Roksana tells me that because she is a poorly paid teacher, she and her husband can only afford two helpers. 'Beside, servants take a lot of your time,' she says. 'I value my privacy and I don't like them asking questions and gossiping with other servants in the street.'

Hamida on the other hand has ten servants and half of them have been with her for ten years. There is a cook, an assistant cook or 'cooknie' in Binglish, maids for her daughters, a sweeper boy, a boy who runs messages and does odd jobs, two bearers who serve tea and set tables, and then there is the cow herd and another casual boy now on leave. Oh, and of course she forgot the *mali* (gardener) and his assistant. Altogether three adults live at home, with her two married daughters, who live overseas, visiting once or twice a year. 'If I didn't have to entertain my husband's clients,' she says, 'we could do with just three or four servants.'

And these are decent and generous women. They pay higher wages than most, are benevolent with gifts for Eid time, give holidays and never raise their voices. I don't doubt for a single minute that their 'domestic helpers' are much better off than anywhere else.

There are no real laws to protect domestic workers from the whims and idiosyncrasies of their employers. They have no rights, and if their employers wish to lock them inside the house, withhold their pay or beat them—they can with impunity. Salaries range from TK 200 for children (less than US$7) to TK 500 a month for adults (less than US$17 per month). Some child workers receive no money. Generous women, like my two friends, will pay TK 1200, or US$40.

A recent university study by Dr Selim Jahan of Dhaka University reports that 96 per cent of housemaids have unbearably heavy work loads; 80 per cent come from families forced away from their village homes by natural disasters or other circumstances; and 95 per cent don't get fair treatment, eat leftovers and sleep in hot cramped kitchens with no fans. The study also goes on to say that 90 per cent of housemaids are physically assaulted by the mistress of the house and that regular physical and verbal abuse is common. There is also a level of sexual abuse that is frightening to think about. True, there are many exceptions where these workers are treated decently and eat the same food as their employers, where they are looked on with affection and kindness, where their pay is not withheld to ensure they don't leave, but this is not the norm.

Yasmeen was one of the lucky ones, we are told. We are left to imagine then that loneliness, homesickness, some dreadful feeling of wretchedness drove her away. Whatever motivated her, she needed courage to leave. It was the act of a desperate girl, to move alone, to step outside the protection which encircles women like the bangles they wear around their slender wrists. They learn from an early age to stay within this circle for their own good. It is a lesson in fear; a lesson in dependency. Voices whisper incessantly, 'Women need protection. Women should behave decently.'

*   *   *

The opportunity to meet Yasmeen's mother, Sharifa Begum, filled me with a feeling of dread; if the truth be known, I was frightened. Far away in Dhaka it had been possible to keep Yasmeen at arm's length and imagine tragedy. But here in Dinajpur there could be no more conjecture. Playing the voyeur to peer behind the veil of someone's grief concerned me—it shamed me in a hundred small ways I couldn't begin to express. I was not a journalist, I had no training, but I knew I had to do this—I had to probe, I had to ask a mother terrible questions.

We sat in the open in front of a small, one-roomed hut made

of plaited reed walls held together with bamboo supports crowned with a flat rusty tin roof. The interior was small and dark with a stamped earth floor and no furniture that I could see. Two wooden chairs were fetched by a neighbour, one for Sharifa Begum and one for me. Shima, and Razia stood behind Sharifa Begum while her neighbours surrounded her in a semi-circle, a living wall of sympathy, or perhaps they were there to protect her from me.

There is no privacy in a crowded *mohalla* or neighbourhood like this, where people share cooking fires and water pumps, and dwellings are so close together that secrets seep through the walls. At its best, this overcrowding produced a fierce camaraderie and a will to survive.

'I was married off at a very young age,' began Sharifa Begum. 'I can't tell you exactly how old I was at the time, but I know I was a very young girl.'

Seeing her face to face for the first time, she seemed incredibly young—but she must have been in her late twenties, I think. Later when her face convulsed in grief her appearance took on that ageless, universal quality which cloaks women who have suffered unbearable losses. Bangladeshis would describe her as fair—of light complexion. She was slender without being thin and dressed in a pale pink and white sari pulled carelessly around her body.

'A year after my daughter was born, I had a son, but my husband left us; he left when the baby was aged four months and fourteen days. After the marriage was ended I had to earn our living and I worked as a part-time maid for two families. I had to feed us you see.' Her words flowed effortlessly and her voice sounded sad, but calm.

'I put my daughter into school but I was unhappy that she could only study up to class five. I wanted more for her, but I could not afford to keep her there,' she told us. 'So you see, I thought that since I couldn't provide for her properly any more, it would be better if I sent her to work in someone's house.' Her voice broke and tears welled in her eyes, her stoicism crumbled. 'You see, apa,' she said, pleading for understanding, 'she was growing up, she was twelve. I thought she would be safe if she stayed with them.'

She told her story without interruption with only the sound of children's voices and babies crying as a background. She cried and cried, sobbing and gasping for air, but the words never stopped. I had never before witnessed a woman so fixed in grief and anger.

Months went by ... the Eid holidays came and went, but Yasmeen did not return to visit her family in Dinajpur as expected. A worried Sharifa Begum went to see the elderly mother of the Dhaka family who were Yasmeen's employers. The mother lived in Dinajpur and had acted as go-between, arranging for the child to work for her daughter and son-in-law in the city.

What was wrong? Sharifa Begum asked. Almost a year had passed; why hadn't her daughter come home to visit? What did her daughter look like now that she had turned thirteen—had she grown? 'If you just brought her to me for a little while, that would be some consolation. I know she cries for me! She would feel happier in Dhaka if she could see me—she wouldn't cry any more.'

'No,' said the old lady, 'she doesn't cry, she's very well.' She calmed Sharifa Begum and gave her advice. 'It's not as if your daughter is old enough to get married yet. You keep on working and let her stay where she is for now.' The argument seemed to make sense. 'You can keep on saving for her dowry and we'll also provide something when she gets married. Remember, we can make sure she is married into a good home.' Her words played on Sharifa Begum's dreams. 'Your daughter is quite happy. Anyway we are going to Dhaka soon. We will take you with us and you can see her,' she offered.

Saving for her daughter's dowry meant everything to Sharifa Begum: it was the key to her daughter's future and the only safeguard she had for her own old age. Everyone knew maids had a hard time finding 'respectable' husbands; without some kind of a dowry Yasmeen would never find the protection of a man, and they both needed male protection. Respectable husbands for maids were drivers of cars or baby taxis—certainly not a rickshaw driver! Even a mali was higher than the lowly pedaller of the rickshaw cycle; because they often worked for wealthy families, they could bask in the reflected glory.

But for Sharifa Begum, the burden of saving for dowry was not the immediate problem, although it couldn't be postponed for much longer. She began to worry day and night: how could she raise the money to go to Dhaka with the old lady to see her child? The capital city is more than 400 kilometres away and a long, difficult trip. She wouldn't dare set out alone.

'I tried to save the money for the trip but the rent was two months in arrears, so even though I was desperate to get the money together I couldn't manage it.' She blamed herself, she sensed something was wrong, she tried, but she had her son to feed.

She stared at me blindly, tears running down her cheeks, strands of hair plastered to her wet face. With the edge of her sari, we wiped away the tears as she talked; she seemed unaware that she was sobbing steadily, gulping for air—tears, saliva and words mixed together, but not once did she pause, although there were times when she talked more to herself as if in a trance.

'I kept thinking of the child, my thoughts kept winging back to her, but I could never get the money together . . . And then I heard this news,' she moaned. 'I know now that my daughter got on the bus on Wednesday and died on Thursday. Friday passed, but it wasn't until Saturday night at ten o'clock that neighbours told me she was dead.' She found it unbearable that her daughter was dead before she even knew she'd gone missing in Dhaka.

'I ran and ran and I banged on the old woman's door. I told them to open the door, that I was Yasmeen's mother. "Oh my it is you. Come in and sit down," the old woman said. "Your daughter has run away with my son-in-law's driver. This dead girl everyone is talking about is not your daughter."'

'I knew in my heart that my daughter would never run away with a man, she was too young and she would never do such a thing!' The distraught woman asked the family to go with her to the police thana so that she could at least see the body with her own eyes, just to be sure, she said, but they refused. 'So I got a rickshaw on my own and went to the thana.' She arrived there to find a pitched battle taking place between the police and local people—she couldn't get through.

*   *   *

The whole town was in an uproar—thousands were out in the streets. The district people were tired of suffering under a corrupt local administration protected and exploited by local elites and bureaucrats; and buttressed, it was alleged, by a sycophantic local press. No-one, especially the lawyers, trusted the local judiciary system. Justice was expensive in Dinajpur and local people were always paying someone in the hierarchy. On 25 August thousands poured out into the streets, marching and calling for justice for this young girl—nobody knew her name, but they knew she wasn't a prostitute. Rumours spread and there seemed to be rallies everywhere, until finally on 26 August the police opened fire, killing seven people and injuring hundreds. Dinajpur and its 80 000 inhabitants exploded into three days and nights of pitched battles and riots. A three day dawn-to-dusk curfew was imposed by shaken local authorities and the paramilitary Bangladesh Rifles moved in to restore order. The police force was nervous: more than 100 men were transferred and a completely new force had to be drafted in from other districts. After delays, the three policemen accused were finally arrested, but not until after the protests and violence.

There were two sides to the Yasmeen affair: genuine feelings of outrage for a defenceless young girl, attacked and dragged down by those who should have protected her but the 'Yasmeen affair' had also become a symbol of everything wrong with Dinajpur. It was the final straw. After the deaths on 26 August, mobs attacked and burnt down four police stations, the customs house, newspaper offices and the press club.

Frustrated in her attempts to get through to the police station that night, Sharifa Begum was forced to return home. 'The night was endless,' she said. The next morning she continued her search. 'I went from place to place like a madwoman ... I couldn't find her ... and then I saw a newspaper with my daughter's picture, and that's when I knew ...' Four days before she knew her daughter was even missing—five days before she knew that Yasmeen was dead.

Yasmeen's body was exhumed on 29 August and a second postmortem conducted; the first examination, five days earlier, only confirmed that she had died of severe head injuries—no mention of rape. Only now could her mother see her dead child's body for the first time, but even then she had to fight because the doctor wanted proof that she was the dead girl's mother. It took the combined efforts of Razia and senior leaders from the women's organisation who had taken her under their wing to force him.

'What kind of identifying marks did your daughter have? Is

there anything you can remember from her childhood?' the doctor asked.

'I told him she had a crooked nail on her left hand and a long scar on her right hand where she'd fallen down and cut herself once as a child and had to have seven stiches.'

The police released a press statement that claimed the body was that of the prostitute called Banu—they had even called in the local madam to identify the corpse as one of her girls who'd gone missing (later Banu turned up and was thrown in gaol so nobody could talk to her). If a body was not identified it had to be kept for three days, so this ruse enabled them to bury the body quickly. Nobody would care if a prostitute was raped. No need for an autopsy, just a quick burial. They used one of the local papers to print the prostitute story, which is why newspaper offices soon became the targets for the public's anger—even the innocent ones.

'By the time they gave me her body, after the [second] post-mortem, there was nothing left, just the bones, and I couldn't even bury her properly ... How can I still be alive after this? How could any mother bear her child to go in this fashion, without a proper burial, without a whole body ... I can't bear it ... I think about it all the time. I can't find any peace.

'I keep thinking that she will come back. If I could hear her call me "Mother" just one more time; if I could hold her close, I would be able to find some peace, apa.

'All I had were my children!' she cried. 'I had so many hopes ... that my daughter would be here; she would grow up and I would stay with her for the rest of my life,' she whispered. 'And now I spend my life like this ...'

Shima and Razia stroked her hair and tried to halt the tears which rolled down her cheeks. I felt I'd been turned to stone. I had reached a stage where I just could not absorb any more, for my own protection, but I knew I would have to stay and suffer

151

with her because she wanted me to hear her story; she wanted everyone to listen. Her grief was an awful thing, but it kept her alive.

'Then after doing this terrible thing . . . they tried to claim that my daughter was a prostitute! That she was a bad woman! Does that mean that the daughter of a poor woman has no value in the eyes of the law?

'How could this have happened? After I worked so hard to support us, to scrape together our meals; how could such bad things be said about us? Now I finally understand that girls are considered worthless! The poor are considered worthless! There is no justice! There are no laws!'

Inside her there was a spring of hatred that would never dry up. So much time had passed. 'They have been gathering evidence, they say. They have been gathering it and taking it away with them. Where have they taken all the evidence? Why is it taking so long?'

She wanted revenge on the men responsible: she wanted them hanged for the way they murdered her daughter—nothing else would do.

At last she stopped and we were relieved that she'd finally exhausted herself. We embraced and I begged her forgiveness for causing her more pain. Shima and Razia told me that she didn't mind; she wanted people to know, they said.

'I don't want anyone else's heart to be torn out the way that they have torn my heart out. Let that not happen to anyone else,' she said.

'Thank you, madam,' she added in English as I left.

'Who takes care of her?' I asked as we walked away. I looked over my shoulder. Sharifa Begum was still standing by her small hut, gazing after us. She didn't care about the money, she insisted; she didn't care about the compensation. Prime Minister Khalida Zia had already visited her and presented her with a cheque for one *lakh* taka (A$3400) and promised her justice.

Her neighbours looked after her, Shima said. What did she do all day, I persisted, for I couldn't bear to think of her sitting all day long, embracing her pain with no distraction.

'She still works as a maid,' Razia told me. 'She cooks and cleans for a good family; they are kind people and they look after her.'

I hoped that my informants were right: I hoped that they would be kind to Sharifa Begum—for a long time . . .

✳   ✳   ✳

In Dinajpur there were women bereft and unable to comprehend why their husbands were no longer by their sides. The next day I met two young widows. One of them was the wife of Shamu who went out one terrible day to order a cake for his three-year-old daughter's birthday and never came back. He was shot by the police as he stood watching the fighting, or so we think, for no one is sure if he was part of the protest march or not—it seemed unlikely and it doesn't seem to matter anyhow, now that he is dead. Shamu's wife, even after three months, was still in shock—her life was over she said in a dull, expressionless voice; she wanted to die.

Older women sat with her, trying to coax her out of her depression. They told me stories of corruption and violence. 'When police are like wild animals, then only the people can protect themselves,' Razia said angrily.

Everyone who came to watch me talk to the young widow emphasised that the first march had begun spontaneously: no activists, no political parties; just the ordinary people of Dinajpur. In fact so often did people tell me this, including my local guides, that I became curious and even sceptical, until I realised that the government and local authorities had tried to paint the demonstrations, protests and riots as politically motivated. And then I accepted what I had been told: that the early protests were unrehearsed and unprompted, perhaps started by the young men from Dosh-mile who rushed ahead to Dinajpur to tell all their friends of the latest police cover-up, to spread the word about the young girl they had seen—one minute alive and well and then suddenly a broken doll lying by the road. The long road between Dosh-mile and Dinajpur was like a river with ripples of shock and anger flowing from one to the other. One had to know just how deeply the police and the local administration were hated to understand how the crowds would have swollen until the anger and the contempt burst out into open confrontation and finally violence—but only after they were attacked by the police. Obviously, within twenty-four hours however, local leaders did emerge with a game plan and began targeting the press club and the railway station and the local newspaper offices.

But Shamu's wife didn't care about politics, she only knew that her tall handsome husband was dead, leaving her to bring up their young daughter, Shuchana, alone. By all accounts they must have been a striking couple. Shamu's wife was lovely; taller than average, with an expressionless face which if it ever smiled again would be beautiful.

'He went out without eating his lunch.' She was bothered by this. 'He wanted to buy the cake and things for the birthday celebration and to invite friends to come for Shuchana's birthday, she turned three on that day. He never came home,' she whispered. 'My daughter kept asking me "Ma, where has *Abbu* [father] gone? Where has that silly boy gone? Isn't he going to feed me?" You see her father was the one who always fed and bathed her.' Her eyes were dry and the women around her told me, in soft respectful tones, that she was still unable to cry.

'On the Sunday that we heard of his death, it was very strange, but my daughter didn't say a word; she suddenly stopped asking where her Abbu had gone. She must have heard what everyone was saying.' Her small daughter jumped up and down on the double bed, talking to herself. With her shaven head it was hard to tell if she was a boy or a girl. The room was sparsely furnished: the bed, a table, a small television set, a calendar hanging on the wall, clothes hanging from nails in the wall, but it was large enough for the six or seven of us seated on chairs hastily borrowed from neighbours.

'My husband loved me very much; he loved me more than anyone could ever know.' Shima whispered quickly to me that the young pair had been in love since their school days.

'We had a love marriage and I think he would have given his life for me. When I was a little angry or if I missed a meal, he would really pamper me, I can't explain it in words.' She talked about their feelings for one another in a voice that seemed as dead and as removed as her young husband.

'I am now destitute. We had a separate household you know, and my husband hardly left me anything. What he earned was barely enough for us to live on.' I looked around the room again. Compared to Sharifa Begum's dwelling, this house seemed much more solid, able to withstand the vagaries of unpredictable storms and cyclones. Other houses standing nearby were also cement rendered with hard floors; she had not been forced outside the house to work, but still they had lived from day to day.

'When the Prime Minister Khaleda Zia, came to the house, she offered a job. She promised that she would give a family member a job. When we went to the Commissioner to talk about the offer, he said we would have to go directly to the Prime Minister's office.' But there was no way that the PM's office in Dhaka would be open to her—we both knew that.

Photos in the papers showed a compassionate-looking

Khaleda Zia and the Opposition Leader, Sheikh Hasina, comforting Sharifa Begum and the Dinajpur widows. They were pictured placing their hands gently on the widows' heads, in the traditional gesture which means, 'You are under my protection, I will look after you'. Money had been given by the different political parties to those who had lost relatives. This assistance is essential in a country without widows' pensions and other forms of insurance.

'The PM has promised me a cheque for one lakh TK, but she said nothing about justice. I was the one who said that I wanted justice for my husband's death.'

I wondered who had advised the PM to fly off to the Beijing Women's Conference without making any public statement about Yasmeen. Might it have been her sister, the local MP? It was certainly bad advice which came back to haunt the PM, who was seen as callous and uncaring in spite of her quick dash to the northern town as soon as she returned from China. But the accusations were hard to erase. 'She's gallivanting around in Beijing while we are dying in Dinajpur,' people said.

✳   ✳   ✳

The gathering reminded me of an afternoon tea at a meeting of the Country Women's Association. A group of twelve or so women came to the Mohila Shikkha Kendra (Women's Association) dressed in their best afternoon saris with a little jewellery on display, to meet me and to talk about dowry, a major problem for women and their families regardless of class. These women had eased my way in Dinajpur by acting as interpreters and go-betweens. Good solid middle-class women, in their thirties and forties, who ate three meals a day, women with varying degrees of education, the wives of respectable burghers—women with maids and cooks, I thought to myself, now that I was wise to the world of 'domestic helpers'. But as country women, I could also see them rolling up their sleeves and doing work around the place, they didn't have that smooth indolent quality I detected in certain women in Dhaka. Of course Shima proved the centre of attention, as nobody had seen her for so long.

Then Shima explained to everyone present that I wanted to find out about dowry problems. Unreasonable dowry demands often destroyed poor families who could not possibly accommodate them—unlike my present company. 'She wants very frank replies,' she warned them all. Everyone sat up like naughty school girls and tried to look serious.

Jamila's family had been tricked into paying dowry. 'My father never believed in dowry, he always told us it was not Islamic; a Hindu custom which we have adopted here in this land, he said. My husband's family said they didn't expect any dowry—well, that's what they said at the beginning ... When everything was finalised they started acting up. "Remember," they said, "you are getting a boy with an MA. How can you not give him any presents?" Suddenly they were calling dowry, "presents" and dropping the word dowry as if it didn't exist! They wanted a bed, a motorbike, a television, a watch, furniture—the list went on and on. My father wouldn't budge and every five minutes a relative from their side would whisper in my ear how lucky I was to get such a highly educated husband. Every day of my married life I was punished and made to pay for not having a dowry. I finally decided that I could not live with a man like that and I divorced him,' she finished off defiantly.

Another woman, from Comilla in the south, took her turn. 'In my family there was never any tradition of dowry. The husband had to pay the *mehr* or dower to his wife as Islam dictates. So when I got married my husband had to give my parents ten units of gold—yes ten *bhoris* of gold!'

'My father did not give dowry,' said the next woman called Mariam, 'but he gave my husband a motorbike, a watch and a television, because he said it pleased him to do so. He didn't have to do it you know, he chose to give those presents,' she said staring hard at her friends. 'After all I was his only daughter. He made it very clear to the go-between that he would have no part of dowry.'

'Why did everyone laugh at the end of Mariam's story?' I asked Shima. 'Because what she's saying is a very middle-class kind of thing to say,' she replied. 'She won't admit it but her father was really paying dowry. We all know it but some women feel better this way. Practically all of the women in this room have been telling you exactly the same "white lie".'

Everyone is so greedy now, one of the senior women told me. 'They all want these consumer items they see on television so the dowry demands have gone overboard. Families even demand an air ticket for the son to go to Saudi Arabia or Malaysia to be a guest worker—he may stay there for years, separated from his new bride. A father often ends up in the hands of the money lender—he has to put the whole family in debt just to get his daughter married. God help him if he has only daughters and no son. He will sell off a plot of land, his cows, anything—he will even turn himself into a man with only his labour to sell. No wonder that many families say, "Why waste education on a girl? Dowry is expensive enough!" A poor woman can be turned out of her home or physically harmed over dowry matters. At least our families have more money and a name, so dreadful things rarely happen to us, this gives us more protection and we can always go home—we have our fathers or our brothers.'

Now I better understood why many sisters handed over their inheritance rights, granted to them under Muslim law, well in advance to their brothers in return for the right to return home whenever they wished. They were buying a kind of insurance policy.

'But what can a poor woman do? What can she fall back on?' the woman asked me. 'Dowry is illegal in Bangladesh but no-one obeys the law. Custom is stronger than the law.'

A woman who walks alone, as they say—a woman without a husband—is nobody in Bangladesh society. She can only do what Sharifa Begum tried to do.

*　　*　　*

Rijia was the young wife of the rickshaw puller, Shiraj, who was also killed by the police during the demonstrations. She was tiny—tinier than any other woman in the room at the women's centre, the result of chronic malnutrition, a lifetime of never getting enough to eat so that the body never develops to full size. Her bare feet dangled, not quite reaching the ground as she sat by herself, eyes downcast, well away from the laughter and conversation. Although someone put a cup of tea in her hand, no one else at our refined tea party spoke to her and I began to feel uncomfortable. They ignored her not out of unkindness, they just didn't seem to notice her. I pointed this out to Razia and she immediately reacted; the three of us left the room to find a place where we could be alone and where Rijia would feel easy.

She sat down, automatically drawing her thin, worn cotton sari over her head into a dignified position; Razia said that someone was looking after her small baby. Shiraj was a rickshaw wallah, a hard job, for the poorest of men; he leased his three-wheeled bicycle from someone who was better off—almost anyone seems better off than a rickshaw driver.

Watch a rickshaw wallah's thin frame as he tries to drum up the energy to cycle his passengers, or even boxes of broken glass loaded high; look at the perspiration running down his back as he cycles you around in the heat and the wet. Men last ten or twelve years before they are brought down by muscular or respiratory diseases. Even maids don't want to marry rickshaw wallahs . . .

The rickshaw business is run like a taxi industry with shifts and leases to be paid. In Dhaka a man is lucky if he can make TK 120 gross (US$3) from which he pays about TK 40 (US$1.20) a day. Maxwell, the American nutritionist at the Mona Lisa, told me they were so thin and wasted because most have families and they can't afford enough food to give themselves the fuel they need to carry out their hard physical work. They come from the slums and are the victims of river erosion which has left them without their small plots of land or without work—about 1.4 million people are dependent on this industry in Dhaka alone.

Rijia Bewa with three children, married for ten years, who looked fourteen but was really twenty-five, insisted, softly, that the family never wanted for anything. The rent was always paid, there was food—even extra food for the children. 'The last time I saw my husband Shiraj,' she said, ' he was going out to try and earn some money, so that he could buy the day's food for us.'

Razia sat next to her coaxing each sentence from her, reassuring her in Bangla and stroking her arm when she faltered.

Razia explained that they subsisted on what he earned from day to day and that he would buy rice, lentils, a little oil and some spices with the money he'd made that day. 'On 27 August,' Razia said, 'a demonstration had been planned to protest Yasmeen's death. A group of young men had organised this protest to demand justice for the dead girl. The demonstration headed for the police thana: people were angry with the cover up. The events of the last three days had led up to this,' she explained. 'The police took the attitude that this was not a serious matter. "We have seen many cases like this," they said.

All kinds of people joined the march, thousands filled the streets when without warning the police opened fire. Shiraj was shot twice—once in the leg and then in the chest. They say seven people were killed including a small child named Nannu whose body has never been found.'

Rijia said, 'My husband must have joined in because he had a daughter too. He must have thought something like this could happen to her—that they could rape and murder our daughter and get away with it.' The bereaved women seemed to take some comfort from thoughts like this; there was a strong need to make some kind of sense out of their husbands' deaths.

'Did you know Yasmeen at all?' I asked Rijia, through Razia.

'No,' she answered in her child's voice, 'I didn't know her myself, but I know her mother. We both used to do embroidery work at the women's centre to try to make extra money.'

The government had given her some compensation and additional gifts of money were given by the opposition parties, the Awami League, Jamaat-i-Islami and the Jatiya Party. The little widow now owned two rickshaws which she leased out. She sobbed quietly. All this money but at what price? She now found herself in the middle of a tug of war between her own family and her in-laws for both sides had their own ideas of what she should do with the rest of the money.

✳   ✳   ✳

We left Dinajpur the next morning. Two women whose names I never knew came with us to the airport. One was an aging widow with an exquisite face and calm shining eyes. Razia told me she had been a great beauty in her day. The small widow swept and cleaned the women's centre. Without this she would be destitute—her husband and son died long ago in the War of Liberation.

161

Her face comes to with me whenever I think of Dinajpur—it is a portrait of harmony and dignity. The memory stays with me because there are still times when I need to blot out the face of Sharifa Begum.

The second woman was small and dark-skinned and there was something wrong with one of her eyes. Her tiny thin teeth looked as if they would snap if she ate anything harder than rice and dhal. She was badly beaten by her husband; the other women thought it was deliberate, to make her leave so he could live peacefully with his younger, prettier second wife. He took a second wife because the first had produced no children after six years. He would show everyone it was not his fault. Besides he could insist on another dowry from his new wife, he had told his neighbours—perhaps a bicycle.

Meanwhile his first wife swept and cleaned the house of the director of the women's centre. She was starting to gain a little weight and seemed happy without him.

'These women have never been outside Dinajpur before in their lives.' explained Shima.

Never once had they strayed more than five minutes away from the two or three lanes which contained the local stalls and the women's centre. This was their world. Now they sat together holding hands in the back seat and never stopped smiling as they munched on bananas and watched their small world grow larger by the minute.

On our way we stopped at Dosh-mile to say goodbye to Javed Ali and his friends. As we drove off I looked back over my shoulder at Yasmeen's memorial. Three goats were nibbling grass at its base, two buses had arrived and passengers were busily getting off, others were waiting to board while small boys clustered around offering bananas, nuts and sweets.

❋   ❋   ❋

Months went by and no trial was scheduled. After I returned to Australia, friends wrote to tell me about the uneasy calm which had settled over Dinajpur. Everyone was still waiting, they said. The evidence and the mountains of paper are piling up, 'Why are they taking so long?' I seem to hear Sharifa Begum cry ...

Now there is another report to wait for—the official investigative report required by the courts, under the Special Ordinance Against Women's Oppression 1995, must be submitted within 60 days of the incident—150 days have passed; the report is long overdue. Sharifa Begum and the widows of Dinajpur, continue to wait ...

❋　　❋　　❋

On 13 December 1995 a large photographic exhibition to mark Victory Day and the participation of women in the country's cultural and nationalist movements was held in Dhaka. It was dedicated to Yasmeen. I had already left—there was no knowing how long the latest hartal would last, and everyone, including officials at the Australian High Commission, urged me to go before I found myself trapped, unable to reach the airport. Everyone expected the violence to worsen. It was time to make my goodbyes and leave.

Looking back, I have often wondered about my own role in the Dinajpur drama, about how I tried to make some kind of sense out of what was essentially disorder and despair. I had simply wanted to tell the story as best I could. I was angry that this story had never gone beyond Bangladesh, never been reported by the foreign press. Yasmeen Akhter was powerless and 'invisible' to the Western media, with no friends in high places. I tried to resist the temptation to create a moral drama out of a young girl's death and to politicise the grievances which boiled

163

over in Dinajpur. The story did not belong to me, I reminded myself.

Who owns the story now I wonder? Has a mythology developed around Yasmeen's death and has it come loose from its Dinajpur moorings, part of a powerful national allegory, and part of the feminist arsenal against *nari nirjaton*, or violence against women.

While I was there everyone talked about the Yasmeen movement; the anger was still alive and her image was being used to draw attention to police brutality and to fight a police culture from within a state ideology which reinforces, in so many ways, society's strong patriarchal views.

I can understand how necessary it is to change these values when a senior police officer can admonish a group of women at a seminar organised specifically to discuss police harassment: 'Women must be responsible for their behaviour. It is up to them to behave like decent women. They should understand that policemen are in their barracks away from their wives ... Women should know how to behave decently.'

But I am still troubled by unanswered questions and my need to know why Yasmeen ran away from Dhaka that day.

Meanwhile, Sharifa Begum still waits for her answer and her concerns trivialise my own musings and silence me. 'What value,' she pleads, 'does the daughter of a poor woman have in the eyes of the law?'

PART TWO

House of Mirrors

* * *

I once told my mother:
I hate you.
I was proud of my courage
Until today.
Today, my son told me:
I hate you.
My childhood
Flows in my veins
Like mercury.

—Kishwar Naheed, 'Deja Vu'

CHAPTER 7

Familiar Faces

✳   ✳   ✳

I have no memories of elsewhere for I was born in Australia. Yet my Pakistani ancestry is plainly etched in my face and in my skin colour and I grew up listening to Punjabi folk tales, Qur'anic verses and homilies about how girls should, or shouldn't, behave and how sons were the centre of the universe. The tussle between the old loyalties of my father's world and the pull of my own was resolved in late adolescence, so many years ago. I won—but at a price.

In a ritual that we secretly enjoyed, certain questions always triggered off family arguments, some more heated than others, certain topics always led to another round of teasing. 'Two girls equal one boy,' my father loved to say, just to infuriate me and make me yell at the top of my five-year-old lungs, 'No! Two boys equal one girl! Two boys equal one girl!'. But even when child number three turned out to be a boy, called Jon Muhammad, and my father gave up smoking as part of his arrangement with Allah, I never for the life of me understood this preoccupation with boys.

By the time I reached adolescence I'd stopped screaming but never gave up protesting. I wanted to know why men were promised a paradise where nubile *houris*—those young, delightful virgins—danced attendance. 'What's in it for the girls when we go to paradise?' I raged. Now I can smile when I think of the compromises we silently negotiated and I understand how spoilt I was and how my father allowed me enormous latitude. No, I never repudiated my past, but I was definitely more interested in the here and now. My poor father was a failed alchemist, for he could never turn me, his base-metal of a daughter, into the pure silver and gold of his dreams. After another of our circular religious debates, he could be heard muttering to himself, 'This is what happens when you bring them up in this country!' And he was right.

My Australian roots go back more than a hundred years now, for both my grandfathers first settled here in the late nineteenth century on opposite sides of Australia, a Punjabi and a Kashmiri who never knew of one another's existence but who came here with the same dreams. Fortunately they were part of a small band of travellers who entered well before the 'White Australian' policy of 1901, officially known as the 'Immigration Restriction Act'; a sorry piece of legislation and a sad way for a new country to mark its independence.

I had always known that my place in Australia had been determined by an accident of history. And as a child, in the back of my mind, I harboured the feeling that I wasn't really supposed to be here. Finally my identity crisis melted away, once and for all put down in adolescence, when I realised that the Indian subcontinent held no permanent allure for me either, and so I got on with my life.

When I first went to Pakistan with my father, to visit my many relatives, nearly thirty years ago, I felt no sentimental yearning to go back to my roots, just simple curiosity. I had a wonderful time, slaked my thirst for as much family history as relatives were willing to reveal and left it at that. I felt no pressing need to revisit, and then the dark years of the Zia martial regime descended, like a curtain, in the late '70s and I turned away.

For all those years I successfully kept Pakistan at arm's length. My feelings were always ambivalent, and I watched from a distance as Pakistan seemed to lurch from one debacle to the next: a civil war with its Eastern wing culminating in the birth of Bangladesh, the hanging of Zulfiqar Bhutto; the Zia-ul-Haq years, the creeping cancer of the Afghan War with its drugs and gun trade which would one day devastate Pakistani society.

Prime Ministers came and Prime Ministers went: Bhutto the father; Zia the dictator; Bhutto the daughter; Nawab Sharif the Punjabi and yet another hasty appearance by Bhutto the daughter; stumbling through the revolving doors of Pakistani politics. The people in retaliation turned their backs and became an alienated under-class of cynics. The first generation's sense of idealism after the birth of Pakistan was not passed on to the following generations. The relay team had not dropped the torch, but the race had been lost—rigged by the 'judges' no less—everyone suspected.

What a mess, I decided petulantly. But Pakistan refused to go away. And one day my imagination started up, taking over, daring me to speculate about the might-have-beens of my life: if my parents had been wealthier; if they'd sent me to Pakistan to be educated; if I'd agreed to an arranged marriage—my father's dream and my own personal nightmare.

*　　*　　*

Three months had passed since my trip to Bangladesh; it was now March and I was in Karachi. The weather was in the high twenties and low thirties, already in training for the onslaught of summer.

I'd come to Pakistan driven by no particular agenda. There

were no academic research needs pushing me down one particular track, no puzzle I wanted to solve—unlike my visit to Bangladesh. I hoped to gather impressions, meet interesting women and learn from their stories. There were some questions in the back of my mind, but the rhythms of this journey were slower and as usual it seemed more important to ask the right questions than find definitive answers. Admittedly, I was curious to learn at first hand if any advances had taken place under a female PM—the formidable Benazir Bhutto or 'old Iron Pants', as Salman Rushdie wickedly lampooned her in his brilliant satire *Shame*, written in the days when he was free to roam the world. Pakistan, like Bangladesh, was another Islamic country with a female head of government. How did this affect women at the bottom? After Bangladesh I was sceptical. But I hoped that things would just 'happen' as they often did when I went off on my own. I wanted to make friends with Pakistan again after a long absence.

In the weeks to come I would find myself surrounded by images of women whose sense of duty and love of family were overwhelming. These were women I could never imitate, yet women I admired. And I think I envied them their sense of purpose and fortitude in keeping at bay the chaos swirling outside their doors; other aspects of their lives I didn't envy for one moment. Although all societies are patriarchal and in the end it becomes a question of degree, I knew that women's sexuality, intellect and movements were far more strictly controlled in Pakistan than in my own society and I was surprised later to find this premise contested by a number of the middle-class women I met.

And when they looked at me, what did their eyes see? The anomaly of a completely Westernised woman of Pakistani ancestry? Yet the role of half sister–half stranger, sat comfortably enough with me. I knew this intimacy gave me an advantage.

I stretched myself like a lazy cat uncurling from a long sleep in the sun, for the moment happily caught up in a society where I 'passed' as a local: a place where there were so many replicas of myself that I felt dizzy. I only became unmasked when I opened my mouth or when someone spoke in Urdu or Punjabi to me and I was unable to answer. When I grew up in Western Australia in the 1940s and '50s, there were no other Pakistani or Indian families and certainly no government-subsidised ethnic schools where children went to learn the language of their parents. My parents spoke English to one another, an outcome of my mother's mixed parentage; her Kashmiri father's English was poor, but it was the only way he could communicate with her Australian mother of Welsh-Irish ancestry.

✳   ✳   ✳

'How many children do you have?' the curious taxi driver asked on route from Karachi Airport to my hotel. And it was then and there, in the back seat of the taxi, that little Halima Bibi and Abdul Majeed were born.

The family is everything in Pakistan and children, especially sons, are the lifeblood of the family. Sooner or later everyone you meet—even casual strangers—will ask you how many children you have and expect you to return the compliment. All those years ago when I had first visited relatives in my dad's village, my aunts and female cousins were dying to know how many children I had. Children were the mainstay in their lives—it was a very natural question.

'None,' I replied, bracing myself for the next question.

'Why hasn't your husband divorced you?' they asked in amazement.

'How do you know it's my fault?' I shot back. When this was interpreted, everyone collapsed in giggles and there was a lot of metaphorical digging in the ribs and 'tut tutting'. I swaggered around enjoying my image of the brazen woman from the West, until I started worrying about my father's reaction if someone relayed stories about my shameless behaviour.

But that was years ago and now I was older and more pragmatic. A woman travelling alone in Pakistan, especially a woman who doesn't look like a foreigner, is already an oddity. 'Where is your husband?' curious officials may ask you at the airport.

On this visit there would be no doting father to ease the way. I would travel alone from Karachi to Lahore; from Lahore to Islamabad, from Islamabad to Peshawar and then back again; it would be an arduous trip and I knew that the airports were all going to be tough.

So that night when the taxi driver asked me about my children, I made up my mind on the spot to invent little Halima Bibi (my sister's middle names), and little Abdul Majeed—named after my father. Only a small fabrication, I told myself; one that made life easier. How could I expect the average Pakistani to understand that my husband and I were child-free by choice? They were already adjusting to the news of a *ghora*, a white German husband—obviously a bit of a strange customer—who 'allowed' his wife to wander far afield without chaperone or male protector. Why jump on a soap box to promulgate a message to people I would never meet again? To the women I met I would drop the fiction of course, but to the casual once-off strange male, up would pop my two children like characters in a child's pop-up book, and if they asked me for photos—why I would say they were locked away in my suitcase! During the eight weeks I spent in Pakistan I grew rather fond of my two children—little Abdul was so good at cricket and Halima Bibi on her way to a successful medical career. I grew bold and toyed with the idea of inventing grandchildren but decided it was better to travel lightly down the path of deception.

Later that night after checking in at the Holiday Inn Crowne Plaza (expensive, but safe, everybody said), I sat in my room, reading a local English-medium newspaper and eating a bowl of spicy mulligatawny soup, when I suddenly realised that I'd arrived in Pakistan on Bangladesh Independence Day, 26 March. Spread out on double pages were all the congratulatory messages from Pakistan to its former Eastern half. I wondered about the feelings and thoughts behind the congratulations. Was a quarter of a century long enough to erode the bitter memories on both sides? I doubted it. Were the two nations, now separated, reconciled in any sense?

In her 1988 autobiography, *Daughter of the East*, Benazir Bhutto writes that she was too young at the time to understand that the majority province of East Pakistan was treated as a colony by its Western wing; that the army drew 90 per cent of its forces from the west and 80 per cent of government jobs were taken by those in the Urdu-speaking wing. She was too naive and young at eighteen, she confessed, to understand that the Pakistani army was capable of committing the same atrocities as any army let loose on a civilian population; her image of heroic Pakistani soldiers is not the memory that Bangladesh women and their daughters and grand-daughters recall. This passing reference might be as close to an official apology as Bangladesh would ever receive in this century at least, I thought. A woman fighting for her political life would hardly make the kind of gesture that would brand her a traitor; it came as no surprise that her biography only blamed the Pakistani generals for the birth of Bangladesh—loyal daughters tend to overlook the role of politician–fathers when reviewing history and loving daughters the world over can find it hard to see the darker side of the first man they learn to love.

❋   ❋   ❋

'Nobody loves Karachi,' Pakistani expatriates warned me before I left Australia. 'People love Lahore, the bureaucrats adore

Islamabad and everyone feels very strongly about Peshawar, but nobody loves Karachi.' They sounded very maudlin but, as I found out, there is nothing sentimental about Karachi!

Certainly, heat, dust and danger are not likely to attract your average tourist to this mega city of over nine million. Karachi, the country's largest city, lacks the romance of old Mughal capitals like Lahore, or the frontier history of Peshawar. But those critics who claim the port city has no soul—only a strong commercial drive—and is hell bent on self-destruction—underestimate the energy and tenacity of the Karachiites.

Nevertheless, the contradictions are deeply divisive and none more so than the ethnic-political divisions between the indigenous Sindhi speakers and the *muhajirs* or Urdu-speaking refugees (and their descendants) who fled to Karachi, from India in 1947. Their political party, the Muhajir Qaumi Movement (MQM), has been a thorn in the side of the Progressive People's Party (PPP) under Benazir Bhutto's leadership and has been locked in terrorist activities with the army and the police for a number of years. The regional political standoff and violence has become a feature of Pakistani life.

During the time I was there at least, the violence usually associated with Karachi—the political kidnappings, the shoot-outs with the police and the paramilitary forces whose search and siege activities were taking a toll on ordinary citizens—had ceased and there was a lull. Journalists called it a sullen peace. Everyone breathed a sigh of relief for this was the closest to normalcy that Karachi had come in many months. The violent eruptions were never good for business, and after all, that is what Karachi is about. If you want to make money in Pakistan, Karachi is the place to do it . . . so the rich become richer and the poor continue their daily battle for survival against a backdrop of gun-running and drug-trading.

174

✳   ✳   ✳

Karachiites are cosmopolitan and full of contradictions, but I had no idea that the first woman I talked to in Pakistan would belong to a world of sugar plum fairies—a far cry from the feminists I'd expected to meet. Still, I learnt an important lesson that day and it was all to do with class and social status.

Sonya was her name and manipulation was her game. She floated towards me across the lobby of the Holiday Inn and every male head turned in her direction. She oozed confidence and style and I admired her elegantly cut shalwar kameez and the dupatta nonchalantly caught in a little device on her shoulder which allowed it to waft in her wake, leaving her free to wrap the other end around her slim wrist like a 1940s torch-singer. Suddenly I felt glad I wasn't letting Sonya down by staying at a lesser hotel. Hotels like the Holiday Inn were the hub of leisure activities for wealthy Pakistanis and aspiring yuppies. Wedding parties, fashion shows, jewellery exhibitions, seminars and conferences were popular fare and Sonya seemed completely at home as she headed towards me where I sat waiting in the hotel restaurant.

She recognised me immediately she said; it was the sunglasses which gave me away.

That morning I had telephoned one of Karachi's leading news-papers just on the off-chance of speaking to any female journalists with time to spare, when, as luck would have it, Sonya answered the telephone. I wooed her gently with exotic tales of Australia and when I mentioned my address she agreed to meet me for lunch. I had the feeling that she was a little bored and welcomed the distraction.

'I suppose you could call me a spoilt princess,' she said, as she idly flicked through the menu and sneaked a sideways look at me through long, lightly mascara-ed eyelashes. She was very young and spoke English with an American accent picked up during her

175

early adolescence and college years; ten years of living in Chicago, where she let drop, she'd even had her own apartment.

'I come from an upper-class family,' she said and I took it as a warning although she was obviously just educating an ignoramus like myself.

Sonya now conformed to a life which seemed a curious mixture of Pakistani tradition and American modernity, heavily laced with refined doses of luxury and privilege. There were no signs of discomfort or conflict on her petal-smooth face, its pale pink mouth ready to smile or pout on command.

'I love my life here', she said. 'I'm glad my father decided we should return to Pakistan.'

I didn't doubt her for a minute. As they say in some circles, 'What's not to love?'

Sonya worked with a daily newspaper, 'Celebrity interviews only,' she informed me, just in case I mistook her for a run-of-the-mill newspaper hack. Sonya just adored Imran Khan's bride Jemima, but then she was also in love with the British royal family and believed fervently that Jemima was a great asset for Pakistan as she provided, according to Sonya, an 'entrée' to the House of Windsor, 'Jemima may restore our lost pride,' she concluded, looking a little misty-eyed.

An entrée for whom? I wondered.

For the nouveau riche of Karachi and Lahore, generally snubbed and looked down on by 'old money' and 'good families', seemed the obvious answer. Sonya told me that she and her parents had flown to Lahore the previous month to attend a dinner organised by Imran and Jemima Khan for Princess Diana; a simple fund-raising event for 500 guests. Businessmen, bank presidents and their wives and daughters dominated the function. Donors (as they were called) could pay RS 80 000 (US$2500) for a table of eight. Sonya and her mother were disappointed that they could only see the top of Princess Di's head. Thanks to the popular Pakistani magazine, *She*, I knew that the princess had been mobbed as the ladies shoved one another in their rush to meet her at the end of the dinner—queuing is not a Pakistani custom. The reporter had written that Imran's sisters could be heard shouting at the mob of rich ladies to be more civil, but alas . . .

A waiter suddenly appeared from nowhere and solicitously asked Sonya if madam was ready to order. She cocked her head at him like a cheeky sparrow, wound a shiny black curl around a lacquered nail and wondered—just wondered— if she might not have a grilled cheese sandwich (which wasn't on the menu); it was the only thing she could possibly eat, but it had to be grilled, not toasted, and it had to be cooked in oil, not ghee. He fell completely under her spell and spent minutes telling her how he would personally tell the chef exactly how she wanted it made; how he would supervise its hatching. He walked away in a daze, quite forgetting to take my order, but as the slighted older woman would eventually pay the bill (and his tip), not his twenty-year-old pin-up, I knew I could wait for my revenge. *Patience is always on the side of the older woman.*

'You're flirting with the waiter,' I said. It was meant as an observation, but sounded like an accusation. 'It's the first time I've ever seen that in Pakistan,' I told her.

She smiled back at me—did I detect a note of pity? Her face flushed delicately. *How good it is, to wield such power*, it said. Then she told me very seriously, 'Oh, but there's a way of flirting in Pakistan which is permissible you know.' I didn't, but then I'd not had much contact with the upper-classes before.

Sonya, as I said, was a strange mixture of modernity and traditional custom all tied up with a privileged, satin bow. 'I'm so lucky; my fiance's so broadminded,' she sighed. It was a phrase she used repeatedly. 'I'm so lucky: he's so broadminded and he's a stock-broker! Our marriage is arranged. I'd never met him before, but he's so cute!' Her wealthy parents had insisted on choosing her husband-to-be, and Sonya had acquiesced readily, putting her bachelor-girl days in the USA behind her, never doubting that her parents would make the right decision for her.

'He's not a relative then?' I asked her, knowing that cross-cousin marriage is often the case in many families, although I wasn't sure if this was the case with people from Sonya's background.

She pulled a little moue of disgust. 'Ooh!' she cried. 'I couldn't! How could I marry any of the boys I played with when I was young? The boys I caught frogs with when we were just kids? They are like brothers. I couldn't French them,' she said.

'I beg your pardon?' Had I heard her correctly?

'I couldn't French kiss them,' she explained once again.

The collision of cultures was starting to give me a headache, so I changed the subject by asking her about wedding palaces, the large, garlanded, brightly lit reception houses I'd seen on my way from the airport. 'Is that where you'll hold your wedding function?'

'Oh no!' she said, laughing at my faux pas. 'Those commercial wedding palaces are used by the middle-classes, even the lower-classes. It's the only way they can ape the glamour of our upper-class weddings, you know. We rent hotels or public gardens for *our* affairs.' She flicked an amused look in my direction and I felt gauche and terribly middle-class.

I learnt many things over lunch that day. For instance, Pakistan I was told, had 'the richest beggars in the world'. When I disagreed, saying that it sounded like a denial of national poverty which after all was well documented, Sonya didn't take offence—instead she changed her mind, a habit of hers I found disconcerting. 'Yes, we are into denial,' she nodded and neatly closed the door on that conversation.

I tried my best to lure Sonya into a discussion about the kind of influence Pakistani wives wielded in their day-to-day lives; what say they had in important decisions to do with their own lives and their family's welfare. I was skirting around the question of power, not wanting to use it in the Western sense of the word. It seems to me that there are two different ways of looking at power, status and male–female relations. One stems from a white, often middle-class framework and causes problems when applied gratuitously outside its own historical and social contexts. The other way is diverse, complex and bound up with the constraints of feudal and traditional power structures and the shrugging off of a colonial past.

'Who decided that you would go to university? Who agreed that you could have your own apartment? Who arranged your marriage? What influence did your mother have in these decisions?' This was the information I was after.

'My mother's different,' she answered, neatly sidestepping my questions again. 'She's economically independent and my father respects that. He knows that if he hadn't agreed to go to Lahore with us for Imran's dinner, my mother would have gone anyway—with her brother.'

It was no use trying to explain that this was not the kind of decision I'd meant, I thought to myself, and then I suddenly realised that Sonya had given me an answer after all. Freedom of movement and removal of social walls were important considerations to women, no matter what their class.

She hesitated. 'You really need to meet my friend Majida, editor of the women's supplement where I work. I guess you'd call her upper middle-class,' she said.

Within half an hour we were in Majida's office. I knew straight away that Majida was a 'modern' woman because she wore a sleeveless tunic over her shalwar—one hardly ever saw bare arms in the workplace. The office was full of fashion-conscious young women working at their desks, answering the telephones (English was the language of choice), editing stories on their computers. Sonya quietly slunk away, promising to pick me up later.

'What influence do wives have? That's an easy question to answer,' Majida laughed. She was dressed in crimson and orange with wavy black hair down to her shoulders. Sonya had told me that Majida knew every socialite worth knowing in Karachi and Lahore.

'Take my mother for instance, now she's turned manipulation into an art form—she always gets her way,' she cried out in a sing-song voice.

Although I kept my expression carefully under control and stayed quite stumm, she sensed my disapproval. Suddenly, she swivelled her chair around to face me, flung a hand dramatically in my direction and began to harangue me.

'Look, if I'm presented the cake on a bloody silver platter of course I'm going to eat it! I learnt this by watching my mother,' she said loudly. 'You should see her when my father walks in the door. She starts running around; she takes off his shoes, does the pipe bit and of course, when she wants to go out later that night, he can't refuse her. "The poor woman," he thinks, "slaving at home all day." He really believes this even though we have six servants!'

Here was my introduction to the art of 'how to control your man' as practised in Pakistan, and it wasn't learnt from the pages of women's magazines, but passed down from mother to daughter. The 'unofficial manual on manipulation', learnt by women of all classes, was full of cunning contradictions. Women everywhere have to struggle with their feelings of respect and contempt.

Rule 1. Treat your husband, brother or father like a god;
Rule 2. Play the ideal wife and behave like an obedient and submissive wife or daughter;

Rule 3. Never forget the 3 Fs—food, sex and flattery, for after all, your husband–god has feet of clay.

The next day a friend from Karachi University elaborated further on how upper middle-class women used the art of psychological and sexual manipulation to influence their husbands.

'Oh yes, this is very typical,' she said. 'Women from this group will use themselves as objects—they see themselves as objects and of course they don't denigrate this: "That's what we are and that is where our power lies."

'They keep themselves beautifully dressed, they pose and they posture and sometimes they use sexual manipulation for really important things like getting education for their daughters. I know of one such case,' said my friend, 'where the wife is married to a feudal and she's used everything in her power—and I do mean everything—to get her young daughters (one girl is five, the other seven) out of the *haveli* into a boarding school in Lahore.'

The haveli, a feudal institution in rural areas, is the women's house where upper-class women, young and old, live together and in the past rarely left its walls. In many ways it's similar to the Arabic notion of harem. The haveli is a part of purdah, and a woman simply vanishes from public sight, leading a life of modern luxury but intellectual and sensual deprivation.

'At first I thought she was cruel to do this to her young children,' the university woman said, 'but now I can understand how desperate she was to get them out of the haveli. All their relatives kill themselves laughing (behind her husband's back of course) at how she's engineered it, but it was all she could do. She was an air hostess, so I suppose she knew a bit about how the world runs.'

'Knowing how the world runs.' It seemed to me that women everywhere were socialised to use their beauty or their sexual wiles while they could, like Eve on her poor unsuspecting Adam (did Eve also perform an emotional juggling act, keeping respect and

181

contempt spinning in the air without dropping one or the other? I wondered.) The promotion and commercialisation of women's bodies through beauty contests, the catwalks, movies, video clips, magazine covers and advertisements is such a part of Western culture that we are becoming blasé: turning a blind eye and pretending exploitation isn't there any more, because supermodels are managing their careers like canny business-women.

Of course even career women in the West are hardly immune to using sexual manipulation and have been known to 'flash the thigh' when the need arises. I once knew a public servant working in the equal opportunity area in Melbourne, a charming intelligent feminist who, if things were not going her way at any meeting where men were holding forth, would deliberately take out her compact and apply a thick coating of glossy red lipstick. She usually swung the meeting around to her point of view.

In Pakistan and elsewhere in the region where the female body is not an obvious or celebrated part of popular culture, women who feel they have no other choice or whose self-esteem is intrinsically damaged (like a hairline fracture that you can hardly see) will use sexual manipulation, quite literally, with a vengeance.

❋   ❋   ❋

Female journalists seem to thrive in Pakistan, unlike Bangladesh where female journalists are usually found clinging to the edges of their profession. From the columns of their papers and the pages of their magazines, Pakistan's regiments of brilliant women journalists expose the hypocrisy and indifference underlying patriarchal values which we are supposed to believe are 'protecting' women.

Razia Bhatti, often described as Pakistani journalism's brightest star, fought for human dignity and freedom of the press. No-one was immune from her pen: from Prime Ministers Zia to Benazir

Bhutto, she exposed human rights violations, corruption and misuse of political power. During General Zia's rule and his tough laws governing press censorship, Bhatti was the architect of the 'blank space'. While she was editor of the *Herald* magazine (1977 to 1986) pages were left blank where she had been forced to pull stories, and readers soon got the message. The government then moved to ban blank pages!

When she resigned from the *Herald* on a matter of principle, most of her female editorial staff walked out with her. They set up *Newsline*, Pakistan's leading investigative magazine, and went on to win numerous national and international awards.

I had looked forward to meeting Razia Bhatti and was stunned to learn when I arrived in Karachi that she had died ten days earlier, aged fifty-three. I sat leafing through one obituary after the other, not knowing what to do. For the moment I postponed my visit to the *Newsline* office.

When Razia Bhatti was setting up *Newsline* she came to Zuhra Karim for advice and support and the two became firm friends.

Zuhra Karim is a feminist and a powerful woman in her own right—the idea of *her* running around with pipe and slippers in hand is comical. Karim is the owner and editor of *She*, one of the oldest women's magazines in the country. An expensive (RS 60 or US$2 per issue) English language glossy, *She* appeals mainly to middle-class urban women. Upper-class women are more interested in Western fashions and designer jewellery and purchase the far more expensive imported Italian, French and American magazines. *She* promotes serious women's issues such as women's health or religion and the role of women, as well as the usual fashion and cooking. The magazine has been around now, she told me, for about thirteen years.

'Men read *She* magazine too,' Zuhra said, 'the younger men like to look at the models.'

The local models are stunning and the traditional garments they wear with just a hint of 'Western decadence' seem right out of a Mughal storybook. Bejewelled, with pouting red mouths and averted eyes—no wonder the men are bewitched!

Zuhra sat back in her office chair, perfectly at ease amid all the noise of the printing presses at work just next door, and led me through the last thirty years of the women's movement in Pakistan. 'In the 1960s,' she told me in her precise British English, 'we had the All Pakistan Women's Association or APWA as we call it. Many of these veterans are in their sixties and seventies now, but they did a lot of the hard spadework, and were involved in the Pakistan Movement before Partition, and later, pushing for reforms like the Muslim Family Law Ordinance when Ayub Khan was president in 1961.'

There is a story that after the women marched up to Parliament one day, urging Ayub Khan not to give way to the conservatives who opposed his reforms, he gave them this advice. 'Be kind to your men,' he said. 'You don't know how scared they are.'

It seemed to me that Pakistani women spent a lifetime being kind to their men.

Fifteen years ago I had read about APWA and from a distance followed them into battle against the Islamists. Because the Qur'an cannot be legitimately challenged, many members relied on defeating the obscurantists through *itjehad* (creative interpretations) of the Qur'an—it always reminded me of the father–daughter arguments we had at home when I was growing up and I grew very fond of APWA.

At about the same time as I was discovering APWA, I'd also familiarised myself with the Women's Action Forum (WAF), a nationwide coalition which took to the streets and defied Zia and his Islamisation program in the '80s. Zuhra was a foundation member of WAF. I felt excited at the chance to meet women I'd admired for so long from the other side of the world who were still struggling to get repressive laws repealed, like the Hudood Ordinances 1979, a set of presidential decrees passed by Zia when he was in power.

These new laws changed the Pakistani Penal Code to the detriment of women. The law which affected women the most was the Zina Ordinance. The charge of *zina* punishes fornication or sex out of wedlock, including adultery, prostitution and even rape. Any woman courageous enough to bring a charge of rape in the first place can find herself being prosecuted for adultery or fornication. As part of his Islamisation process, Zia tried to introduce new legislation in which the testimony of two women became equal to that of one man's, as accepted under Shariah law by some less liberal schools of law. But under public pressure the Government was forced to drastically modify these laws on testimony. 'Two girls equal one boy,' says my father's voice jokingly from the past, and I remember that even a five-year-old girl knew that it was wrong, and must be resisted.

Today half the women prisoners in Pakistani gaols, according to a recent Amnesty International report, are there on charges of zina. They may be arrested and held in prison with their children awaiting trial for years without any evidence being produced. Men find it expedient to bring false charges against their former wives, daughters or sisters to stop them from marrying against their wishes. A favourite way of humiliating or taking revenge on your former wife, if she remarries, is to accuse her of zina. There are hundreds of cases where the husband has divorced his wife verbally and then failed to register the divorce with the local courts as required. The wife, thinking she is divorced, remarries, and then the husband gleefully turns around and charges her with adultery! The law requiring him to register the divorce stipulates no time limit.

But in March 1996, Pakistan ratified the United Nations Convention on the Elimination of All Forms of Discrimination against Women, Article Three. Did this mean that the government would repeal the Zina Ordinance?

'You must remember,' Zuhra cautioned me, 'that the Convention was ratified with the reservation that no provision which conflicted with the country's Constitution would be adopted.'

I was later to learn that Bhutto, who clung to power through a coalition government, had no way of gaining the two-thirds majority she needed in parliament to repeal or amend any of these ordinances, even if she had the political will to do so: her government was weak, the changes controversial and her popularity waning. Most women activists believed that she wanted to, but was powerless to effect change.

Zuhra told me that WAF was no longer as strong as it used to be. 'The organisation always had trouble getting down to the grass roots and now, of course, we have this NGO thing.' She paused briefly to speak to one of her editors who'd knocked on the door. One quick sentence and the problem was solved.

'This NGO thing.' I thought about the phrase. One of the differences between the women's movement in Pakistan and Bangladesh seemed to be that Bangladesh had gone down the NGO road fourteen or fifteen years earlier than Pakistan. The situation of destitute Bangladeshi women in the aftermath of the 1971 war had been one reason; Bangladeshi middle-class women had rallied, foreign aid had poured in quickly and an organised, ongoing, local women's movement had taken off with NGOs providing the infrastructure, the international networks and the funding for programs which concentrated onimproving women's lives economically. I felt that Bangladeshi women were far more collective, less self-absorbed, in their approach.

Pakistani women, on the other hand, were more inclined to the academic or theoretical, or to work at changing repressive laws and introduce systemic change. The catalyst for Pakistan's women's movement had been through its own organisations like APWA and WAF. Then had come the Afghan War with the local *mujahadeen* (freedom fighters) fighting the Soviets and in the mid '80s, NGO funding had poured in to help Pakistan cope with Afghan refugees.

'WAF has lost part of its appeal,' said Zuhra joining me again and taking up the thread of the conversation, 'because NGOs are much stronger and can specialise. In Pakistan, everyone's busily doing their own thing.' She paused and gave me a candid look; she was deciding whether or not to invest more time in her visitor. I tried to look worthy.

'When Benazir Bhutto first came back to Pakistan some years after her father's execution, WAF asked her to agree to a Women's Manifesto and we did the same with other parties. With one or two minor exceptions they all signed up.

'But what has been done over the last five years? What has been done for women in this country since 1988?'

I took this as a reference to Benazir Bhutto, as 1988 was the year BB won her first election. Benazir was often referred to as 'BB'—or 'Big Ben' because of her height and her pompadour hair style which delighted the country's cartoonists.

'You're going to discover many things while you're here in Pakistan,' she warned me. 'You've probably already discovered that this country is totally disillusioned with its politicians. We don't expect the government to do anything for us any more, therefore each organisation concentrates on doing its own thing. At least that way you may get something done!' Her comments were sombre, there was none of the optimism of Bangladeshi activists.

Before I left *She* headquarters, Zuhra presented me with a special back edition marking the forty-ninth year of Pakistan's independence.

'Don't look at it until you reach your hotel,' she said. 'You'll understand, I think, why my secretary monitors all my incoming calls,' she laughed.

As soon as I read the feature article I understood. Forty-nine women were selected by *She* to mark the forty-ninth year of Pakistani independence in 1996. The magazine had drawn together a 'Who's Who' of the women's movement in Pakistan; a gliteratti of female activists and I wouldn't have been in Zuhra's shoes for a minute! For every woman honoured, another twenty must have felt slighted—along with brothers, fathers and husbands. Selecting forty-nine women seemed an impossible task for there were so many brilliant stars: intense, intelligent, determined women.

Benazir Bhutto was there of course, so was the animated face of the late Razia Bhatti side-by-side with Hina Jilani and Asma Jahangir, the two famous human rights lawyers—sisters whose names were synonymous with defending minority rights ... I flicked through the pages ... the list continued, and then the name of Nafisa Shah appeared.

Nafisa Shah was the woman I was going to meet the next day, the *Newsline* journalist who'd exposed violence against women in feudal Sindhi society. Her special investigative work into *karo kari* murders three years earlier had rocked urban society in Pakistan.

❋ ❋ ❋

Newsline's location was one of the best kept secrets in Karachi. Considering their tough style of investigative journalism and the enemies they made, it wasn't surprising to find them hidden away in a lane with no name, in a house with no number. Three trips were necessary before I finally tracked them down: three nerve-wracking trips, where friendly shop keepers gave my drivers different directions. If only I'd persevered with my own investigations and looked beyond an innocent-looking herd of goats I would have found them a lot sooner!

Nafisa Shah had the impudent look of a woman who would dare almost anything, but there were two sides to Nafisa Shah, I discovered: the city face and the traditional face she put on when she returned to her rural town in central Sindh.

Nafisa's city face was lean and hungry with a broad expressive mouth outlined in dark, dramatic lipstick. We sat virtually on top of one another in front of her desk crammed into a corner of the busy office—there wasn't room to swing a cat. Papers and files littered every surface—desks, chairs, the floor. Out of this chaos came the quality monthly investigative journal which had won numerous international awards. She introduced me to her colleagues as they trundled by. Yesterday they had put a new edition to bed and were all feeling relieved that they'd managed, in spite of their editor's sudden death, to keep on working and continue her tradition.

'People call you the karo kari expert,' I told Nafisa. She grimaced and put her hands over her ears in mock horror.

'Karo kari' (literally 'black') was linked in my mind with honour killings—that was all I knew.

'There's nothing new about these so-called honour killings,' she began. 'They've been going on for hundreds of years camouflaged as ordinary murders. After I uncovered my first story of ritual killing, *Newsline* put out a cover story, in January 1993.'

The village of Khaipur Juso near Larkana still talks about that gory night a year ago when a young Baloch woman nine months pregnant was hacked to death. A young man of the Channa tribe had gone to visit a friend in a neighbouring Baloch village. The friend welcomed him, told his young wife to cook a festive dinner for the two of them, and asked Channa to stay overnight. The next thing Channa knew was that the woman's uncles suspected him of having a liaison with his friend's wife. Channa ran back to his village. The woman had nowhere to run. She asked a lorry driver on the road to take her away from the village. The lorry driver refused. As though driven by intuition, she hid in the graveyard. Her uncles brought her back the next day, collected all the village women, gave the young woman water to drink and just as she was about to drink, chopped off her head with a kulhari. The poor husband helplessly watched his wife being butchered to pieces. The uncles forced the husband to swear that he was the killer and had him sent to jail for murder. The Channa tribesman had to pay two lakh rupees in protection money to save his life.

Nafisa Shah, *Newsline*

'Karo kari,' Nafisa explained, 'is a Baloch tribal tradition which is now practised by feudal Sindhis and Punjabis living in the tribal belts. The dice are heavily loaded against women since the accusations are always made by men who are the custodians of power in the feudal set-up. The killers take pride in what they have done, the tribal elders condone the act and protect the killers and the police connive in the cover-up.'

The ritual has apparently survived all the legal, political and ethical developments of the time and is now a convenient cover for all kinds of murder.

Nafisa was totally immersed in her work and was used to briefing neophytes like myself, who wandered into the world of karo kari and wandered out again, while she remained behind absorbing stories which still had the power to anger and upset her even after years of listening, years of interviewing grieving families.

'Men get back at their enemies by killing their own women and then accusing their opponents. Killing a woman can also help you out of financial difficulties,' she said, and told me about a case where a man murdered his eighty-five-year-old mother, calling her a kari, and then demanded 25 000 rupees which he badly needed from the man he accused of being karo.

There were so many excuses for disposing of women and making a profit.

'The only hope for a woman is if she can claim sanctuary in the *kot*, or house, of the *sadar*, the lord,' Nafisa said. 'She is given refuge till the tribal court pronounces its verdict. But in most cases, of course, even if cleared they dare not go back to their families and become the property of the sadar. If they are lucky they build a new life for themselves, but the stigma of being a kari remains.'

I was horrified by the obscenity of what she was telling me. Why had this been hidden for so long? I felt my throat tighten. I was beginning to sound strident.

'There's a sharp line between urban society and rural society,' Nafisa explained patiently. 'There's always been an urban bias in our media and when the media did take up rural issues, there was little understanding of these cases. It was just seen as a husband murdering his wife, you see. And of course in rural society it was a part of life. Men killed women because if women were subversive then they had the right to kill them.'

The background din had faded; I concentrated on what she was telling me, focused on her eyes and her voice, trying to comprehend the level of contempt for women underlying this kind of practice, and I wondered at her perseverance in the face of so much cynicism.

'And if a man kills a woman it is always a private matter,' she told me, 'because it happens within the four walls of the home and is always hushed up—a family problem not to be discussed in public. Even when, now and then, they were reported, the headlines were always shown as "MAN KILLS WIFE FOR ADULTERY!" The ultimate sin for a woman is extra-marital sex.' Guilty or innocent, lower-class women pay the price; it does not affect middle-class women.

Nafisa had exposed the karo kari murders by lifting them out of the 'MAN KILLS WIFE FOR ADULTERY' context.

'I focused attention on the custom which provided the space for these killings to occur.'

'How could people be so blind!' In the back of my mind I remembered that the Prime Minister's home province was in Larkana in central Sindh.

'In the rural areas people have always known,' she said soberly. 'In one sense there is nothing new in what I'm writing, but then again, even the regional press never thought of extracting it and writing about the custom.

'But in Sindhi literature you find mention: in short stories and in plays. I come from an area where it's quite common and I never knew, because it was so secluded and as women in the haveli, we were so protected from what was happening outside. I think my first exposure happened when I watched a short teleplay. I saw all these men screaming "Kari! Kari!" and descending with axes on a woman.'

We stopped for the customary tea, the ritual of politeness and hospitality, turning our backs for a second on the ritual of honour killings. When we resumed our dark discussion, Nafisa reminded me that karo kari was a tribal custom, not a feudal custom.

I couldn't restrain my curiosity. 'There are so many customary practices which need changing, Nafisa. Why did you choose karo kari?' My words sounded clumsy and perhaps I was wrong and karo kari had chosen her.

'It was the sheer brutality of it,' she said simply. 'There are customs which are dangerous and deeply entrenched, but the brutality of karo kari paralyses you, and then I heard of a case which still haunts me.

'A seventeen-year-old girl eloped with this boy and they married, but they were brought back forcibly by the traditional court system. In matters like this the families prefer to have it settled by village or tribal heads or feudal lords. They think it will do more harm to their honour if they go to the courts. The mullah is not involved because it is not a religious thing.

'So the couple was brought back on condition, said the court, that the girl's parents promised they would not harm the girl. Well, it was the last day of Ramazan; she was fasting of course and her uncle came with other men and he just chopped her in front of everybody . . . they took her young husband away and held him prisoner. They still swear they will kill him.

'Now the uncle is out on bail, walking around freely. Of course there were witnesses and he could have been tried and convicted. There's a rumour that police were bribed.'

I asked her where the problem lay.

'I don't think the courts are so much the problem,' she answered. 'There are cases the police have registered and the courts have taken them up but—' and she paused, stabbing her forefinger in the air, '—witnesses will not testify, so it becomes a matter of evidence.

'The women's families worry about their honour. They will be called *beizzat*—without honour—for the rest of their lives. The men say it is their right . . . it is so deeply rooted and it happens within an honour system which justifies it.'

I asked Nafisa how she found her stories. Once you started, she said it wasn't difficult. 'There was heaps of material around. But before everyone just looked at the crime and not the custom. I remember talking to a friend, who told me, "In my area it happens several times a month". And when I went there the stories were so strong.'

Nafisa had unmasked karo kari for everyone to see, but what was the next step?

'You need the State to take it up. But here you have a problem. What can the State do?'

For a moment I heard Zuhra's voice, 'We don't expect the government to do anything any more . . .' she had said.

Nafisa continued, 'When my story first came out everyone was horrified, but there's been no action, no public condemnation of the custom nor any government action against it.' She sighed. 'The only difference is that now you read more stories about it in the press.

'It's so entrenched. A policeman said to me, "Karo kari is big business now. You can solve any of your problems, any fines that you get under tribal law, by killing a wife or a daughter on charges of adultery or fornication".'

There were so many instances where customary laws were in direct confrontation with the secular law of the land. Pakistan had the laws in place, but it was a question of implementing them. People in the rural areas accepted the customary laws (some called them 'living laws') and how did you change this acceptance? It seemed unlikely that the regional or central governments would be interested in stirring up social unrest. Both assemblies were full of politicians with feudal backgrounds.

Nafisa didn't know the answer and neither did I. 'Even if you make laws you are not going to stop men from killing women,' was her bleak comment.

'And then you have the international media,' she cried, and I immediately noticed the change in tempo. 'When they fly in to cover a story, what they do is sensationalise our experiences, because they take them out of context. They never do enough detailed research to place it in a balanced perspective,' she complained. 'It is not how we would like to write the story, but they have a different angle and they are only interested in looking after their own audiences. They may even say that karo kari is an Islamic practice. For God's sake it is not!'

But now an NGO called Sindhiani Tehreek was trying to start a campaign. In the last fifteen months, they reported, 246 people, including 148 women, were murdered in the name of karo kari in the Sindh province alone.

'When I ask the tribal people, "Why do you do this?", said Nafisa, 'they say, "What can we do? We are caught in a trap; we are not educated and this is our tradition." They say to me, "We have hot blood, we are not like you. Schooling and education, it makes a coward out of you and so you think twice before doing this, but we people are dogs and in an instant we take up an axe!"'

'They actually call themselves dogs?' I couldn't believe it!

She quickly corrected herself. 'No, but their womenfolk do . . . There are also men who want to change this custom for they are also a prisoner of this system. A man comes up to a husband and says "I saw your woman talking to such and such a man". And if the man doesn't kill his wife or his daughter or his sister, or do something, then he has no honour, he has to live without honour for the rest of his life.

' "Murder is not murder if you do it for honour," they say.'

'Everyone I meet tells me that feudalism is the curse of Pakistan,' I suggested.

'It's such an empty term,' she answered sharply. 'I see feudalism in the urban areas, in people's mind sets, in the way NGOs are run. I see it behind the whole notion of power and wanting to dominate and rule; it hides behind property issues and industrial settings. It's more than landlords with big landholdings. I see it everywhere.' She shrugged her shoulders and I grew quiet.

'I come from a feudal family that is middle-class in an economic sense, but politically powerful. As a journalist in Karachi I have personal freedom, but when I return to my family, I am only a degree better than my cousins in the havelis. I still hide from strangers that come by, so I live in two worlds. At work I am myself, but at home I am a feudal's daughter. I dress differently—I put away my jeans and put on my *chador*. As soon as I move into the shadow of my family's circle I observe the standard of behaviour and dress which is part of that.'

I wondered if haveli women were able to influence the passage of their lives or the lives of their daughters.

'Even now,' Nafisa said, 'I move between two worlds. You expand in the city and then you visit your home and your whole world shrinks. But changes are happening; men have realised that economically it is sound for a woman to come out and take up traditional jobs like teaching and medicine. My own haveli has changed a lot.

'Look at Benazir,' she said and for an instant she seemed to brighten up. 'She comes from a haveli family, although her family is an example of a very modernised feudal–industrial family. But if you look at her father's first wife, BB's step-mother, why she is like any haveli woman! An amazing woman; marvellous, but still a victim of that system. Bhutto, as a young man, was forced to marry her; it was a cousin marriage again, and then he found another wife for himself who could relate to him mentally, was more attractive, more of a companion. But his first marriage is very typical of the upper-class and the middle-class. He didn't divorce his first wife because she brought a lot of property with her,' she explained sagely.

Nafisa looked up to Benazir. 'I don't see her as an agent of change for women, I admit, but when I go into the rural areas and I ask the women, who will you vote for? they answer Benazir. "Why?" I ask them. "What has she given you?" They say, "We want nothing, but she is a woman like us." I agree some of her measures have been cosmetic but she is such a tremendous role model and even the fact that she is voted for by men gives you a powerful feeling when you go to meetings and the men are all cheering for her—a woman! Yes, I like her because she's a woman—and then of course she's a Sindhi, like me.'

CHAPTER 8

Anarkali Tales

* * *

People may snub Karachi, but who can resist Lahore? For nearly a thousand years, Lahore has been the capital of the Punjab, land of the five rivers and the most fertile, heavily populated province of Pakistan.

But the key to Lahore lies in its Mughal history and the city exhales the romanticism of the past. How the Mughal emperors loved their fountained gardens and their palaces! Emperors Akbar, Jahangir and Shah Jehan all favoured Lahore.

And then came the British who built for longevity and their own Empire, with India as the jewel in the crown. The empire has gone, but their Gothic-style structures remain standing and people still murmur admiringly to themselves, 'Those damned British knew how to build!'.

In Lahore there is a love story people remember. It's a legend not as well-known to the outside world as Shah Jehan's love for his wife Mumtaaz, expressed in the Taj Mahal, but a tale which still holds all the elements of a royal tragedy.

The story is about Anarkali, or Pomegranate Blossom, and the Emperor Akbar's son, Prince Salim, later called Jahangir. Legend has it that the dancing girl was buried alive in a wall as punishment for daring to love a royal prince. Anarkali's tomb, built in 1615, bears a mournful inscription said to have been added by her lover Jehangir. Today the name Anarkali is associated with a thriving bazaar close to the tomb.

But if you are looking for a different introduction to Lahore and the Pakistani way of thinking, one not found in any of the guidebooks, you need only watch the lines of traffic pass by: cycle-rickshaws jostling for space next to horse-drawn tongas and yellow top taxis showing off their dents and scratches like wounded warriors; donkey carts locked in combat with BMWs and Corollas. Nobody gives way. Everyone wants to be first. This is the Pakistani character—this is the Pakistani way. Yet Lahoris know how to enjoy life better than anyone else in Pakistan. Time is their friend—almost a relative! They live to eat, shop and talk politics. The city is also famous as the location where Imran Khan—Lahore's most famous son—has built his community cancer hospital, the Shaukat Khanum Memorial Trust Cancer Hospital in memory of his mother.

Lahore is the intellectual, educational and cultural centre of the nation. About five million live in crowded Lahore and there is always something to do, places to go and be seen. Life has been good to both the upper- and middle-classes in Lahore.

✳   ✳   ✳

I met a woman, an attractive woman in her late forties with short, reddish tinted hair, and a habit of lifting her chin and staring at me as if we were on opposite sides of the room which gave her a strange unfocused look. Her voice was low and her words swift and hard to decipher although her English was flawless. But while the words poured out, she was holding something back and I worried that I might have been there on sufferance, but I was wrong, it wasn't impatience or disinterest or even wariness on her part; the greyness hovering overhead was something else.

Ayesha Saeed swallowed her words like she swallowed her rage and I wondered why a well-educated, successful woman from a progressive family, who seemed to have everything, was so obviously unhappy and so intent on locking me out.

A friend of a friend had brought us together. Smart women in Lahore 'did lunch' and networked with all the aplomb of professional women. The Pakistani upper middle-class in Lahore is affluent and sophisticated with a self-assurance stemming from the best education money can buy, post-graduate qualifications from prestigious institutions and a feeling of belonging to a city famous for its culture and history. These attributes make them a formidable lot: an impressive crowd of women and men who can hold their own, I imagine, in almost any forum in the world.

Outwardly at least, the women I met seemed very sure of their place in the world. They were far more Westernised, certainly wealthier and better educated than most middle-class Bangladeshi women. They wore their material accolades like garlands—there were times when I felt like a country cousin surrounded by glamorous relatives, lurching around from one location to the next, forever dependent on the 'kindness of strangers'.

We sat together in Ayesha Saeed's office where she said we wouldn't be disturbed. At first we discussed neutral topics, and like a good little foreigner I listened to a potted history on Pakistani television. Ayesha still remembered the ten golden years of television in Pakistan, as she called it, between 1967 and 1977.

Ayesha was a senior script writer and also a well-known author of children's stories. Forty years earlier her father had been in the diplomatic corps and she had spent her infancy in Malaysia.

I asked her what kind of impact General Zia's policies had on television. To my ears it sounded like a fairly neutral ice-breaker. Start slowly, I warned myself, don't frighten her away.

'We had twelve bad years with Zia,' Ayesha answered, 'and there were certain rules which had to be obeyed. Nothing appeared on television that could be interpreted as anti-Pakistan, anti-Islam, or vulgar or obscene. We were hemmed in by stringent guidelines and government censorship. Women were mostly out of sight and if there was a working woman, she was always someone who neglected her children, or ignored her husband—definitely a bad woman, no two ways about it,' she told me in her flat, rapid monotone. She paused for a few seconds and gazed at a spot on the wall above my head. I waited for her to refocus.

'Women didn't disappear from the screens but even the news announcers had to cover their heads and ads were scrutinised for any signs of "indecency". Women generally became more submissive.' She looked at me and then looked away again, and I wondered if I offended her in some way.

'Then in 1988, BB won the election and I think that's when the policy towards women became pro-active. Today everyone is talking about women—all our women's programs focus on awareness, education, health—and everyone is talking about how women are suffering. In practically every drama, you find a woman in the forefront—she is the power and it is almost becoming nauseating!'

Now that made me sit up, and I noticed that she seemed to be waking from a long sleep, changing into another person right before my eyes. 'It's not real any more,' she continued. 'This is not the real picture outside. TV is trying to undo all those twelve years of the Zia regime which is not easy and it can't be done overnight! It's almost propaganda, and I worry that it will produce a backlash eventually,' she finished off and for the first time we made eye contact.

Her outburst puzzled me: her response was the opposite of my Bangladeshi friend Shireen, who struggled to get stories of strong dissenting women broadcast without the censor's guillotine coming down hard. Didn't she think television could shape attitudes and set up role models, I asked her. Couldn't it act as an agent of social change?

She lifted her chin and frowned at me. 'There is no way you are going to break down feudal barriers through talk shows,' she scoffed. 'Let's be frank. We are talking about breaking taboos and customs going back hundreds of years. It's madness to think you can transform society just by putting on soaps and dramas with "feminist-correct" plots. I don't think TV is going to bring about any revolution or any evolutionary change in this country. Television can be socially critical, but it has to be real and if the courts are dishonest it must show the courts as dishonest. Too often,' she said, 'too often in Pakistan, television is used as a propaganda tool.' She went on to tell me that Pakistan had two government channels and a third private channel in which the government held a large number of shares.

'What happens now, goes something like this: the PM sends down the word from all high, telling us that television news and programs are currently overdoing their criticism of policemen in Karachi; "therefore no policeman in any TV play can be shown as corrupt". Now that's lying,' she laughed bleakly, 'now that's dishonest!'

There was no holding her now. She had suddenly realised she could open up to a stranger: a neutral party who would soon pass out of her life. The remote, unfocused woman I'd first met was gone, and in her place sat this intense woman, showing signs of an angry disillusionment that left me baffled.

'The other day one of our directors was charged with showing unnecessary violence because he did a play about a family held hostage by masked men. Now we all know this happens every single day in Pakistan,' she told me and her mouth turned down at the corners. 'But the play was stopped in mid-air. You may disagree,' she said, 'but I don't find this very different to what was happening in Zia's day. In those days we had to weigh up every word very carefully, taking care to watch how it could be interpreted. Inside you all the time a voice is saying "this is wrong; this needs to be said". This is just as bad as in Zia's time when no figure in a drama, nobody wearing a beard could be corrupt, because men with beards were all maulvis and ...'

I cut in, 'and everyone knows—that all maulvis are pure of heart!' We were sharing a joke at last?

'Yes,' she finished off, 'and negative characters were always Pakistani men wearing Western clothes.'

Movies she dismissed as an escape for poor people—only the lower middle-class or the lower classes went, she informed me, and when I asked her what a ticket cost she said she had no idea. 'We all prefer to watch real movies,' she said, 'on our VCRs.' I understood that real movies meant Western movies and not Indian or Pakistani offerings.

'Ayesha, how does it feel to be a woman in Pakistan?'

She wasted a few moments lining up the pens and paper clips on her desk, before answering me. I caught her eye as she looked up but she refused my half smile. Suddenly she began speaking very quickly in a low voice to the door behind me.

'I hated being a woman in the twelve bad years,' she answered, 'but it's better now. Until Zia took over in 1977 I never felt any different; I never felt I was discriminated against—and then almost overnight, one was made to feel different.'

The reasons for my own 'on-again off-again' love affair with

Pakistan were partly based on images I didn't want to face, although I'd kept up with my reading as a form of punishment for my cowardice. Pakistani women were the first casualties of Zia's puritanical Islamisation programs, with which he tried to appease the religiously-based political parties; a time when he beat back the advancing women's movement to a position from which it has still to recover. Attacks on women in public increased during this period. Despicable actions like hitting women who didn't cover and spitting at them suddenly became honourable, even patriotic. Men and women acting together under WAF's banner took to the streets in protest. They marched against the repressive Zina Law and they resisted lathi charges by the police.

Paradoxically, the anti-Zia agitation gave the women's movement a focus which I think it has now lost. The organisations still exist, individual women warriors fight on, but the days of street power and politics, of marches and confrontations have disappeared. Did the activists expect everything would change overnight simply because there was a woman PM? Whoever I spoke to seemed too politically astute for that.

Where have all the fighters gone? Some women have been co-opted to work with government, others are busily writing, while many have channelled their disappointment and gone their own way into the warm burrows of NGOs, as Zuhra Karim, *She* editor, would have it. Others may simply be resting between engagements, grooming daughters and nieces for the next wave.

'I grew very angry in those twelve years,' Ayesha told me, 'even though I belong to a family which is liberated and emancipated—and so is my husband,' she added almost like an obligatory afterthought, 'but sometimes I feel that in spite of all this progressiveness, inside every Pakistani male there is a conservative feudal lord. Absolutely—no question about it,' she insisted when she saw my raised eyebrows.

'I mean they will allow their wives to work and stand next to them, have their own lives and be professionals, but at the end of the day, it is always *she* who asks *him* how his day has gone.'

If that was the definition of a feudal lord, then the whole world held nothing but feudal lords.

The legacy of the Zia years seemed like a noose dangling overhead waiting to punish women growing up under the shadow of oppressive legislation which even to this day—nearly twenty years later—has not been amended or repealed by successive governments. Zia is dead, but the anti-women laws he created and the climate of female repression which blossomed have surely infected, in hundreds of ways, the behaviour and thinking of a younger generation of men who grew up in these times. A horrible thought struck me—many of this 'lost generation' were the sons of earlier feminists, women now in their forties and fifties, and many of them were also the husbands and brothers of younger women. The repressive Zia years meant that an entire generation of Pakistani men might have been affected by the State's ideology towards women. How could they have been unaffected? Western education was no talisman against discrimination and the Pakistani educational system reflected conservative views. The laws showed that women were not equal to men and man-made feudal traditions used Islam to hold on to their power. Everyone knew Pakistani parliaments were dominated by feudal–industrial interests. Relinquishing power and ruling in the interests of everyone was not an outstanding characteristic of feudal landlords—if so there would have been massive land-reforms long ago in Pakistan.

As if she could see read my thoughts, Ayesha said, 'I know my sons are good young men, but I know they have changed. Psychologically they are not as liberated as the generations before them; I know there are psychological scars. And it hurts me a lot to hear what they say. Their attitudes are conservative, they've lapped up a love of material values at an abnormal speed and I have the feeling that I'm fighting on two fronts.

'Please don't judge the normal Pakistani woman by me, or the likes of me,' she begged. 'We are freaks—pioneers if you like—but we are women who are unhappy, I think, because we are ahead of our times.'

'Would you describe yourself as an elite woman?' I asked.

At times I wondered why I persevered with this question. Nobody ever saw themselves as elite but I always found the reaction interesting and lived in hope.

'I would describe myself as an avant-garde woman, a woman born before her time,' she corrected me, pursing her lips. 'I have lived through some exciting times and I have lived through some horrible times. I have seen the golden period of Zulfiqar Bhutto; I've seen the terrible martial law periods of Zia and then the return of democracy, but there are too few women like me. Look at the silent majority of Muslim women and you will find their lives have not changed very much. But then again when I ask my seniors from the Partition time, those who struggled for Pakistan fifty years ago, when I ask them if they've seen many changes they say "Oh God, yes".'

I was inclined to agree with Ayesha and not her older friends. The changes her friends talked about—who were they benefiting? There seemed to be two worlds: one world for the rising middle-class, in towns and cities, and another world for the majority, a world which never changed for working-class women in the cities and lower-class women in remote rural towns and villages. But these two worlds had one thing in common: they demanded that women be decent.

I told Ayesha a story about a class of young girls I'd met the day before at a college run by APWA.

They looked like a flock of flamingos, I recalled: shy, delicate and neatly dressed in white cotton uniforms with pink dupattas around their shoulders. We talked about their studies and their aspirations, about arranged marriages which they all seemed to approve of.

Their teacher, who was hardly older than her charges, confided to me, in an aside, that she had married a cousin and was very happy. My mind went back to Sonya of the French kisses and the frog chases and I told her that some people believed there was no mystery in cousin marriages. Her face flushed and she hesitated, making sure that none of the girls could overhear. Romantic nonsense, she said, quietly but firmly. Sounding wise beyond her years she told me that the boy who played games with you when you were nine was different from the man who looked at you when you were eighteen.

They allowed me to take a group photo before I left, but I couldn't persuade them to smile or pose naturally. It was that typical poker-up-your-backside, Victorian kind of stiffness that you see everywhere in South Asia.

They won't smile, I complained to their teacher, and by now I'd tried every trick in the book. No, she answered very seriously. People might think they're not decent girls.

Ayesha nodded sympathetically; we were friends again. 'It's a great weapon, this decency thing,' she agreed. 'And of course, restrictions are put on girl children and on women who are always told "it's for your own good". Now a lot of the time I face that restriction too,' she confided—and at last she began to reveal the root of her unhappiness.

'My husband isn't happy when I come home after five pm and the unpleasantness that ensues isn't something to look forward to. "It's for your own good," he says, and I think he really believes it, that he doesn't see how much is imposed on me—on women generally—all in the name of protection.

'Decent women don't do this, decent women don't do that!' she chanted. That distant look in her eyes started to return.

'What will people say?' I knew the song by heart and it was

my way of letting her know that I understood and that there was no need to cut me off again.

'This restriction is with you always; they use it like a weapon.' Her eyes clouded and I could see she was revisiting some unpleasant scene from the past. 'Even women like myself who come from progressive families face this. And it requires an inordinate amount of determination—even ruthlessness—to break through. You have to become an out-and-out radical, almost an outcast in many cases—and that is very painful for us,' she almost whispered, 'how can you turn away from your family, your conscience?'

I kept quiet. I didn't want to upset her by suggesting that the family held the power to ostracise the rebellious one—not the other way round as she implied.

'Day after day, I face that.' She looked at me bleakly. The composed professional woman had retired and in her place was a lonely woman tired of fighting those who loved her.

'In Pakistan,' she said, 'a woman has firstly to live with her father, then with her husband and then with her sons. I was lucky to have had a father who placed no restrictions on me; now I have a husband who does place some restrictions on me and then there is my eldest son, who for all my attempts to bring him up progressively, this son of mine, places restrictions on his wife and keeps her completely under his control. He is a man with a tremendous amount of insecurity in him,' she finished.

And, I said to myself again, part of that generation of males who saw women through Zia's eyes—no matter how liberated their mothers were, they were infected.

'Hanifa,' Ayesha said. 'You will hear a lot of talk about violence as you visit other places, but can you understand that I consider myself violated if my husband restricts me? Can you understand how that leaves scars on my psyche?' She bit her lip, she wanted understanding. 'When my son frowns at me and says don't do this, I feel it is a violation of my human rights, that it is the same as being beaten and it is impossible to bear.'

Now when I think back, I sometimes feel ashamed because I don't think I gave her the understanding she wanted. I stopped playing the neutral party she had a right to expect.

'But Ayesha,' I said, 'surely there is a difference?' Perhaps I was still caught up in the horrors of karo kari, but I felt she had the resources and the freedom to choose, tough though the decision might be. 'Your maid, or the woman in the factory or in the village is uneducated and totally dependent. You make the decision to stay when you could go—you have the money, you have the job and the qualifications. You could fly out of this golden cage you're talking about.'

For a minute she smiled at me, a weary 'if only you knew' kind of smile. 'You look Pakistani, but our worlds are very different, Hanifa.' The village woman was a lot freer, she said, because she didn't have to worry about protecting her family status—this wasn't ingrained into her consciousness—she didn't come from a 'good family', was how she put it. 'They don't have to hide things—they openly fight like cats and dogs, while I am held back by an ingrained feeling of having to protect my family name, knowing that everyone is watching me—a woman from a "good family".'

I was sitting in the office of a woman whose walls were studded with awards and commendations, talking to a professional who'd just won a prestigious writing fellowship. I couldn't help but feel that Ayesha's worries about her background and status made her toe the line when she'd rather not. Somewhere along the way she had made the decision to stay in this arrangement when she could have left, or at least negotiated some additional space. I tried to express this to her, but even while I was uttering the words I tasted their glibness, the tart edge of smugness on my tongue.

But then I thought back to all the Bangladeshi women in the villages I'd met, who stole their education from their husbands; who confronted the conservatives and the extremists and won—and those who lost and faced dreadful penalties. I thought of the Pakistani women struck down by karo kari. The rural women might not have to worry about their family's precious background, but my God, they had to worry about the murderous aftermath of their men's so-called honour being brought into play! Women from the lower classes had to worry about being falsely accused of zina—or adultery and rotting in prison with their children beside them. The bars of the golden cage Ayesha complained about also protected her from any of these extremes and for a second I felt angry with her—couldn't understand why she seemed blind to all of this. I was sorry later. I should have been a sister, not a stranger.

As a sign of faith I asked her to give me more examples of what she meant, why she saw her suffering as more intense than a village woman's.

Ayesha went on to tell me anecdotes about her friends and colleagues who suffered in silence, who put up with their husband's mistresses; women who felt hemmed in, women who were doctors, engineers, businesswomen: women she said who were vocal, who were leaders, seen by their peers as progressive elements. There were clothes she wanted to wear, places she would like to go, changes she would like to make, but—she was paralysed because she came from a 'good family'.

I listened. Many of the concerns she raised were faced by women everywhere—Western women too—the kind of balancing act which women perform fairly adroitly, even if resentment makes them drop a ball occasionally (or hurl it at their partners' heads). I still thought her dialogue seemed peppered with uncomfortable petit bourgeois concerns which couldn't compare significantly to the life and death issues of other women.

'If I want to sleep separately from my husband,' she complained, 'I can't do that because there are servants in the house and they will talk. I know it's artificial, but it means I'm not free. Now a man couldn't care less if he's talked about—part of his Punjabi feudal attitude I suppose; if he's seen with another woman and people gossip he can strut around feeling proud. Now there is no way I can walk out and go and stay at my mother's for a week.'

'Tell me, what have you got to lose?' I begged her.

She paused, my question surprised her, 'I don't know ... it might be admitting to myself that it isn't working, that I'm not satisfied. But you see that's what I mean. My group never vocalises it; we never show it. Maybe we are not conditioned to breaking the mould.'

'Is it fear of the unknown? Fear of ostracism?'

'Yes, yes,' she said quickly. 'What makes me think that life outside marriage is going to be any better? Making it as a divorcee here is very tough—it's an awful life. You'd be surprised at the spiritual unhappiness that comes from women you think have everything: the cars, the house, the social life ... we try to keep the facade alive.'

Suffering in silence also seemed a very British thing to do and it led me to wonder about Pakistan's colonial heritage, a part of its history one couldn't ignore. Most of Ayesha's progressive women friends were brought up in semi-Western lifestyles and educated overseas. They found it hard to talk, even to one another, about their emotional injuries, she said. Some women also kept their marriages intact because it suited them; even if the marriages were boring and conflict-ridden, they had their creature comforts. We agreed that this was very true of wives everywhere.

'How do husbands and wives resolve personal differences?' I asked.

She stared at me as if I was mad and then she laughed loud and bitterly. 'In Pakistan, my friend, it's either an argument or a fight. We don't have the kind of rationality where you both sit down and discuss marital problems or solve slight disagreements. The servants hear everything and the wife is pitied while the husband is seen as a "real man". Now and then you say "to hell with it all, I don't care"—at least your body language says this—' she qualified, 'but if you stay in that kind of situation it means you have buckled down ...'

'A good family.' Now what exactly did this mean in Pakistan? Sooner or later it emerged in everyone's conversation. BB came from a good family, but I knew it wasn't always synonymous with the feudal class; Imran Khan came from a good family but I knew cricketing prowess wasn't a prerequisite ... *Horror of horrors! Was it possible that by these standards that I didn't come from a 'good family' a la Pakistan?*

Ayesha told me, with no show of embarrassment, that the meaning came from the Urdu expression '*quibbla drust*'. 'Praying in the correct direction' was her translation, singling out people who are following the right direction in their lives: someone who comes from a family that doesn't have any scandals attached to it and that is also properly educated. It doesn't have to be a PhD; the value a family places on education is shown by their attendance at a good solid educational institution like Aitchison College, the alma mater of Imran Khan.

'Probably if you trace them back a few generations,' Ayesha said, 'you'll find they were regarded as good people, never corrupt; honourable people who contributed to the Pakistan movement before 1947. They may have been Muslim League politicians who wouldn't compromise at the time with the British or the Indian Congress Party. They are also seen as being politically stable—meaning they've followed a consistent political line and not changed horses in mid-stream for self-gain.'

'And what,' I asked her, 'are their attitudes to women?'

'Their women don't observe purdah to that extent,' she answered, 'and these families don't consider it is such a dreadful thing if their women are professionals. But then again some families have progressive ideas and others do not, so it's hard to generalise. Overall a good family comes from good stock and you must be able to look back for at least a couple of generations.

'Now, I have a friend,' she said. 'She comes from the nouveau riche; a woman who is on her way up and has just been appointed politically to a high position and you turn around and say, "My God! Where does she come from? What is her family background?" and you realise suddenly that you don't know the father, you don't know the mother and obviously you don't know anything else that goes on! So she is not from a "good family".

'Yes, I come from a good family,' she answered my unspoken question. It was a fact and nothing could change it, unless she stepped outside her circle of protection by causing scandal in some way and I imagined there were a hundred ways of doing just that. But I could not imagine Ayesha breaking her 'slave bangles', leaving everything behind her to go in search of a greater personal freedom—the cost was too great. Her family gave her a sense of belonging that nothing else did. Feelings of suffocation and frustration pulled her down; they were the price she paid for the emotional security she couldn't live without. There is no substitute for the family in Pakistan.

✳   ✳   ✳

Bushra Sadiquie felt privileged to be a Pakistani woman and to be part of a family system which gave her so much confidence. 'I'm proud to say that I never dated my husband although I met him at work,' she boasted. 'Two years after I'd left the company, he telephoned me and then a few months later on the phone, I suggested to him that we get married—provided our parents permitted this, of course.'

Bushra was a Harvard College graduate whose father could just afford to send her to the USA. Fortunately he believed that investing in a daughter's education was worthwhile. 'His friends said to him, "What are you doing Sadiquie Sahib? Wasting all this money on a girl—she will be married soon".'

During her Harvard years she promised herself there would be no parties, no kicking up her heels, no drinking alcohol at the college wine and cheese soirees and she kept her word. Her husband came into the room and I met this well-mannered, quiet, curly-haired young man whose mother was English, she said later, and who obligingly took their two children into another room leaving us in peace.

Bushra, the liveliest woman I'd met in Pakistan so far, was very engaging. On closer acquaintance, she seemed a woman of action rather than reflection.

She was the first woman I noticed who pulled faces and shrugged her shoulders, who used her hands and was not self-conscious about her body. Her habit of stabbing a long graceful finger in my face to emphasise her arguments was less endearing, although I admired the spirit behind the movement. Other young women (she was in her late twenties I judged) were far more dignified and self-conscious with newcomers—certainly not given to bold physical movements—but Bushra told me she'd been brought up differently and in her youth climbed trees, flew kites and played badminton and took up karate at her father's insistence, when she was older. This explained why she seemed so at ease with her body and not trapped inside the graceful, yet passive stillness I'd observed in other young women to whom physical activity was a stranger.

Bushra believed passionately, that 'Western society' was a failure and had nothing to offer Pakistan as a social model. The high rates of divorce and illegitimacy, the drug taking—her list was lengthy—the way society was geared towards the individual's happiness and not society's happiness as a whole, convinced her.

'I have seen the destruction of family values in the West,' she insisted, pushing her hair out of her eyes. *She made it sound like the rise and fall of the Roman Empire.*

There is a Pakistani culture outside the home which influences how people behave, especially how men behave. 'You can't blame the West for everything, you know,' I said defensively.

She shook her head vigorously. 'Look at countries like the USA; the countries meant to inspire us. Tell me how many women have been head of government in those countries? You don't find women in our country working as secretaries, office cleaners and sales girls! Hanifa,' she entreated me, 'I've been to the USA, I know what the women are like there. At college those girls live for one thing only: at the end of the day, all they want is dinner and a date. Western women are very unhappy. These are countries much richer than Pakistan and if with all their laws, education and material wealth they do not feel secure, why should we go down that road?'

What on earth was I doing with my back to the wall? What I really needed was a pistol to my head!

There was no way I could convince her that positive change for women had occurred in countries like Australia and that legal reforms and attitudinal change had improved life choices for women substantially, although there was still a long way to go for marginalised groups at the bottom of the hierarchy. Control of reproduction, control of sexuality, of personal space and movement, control of resources—she dismissed all of these and I began to wonder if there was some kind of denial at work making her reject the problems around her.

Bushra was right to question overseas models which were often accepted uncritically, as if they held all the answers, but to close her eyes to the lives of rural women which Pakistani activists spoke of as depressing because so little change was occurring, seemed strange.

She also felt very indignant about societies which provided free health services and social justice programs. This was not the business of government, she announced, but the province of the family, and charitable, philanthropic organisations. The welfare state, she said, was a threat to the family and its Islamic obligations.

Had she been to a Republican Women's Convention during the Reagan–Bush years, I wondered? Is this what she picked up at Harvard?

I found Bushra full of contradictions. 'In Pakistan,' she said, 'the dignity of a woman is to serve as a mother, as a daughter and as a wife or sister or daughter-in-law. She must be humble, self-sacrificing and never demanding. I have even seen women in villages criticised for drinking milk. "She drinks milk", they say, "she should leave it for her children."'

Was she agreeing that these were ideal qualities?

'Now I have a model in my head, Hanifa, a way to keep the family from disintegrating. It should be absolutely mandatory,' she declared, waving her finger in my face once again, 'mandatory I say, that a woman with children should not be allowed to work—she must stay at home.' She paused while I struggled to digest this. 'But she would have financial independence because 50 per cent of her husband's wage would go into a separate account. This would be a law—after all she is sacrificing her career, and her time.'

I found it a strange mixture of ideas although I approved of the idea that women should be paid for working at home.

215

'Mandatory for a woman to stay at home,' I repeated, 'Don't you think you've just violated a fairly basic human right?'

'Then I don't care about human rights!' she cried. By now she was sitting on the edge of the sofa, a beacon of righteous energy. 'It is the role of the woman to be with the kids. I believe that every woman has the power to change her husband if she uses the right method. He will adjust his thinking if he sees that his wife only disagrees with him on one point—doesn't have too many differences of opinion and tries to please him in everything else.'

What a waste of a Harvard MBA!

She promised we would come back and discuss these problems later. But of course we never did.

'I expected to continue my work after we were married,' she said, 'but as soon as I had a child everything changed. I had to fight with my inner feelings and sit at home for four years. I was terribly unhappy.'

'My husband is wonderful,' she protested when we moved on to talk about husbands. By now we seemed to disagree about everything so perhaps she thought I intended to attack him personally. Bushra bounced back. 'Like most Pakistani men,' she rallied, 'my husband hands over his pay packet and I manage all of the finances.' There take that! She waited for my response; the smell of battle filled our nostrils—we were starting to enjoy our differences.

'Most Pakistani men?' I echoed. 'Bushra, darling, I can't believe that for a moment! Your husband's an angel, but the pay packet business!'

'Oh yes,' she insisted bravely, 'the majority of Pakistani men do that.'

'The majority of men who live in villages don't have a pay

packet to take home,' I argued, 'and the majority of men do all the shopping for their wives anyhow.'

Later, just to make sure that Pakistan hadn't changed in the last twenty-four hours, I asked other women. They looked at me and laughed. The next time we met, I passed on my information (a little smugly, I admit), but I could tell Bushra remained unconvinced.

'My husband is wonderful,' she repeated now, changing the subject. 'He's kept a fulltime man to help me in the office I run from home; I've got a very expensive nanny and a very expensive cook—all of this is being paid for by my husband. And when he comes home at night, it is a pleasure for me to take off his shoes and socks and put on his slippers. I do this out of love.

'When I told him I wanted to start a marketing business, he said, "Do you really want to do this?" and when I told him yes, he said, "All right then, but I'll engage a man to go with you to the offices". He did this so there would not be any gossip about me going by myself to offices where I would be dealing with men.'

'A decent woman shouldn't go into a man's office?' I ventured and she nodded back.

'You know, Hanifa,' she said, very earnestly and very sweetly just before we parted. I hadn't expected a final attack and she took me by surprise. 'Here in Pakistan we have this expression, "I am the Queen, I am the Rani of my house!".'

'I'd rather be king of the road,' I fired back. No, I hadn't been the ideal visitor. Perhaps I envied her the cook, maid, driver and personal assistant after all.

The weeks went by as I travelled between Lahore and Islamabad and as I moved from place to place, I began to recognise something I started to call 'the middle-class syndrome'.

✳   ✳   ✳

We lounged around, talking hour after hour in my room at the Continental Guest House, sandals off, feet up on the bed, drinking lime and soda while she chain-smoked. She had recently returned from the USA and seemed to be having trouble settling in again. Azra became my confidante.

With her short dark brown hair, and the muted olive colours she favoured, she had a style all her own. She drove her car wherever she went, unlike most of her friends who always had their drivers on hand.

'People don't see me as being an authentic Pakistani woman any more,' she told me, 'even other women activists think I've been overseas too long. I'm too Westernised, too independent, too critical and at first I used to get very defensive—even apologetic—but lately I've stopped. There are others like me who've travelled around and seen the world, and I don't see why we have to apologise—the women's movement has to be big enough for divergent strands. I can't change my experiences. I don't want to.

'It's strange you know,' she said, 'inside my own country I'm seen as the non-Pakistani, yet I find myself caught up in this strange paradox where I become more "Muslim" once I'm outside Pakistan.

'Normally I would define myself as secular, I'm not religious at all: my national identity, my gender, these are my two main identities, but because of the anti-Muslim hostility I find outside, especially in the USA where I've been studying, something inside me makes me respond as a Muslim—I don't like it at all, it's not really me, but I can't seem to help it.

'And what annoys me most of all,' she added, 'is that someone else has the power to construct my identity: "the other", who looks at me a certain way, decides what I am.'

I knew exactly what she meant and I thought Azra would understand me when I talked about 'the middle-class syndrome'.

She tried to explain it by putting it into an historical and political context. It was all tied up with the phenomenon of Pakistan itself, she said. 'I think we are very insecure about what we are and how we came into being and the kind of state we've created.' There were so many contradictions and Pakistan's political course had been so chaotic.

'Something went wrong at the beginning,' she said. 'In 1947, our founder Ali Jinnah advocated secularism—he never meant Pakistan to be a country for Muslims only. We are riddled with contradictions. Look at the creation of Bangladesh, that sealed our fate. How could we say Pakistan was created for Muslims— here was more than half of our population in the Eastern wing saying we don't want to be part of you any more—goodbye! Look at India—like it or not, there are now almost as many Muslims in India as in Pakistan.'

'So you see our country got created and right at the beginning something went wrong. Something, somewhere, has died,' she said soberly.

While she lit another cigarette, I asked her how this affected the upper middle-class women I'd talked about.

'Well,' she answered, inhaling deeply and breathing out channels of smoke which made me remember my past addiction. 'It gives us a feeling of insecurity. How do we justify our existence? And that is all tied up with questions of identity. National identity and class identity and further down, personal identity.'

There was an inbuilt feeling of insecurity, she explained, and those who could, grabbed everything while they could. And if you wanted to share in the power structure, there was a certain status quo to be maintained. All of these insecurities were part of a whole national psyche.

'People will tell you that the feudals have all the power,' Azra went on. 'No,' she said stubbing out her butt emphatically into an ashtray. 'Don't forget that after the feudals and the army, the middle-class has a lot at stake—they have a big share in the power, especially the bureaucratic power.'

The women I was meeting she said; women with all the privileges of education and all the opportunities you could imagine, were women who failed to question what they saw. It stemmed from their fear of losing their status. The moment you started questioning your own status you had to start crossing that barrier and it was often a class barrier.

'Last month,' Azra said, 'I went to a village near Rawalpindi to monitor an NGO. There were some middle-class women working there and I felt they didn't show much empathy to the other workers: to them it was a desk job which has high status, but there was no commitment and they spent a lot of time complaining to me about the women they worked with.

'"We can't find motivated women to work in the field on aid projects," they told me.

'I had gone there,' Azra said, 'to see what I could do to change their thought process and so I looked at their program which was quite a radical program for change. "You are working with the poorest of the poor [I hate that phrase, but anyway]. Aren't you creating a lot of unrest in their lives? Don't you think you are pushing them a little too hard? There's not much chance or hope of economic change within this generation so you are going to create further awareness of their deprivation. How does this make you feel?"

'They told me, "We want to bring about change and the only way we can see that happening is for these village women to become conscious and angry, then react to their environment and bring about positive change."

'Now these were the same women who at the time were complaining at the NGO that they had to be back at home by five pm, before sundown, and that they couldn't go out to the villages at night because their neighbours gossiped.

'I asked them, "Do you think it's fair, do you think it's ethical, to force other women to change when you don't even question the limitations on your own lives?" They were blank, absolutely blank ... and that's it in a nutshell—"the middle-class syndrome".

'These young women I meet,' Azra continued, 'lead difficult lives, I know. They come under enormous social pressure to marry. The only way they can resist this pressure to marry is to get a highly-paid desk job which validates their decision.

'Our middle-class European sisters,' she said, 'don't understand that and become very frustrated with what they see. They don't understand how powerful the family is in our lives: the concept of family loyalty as we understand it, the familial ties which bind.'

It was nearly midnight and the guest house receptionist had already knocked on my door twice to remind us how late it was. 'How was my lady guest going to get home?' he asked. 'She'll drive herself home,' I told him and noted his surprise, bordering on disapproval.

'Pakistani women don't have the space that Western women have,' said Azra as I walked her to the front door. 'And really, this is the positive thing about NGOs. They provide that space for us to become exposed to new ideas and have the time to think and debate. I know it's a very slow trickle down but it gives us the space to mobilise—and jobs, well paid jobs so that we can fend off marriage—at least for a while,' she smiled.

CHAPTER 9

Not Without My Husband

*　　*　　*

'He was the best looking thing I'd ever seen in my whole life,' Debbie Khan confessed years later.

This was the time of day she hated. She felt such a fool handing out the mail to the long line of foreign students whose Taiwanese, Sri Lankan—or whatever—names mystified her, leaving her stammering and red-faced, sounding like the small-town girl she really was. 'Why me?' she groaned every morning.

' "K–H–A–N" he spelt out. And I thought, "Hey, I can handle that one!", and I looked up and when I did—Wow! That was the lightning bolt—the whole shebang. Just like my mom told me about when she met my dad—just magic—and he didn't even notice me!'

The object of Debbie's adulation looked down at his feet modestly. We were sitting in his parent's home in Islamabad. Every day I found myself a visitor in someone else's home and after a while they all started to look alike: spacious living rooms with

222

beautiful hand-woven carpets, warm glowing brassware, carved rosewood and brass screens, chandeliers, armchairs, brocade sofas—rooms large enough to entertain dozens of people.

Considering we'd only just been introduced, considering his young American bride of five months was pouring out her heart to a stranger, Irfan was taking it all in his stride.

He possessed the kind of good looks and dark melting eyes that I'd always taken for granted in Pakistani men. There is a certain quality which distinguishes the Pakistani male from other South Asian species. It shows itself in the way they stand, in the turn of a head, the way they have of looking down at you over those long well-shaped noses, or the cocksure stride of one born to rule (even the poorest man can rule over his wife and daughters). Their carriage shouts to the world how completely at ease they feel about their manhood. But Irfan's character was gentler, there was a certain offhandedness, even humility, that disarmed you immediately. Because he'd spent most of his life outside Pakistan, he didn't expect to be the centre of attention. A young man who looked at home in designer jeans or well-tailored, expensive *kurta*-pajamas, he stayed by Debbie's side. The husbands of other foreign wives I'd met could hardly wait to disappear into their own masculine world. But Debbie and Irfan were a pair.

The lovers had met in their sophomore year. Debbie was studying languages and working at her part-time job in the Foreign Students' Office to make ends meet. Like most American students she didn't mix with foreign students—there was a general feeling of 'stay away and they won't bother you', she said.

Even if American students had wanted to fraternise, the Director, who sounded like a martinet, wouldn't allow such goings on. Mrs Lowry ran the office like a marine drill sergeant and had two fast rules: no jeans and no dating foreign students. A long time ago one of the girls, so legend would have it, became pregnant and her parents had tried to sue the college, so foreign students

223

were off bounds to employees. The rationale behind this rule sounded peculiar, especially in the 1990s. I couldn't see how any college could enforce such a discriminatory code, even if it was the formidable Mrs Lowry's own unwritten law.

Debbie was how I'd always pictured American college girls from the great Midwest. Fresh-looking, brash, unselfconscious and a fast talker—a little of the cheer-leader too, I guessed. She was twenty-four years old and had been living in Pakistan since her wedding five months ago. She had been at college in a small Midwest town called Kirksville, near Kansas City, St Louis; population 17 000 with a student head count of 5000 including 200 international students.

'We're talking main street, cornfed conservative here,' she warned me.

I'd grown up reading Sinclair Lewis, and his wonderful exposes of Main Street USA prepared me for the kind of small-town insularity she was talking about. And when I stopped to think about my own Australian roots, I recognised the small-town girl in myself as well.

Debbie was about as different from a Pakistani girl as a hot dog is from halwa, and it was more than her red-brown hair and white skin. While Irfan played the exotic stranger in her fantasies, she might well be accused of luring him on with her own brand of 'otherness'. Her down-to-earth streak and lack of pretension readily subverted a young man from his path of duty.

'I just kind of drooled over him every time he came into the office,' she laughed now at her 'shameless behaviour'. Debbie, as natural as corn on the cob, opened up about her love-life in a way that startled me at first, until I realised it was the product of a mind set where nothing was held back, just like American TV talk shows. Reticence was not part of Debbie's nature and she reminded me of the friendly Americans I'd met overseas who presented themselves with all the subtlety of vacuum salesmen. *Within five minutes you knew all about Auntie Flo the alcoholic and Uncle Morty the axe killer ...*

'I knew about the rule,' said Irfan, 'and that's why I didn't look twice at her. But after a few weeks I asked around,' he said, a little defensively, anxious to show that he too had been smitten and the initial attraction wasn't as one-sided as Debbie made out. He was the hunter and not the hunted, he was telling me—and I didn't believe him for one minute.

'Yeah!' Debbie teased, 'After I got promoted to Office Assistant, you did.'

'Are you telling me he only fell in love after you began moving up the office hierarchy?' The three of us were having fun.

'He was terribly shy, he'd stand there on one foot trying to make conversation—I'd never come across anyone so well-mannered in my life. And then I turned twenty-one and I started going out to the clubs with friends and that's where I saw him again. He'd buy me drinks—he never drank himself of course—and we'd dance, but that rule was still there and it was a big thing with all the students. But we couldn't help the chemistry,' her eyes grew into saucers and she mugged a look of helpless love. *And the corn is as high as an elephant's eye.* Debbie was a lot tougher than she looked.

'Nearly three months passed and we were still meeting secretly,' said Debbie. 'Maybe we liked the clandestine edge it gave to our meetings—forbidden fruit and all that.'

Debbie the small-town girl, unsophisticated and with hardly a devious thought in her head. Debbie, side by side with this gorgeous-looking man out of the Arabian Nights. 'The dark stranger, with a hint of cruelty, from another world', in the best tradition of a Mills and Boon romance.

'I always told Debbie I was going back to Pakistan and had no intention of getting married. I wasn't one of those guys after a

Green Card!' said the dark stranger, and I woke up suddenly from my Rudolph Valentino fantasy.

'It was a big love affair that wasn't supposed to go anywhere from the beginning,' Debbie confirmed.

'I'm surprised your parents didn't anchor you by getting you engaged, or even married off, before you went overseas,' I said to Irfan. This popular practice prevented an 'unwanted one' from enticing young sons away. My father's relatives had tried similar tactics seventy-five years ago, just before he left for Australia but my mother's Kashmiri beauty and Celtic-Australian charm proved stronger—but that's another story.

'Yes, that's what they do here,' he answered, 'but my situation was a little different because I went overseas right after high school—I haven't lived at home with my parents for very long periods at all.' Perhaps this explained his SNAG (Sensitive New Age Guy) charm which I'd found at odds with his Pakistani machismo.

Debbie pressed on with their story. 'One day,' she said, 'Mrs Lowry came up to me and said "Debbie honey, we'd better have a little talk". She gave me an ultimatum. "Either you quit seeing him or you lose your job. I've spoken to the Board of Governors and this can't go on."

'I remember I went to the Ladies and cried . . . but I quit my job. He went back to Pakistan for the holidays, but I didn't forget him. I sat by the phone waiting for his calls and when he returned we picked up again, only now we could hold hands, and of course since it's the corn belt of America, we did meet with a lot of stares and a lot of whispers and comments. No, I don't call it racism, I see it more as a lack of education or just plain old ignorance.'

I looked across at Irfan hoping to catch his reaction and was just in time to see the smile of someone who disagrees but wants to keep the peace. There was a side of American life he knew about, a side that Debbie was unfamiliar with, and I think he wanted to protect Debbie, to let her keep her illusions—up to a point.

'Over there,' he said, 'they like you to stay with "your own kind"—that's what they call it.

'They don't like you to go out with one of their women. I expected the worst, but Debbie had never experienced any prejudice before in her life.' Until she started being seen with Irfan, that is.

'We went to a little yoghurt place one day,' she said. 'This woman walked in with her son and she started making rude comments about how terrible it was for me to let a Mexican drive my car. "If *my* daughter brought home a nigger . . ." she said. I was shaking, but Irfan was totally relaxed about it.' Maybe on the outside I thought as I listened to Debbie pass off racist insults as 'rude comments'.

'It was my first time you see and I was so shocked I didn't have the words to confront her. So we just kissed and held hands to show her.

'People used to stare at us on campus and the student newspaper wanted to interview me about mixed couples and I thought "Hey! What are you talking about?" 'Cause mixed couples always meant one of them was coloured, and I thought "He's certainly not black!" After a while Mrs Lowry changed her tune and was on our side, but her offsider hated us! We had broken the rule.'

There are all kind of rules. I told Debbie that they had done much more than simply break college rules. I think she was too innocent to understand that some of the college authorities were deeply affronted by the idea of people of different races loving one another; having sexual relations or any kind of intimacy, maybe marrying and begetting children. Some societies in the course of their history have passed laws against miscegenation: Nazi Germany, South Africa, certain states in America's Deep South and Australia in its racist laws against Aborigines.

'Here they stare at us too,' protested Debbie.

'But here,' Irfan corrected her gently, 'they are staring at the white face and not at the mixed couple.'

And they stared at the white face, I thought, because it was unusual, because it was different, and different didn't mean abhorrent.

'I know you're right,' said Debbie, 'but the staring over here really bothers me. I'm slowly getting used to it, but it makes me feel it's anti-American and I want to stare back and be an American even though I know that ninety per cent of the time it's just plain old curiosity. I'm not used to being the centre of attention.'

Becoming the 'other' almost overnight is something that takes time to adjust to, especially if you've never been outside your own cultural backyard before and you take your national identity and the confidence your passport bestows on you for granted.

Two years passed and Debbie still remained a well-kept secret with Irfan's family. 'My sister living in New York was the first to meet Debbie and she was so surprised. I remember her telling me, "Irfan, she's not your typical Western woman at all!".'

'What ideas do Pakistani men have about Western women?' I asked him.

'Well,' he began a little slowly, 'the ideas all come from movies and the media. And Western women are seen as promiscuous. In the 1980s here,' he elaborated, 'we had a big revival of the old James Bond movies and this fed crazy ideas—that all Western women were like the sexy Bond girls in bikinis. That is why Pakistani and Indian men behave so badly with Western women— because they think it's expected of them; they fancy themselves as James Bond types!'

Over the years, I'd heard many excuses for men behaving badly, but this was a novel way of blaming the victim.

'There's another belief that if you marry a Westerner your marriage will eventually break up—everyone talks about the high divorce rates and the lack of family values, the lack of respect. The family is everything in Pakistan.'

Debbie cut in, 'My parents celebrated their thirtieth anniversary last year, thank you! And my grandparents have been married for sixty-four years!'

I soothed her and made her laugh by telling her that her family must be either a national treasure or headed for extinction!

'My sister broke the news to my parents,' Irfan said. ' "Debbie is a good girl," she said, "she comes from a good family, she's different from other Western women".' Irfan was lucky to have an intermediary acting on his behalf.

'My parents were totally shocked. They didn't come out of their shock for four months.'

They obviously had other plans for their only son, I thought; perhaps they'd even started looking for a girl from a 'good family'?

Debbie's father was more vocal. 'God damn Pakistani!' was his reaction when his eldest daughter broke the news to her parents.

'He thought this guy was just stringing me along and would never marry me. But my mother just adored him right from the start—so charming and polite . . . so my family were behind me even though my father didn't agree with what I was doing.

'Irfan went out one night and rented the video *Not Without My Daughter*. He wanted my mom and me to see the movie and to discuss it with us.'

The film based on the book by Betty Mahmoudi about her unhappy 1980s marriage to an Iranian doctor has probably done more to shape negative Western attitudes to intercultural marriages with Muslim men than anything else in the last twenty years. The film depicts an enormous culture clash and custody battle, emphasising, I believed, the geopolitical tensions between the USA and Iran at the time instead of seeing the drama as a marriage breakdown complicated by many different factors.

'Irfan wanted to show us the difference between Pakistan and Iran—the difference between Sunni Islam and the more fanatical Shia Islam of Iran. Actually,' she continued, 'in a strange coincidence, the real Dr Mahmoudi went to our college, and knew Mrs Lowry. He studied medicine there for four years.'

'On top of everything else—I mean the guy was brutal to his wife—I think he suffered a nervous breakdown,' said Irfan. 'He suffered racism in America, discrimination in his medical career, the Iranian Revolution was happening and he felt guilty that he wasn't there; he had the pressure of his extended family on his back—the guy just cracked. I'm not excusing him, the guy was brutal to his wife,' he repeated, 'but it's not as simple as the movie made it seem.

'Well,' he continued, 'I wanted Debbie's parents to see the differences and so I gave them a commentary as the film went along. "His family was Shia and mine is Sunni, his family wasn't educated and mine is—"'

'You mean the class difference,' I broke in.

'Yes,' he said, 'and I really believe his family had a lot to do with the break-up; there were some strange ceremonies going on in that film.' He spoke with all the suspiciousness a Sunni Muslim can have towards a follower of the Shiite strand of Islam.

'We were still together after nearly four years and by now Debbie wanted to elope. But I couldn't do this. "It must be done the right way", I kept saying—in the Pakistani way—and both families had to be involved,' he said. 'I insisted that it must be done with honour.'

'So,' said Debbie, 'he decided I must meet his family first before anything else happened.'

'With all this toing and froing and the keeping of secrets, didn't anyone get tired? You were certainly treading water for years,' I said, turning to Debbie.

'I was starting to get fed up,' Debbie admitted, 'but after his graduation, things finally began moving along and suddenly his father decided, after talking to some friends, that it was all right for a Pakistani man to marry a foreign woman.'

'Yes,' said Irfan. 'The stalemate was broken one night when we had some visitors to the house and one of the men whose sister was married to an American guy said "Mr Khan, he really loves her—give them a chance."'

A thought crossed my mind. Would Irfan have married Debbie if his family had finally said 'no'? Could he have borne the pain of being ostracised and gambled on his parents one day forgiving them? Would they have been forced to wait until the first child was born? Or would he have said goodbye to Debbie rather than have her become the 'unwanted one' in his family, a woman tolerated rather than loved?

'My father told me to telephone Debbie and tell her to take the next flight out of St Louis to New York, pick up her ticket and then travel by PIA to Islamabad.'

'I had forty-eight hours' notice,' said Debbie, 'and I'd just started a new job the day before, but I'd been waiting two years for this phone call.'

Her parents were impressed by the first class ticket, but her father was still suspicious . . . 'My father even had a code word for me to use, if I was in trouble,' she explained trying to keep a straight face while she told me. 'If I said "I'm fine, I'm fine," then he'd know everything was okay, but if I didn't use the code words, then he told me he'd send in the marines and I don't think he was kidding!' she said.

'When I landed I tried to put away all of my Americanness; I watched my p's and q's—I knew I had to behave differently.'

'We told her to relax; she didn't wear what's she got on now—the shalwar kameez, and my father said, "Just be yourself, Debbie."'

'There's so much respect in this house for his father,' said

Debbie, 'and I tried hard to copy what I saw. When his father talks for instance, you listen until there is a break in the conversation, there's never any interrupting, never any contradicting your father . . . nothing American like that.'

Or Australian, I thought, remembering with a guilty start the arguments I'd had with my embattled father although ultimately his word was law—at least until I found a way around his injunctions.

' "She's not what we expected," my parents said. Debbie wins everyone's heart sooner or later,' he said proudly, picking up her hand and holding it—an act which touched me because Muslim men hardly ever did such things in front of others; they would never dare hold hands in front of his parents. 'People over here are always talking about her. She relates to anyone she meets in a friendly way which is not common over here. She's not acting though—that's Debbie,' Irfan finished off.

'Whether I meet important government friends or poorer relatives, they're all the same to me,' Debbie explained. 'I thank the servants—I know you're not supposed to do that. I have a Muslim name now,' she added. 'It's Sara— pronounced "Shara" over here—and I'm working hard on my Urdu.'

They continued telling me about that eventful first trip which lasted ten days. 'I was still a secret,' said Debbie, 'only the immediate family knew about me. His mom watched me a lot,' she remembered, 'she'd sit there silently and once she began crying when his dad mentioned a ceremony sometime in the future. Tears ran down her cheeks and I thought to myself, "Oh, I hate hurting this woman like this".

'His father told me they wanted their son to be happy and if this was what made him happy, then they'd agree.'

'Yes,' said Irfan, 'it was not what my mom wanted, but in the end they accepted it. And of course Debbie has won my mother over by now. It didn't take too long.'

But by the look on Debbie's face her guilt was a heavy load she hadn't quite put down yet.

They were married a few months later, on 24 December 1995.

Her parents flew over with Debbie, who'd had a heart-to-heart with her father before they left. 'Dad,' she warned him, 'please watch your language; don't expect alcohol; don't sit like this with your foot pointing at someone and pul—eeze practise saying "*Salaam alaikum*" a thousand times until you've got it straight.'

'Meanwhile *my* dad,' said Irfan, 'was trying hard all around Islamabad to get a bottle of Jack Daniels, her father's favourite drink, but all he could get was a couple of bottles of wine, so that had to do.'

I asked Debbie if she'd become a Muslim.

'Yes,' she said, 'the night before we got married. We wanted it to be right in every aspect, although I know,' she said anticipating my next question, 'that women marrying Muslim men don't have to convert.'

I was dying to know what her Unitarian Church parents thought of this, but she explained that in her family religious matters were easy going and you could believe whatever you wanted; it was never a big deal was how she put it.

Irfan intimated that she'd converted to keep everyone happy. 'You know what it's like over here; everyone asks "Is she a Muslim?" and we wanted to keep that kind of talk quiet.'

I asked him if his parents understood that Debbie's conversion was not out of conviction, but simply a matter of convenience and courtesy?

They both answered yes and Irfan went on to tell me that in his family only his mother prayed. 'We are very liberal on religious matters,' he insisted, and I thought to myself, yes my lad, but not liberal enough to decline a conversion which wasn't genuine and not even necessary or encouraged according to Islam. Their concerns were social and status oriented; religion had nothing to do with it. And I wondered why Debbie had volunteered, or had it been her mother-in-law's suggestion? Her feelings of guilt about her new mother-in-law were so tangible that it made her vulnerable.

How could you refuse anything to a woman who burst into tears when she looked at you?

Irfan hurried to reassure me and pointed out that, 'It's like just changing your name on the passport, we're not changing her personality by doing this.'

We went on to talk about children and they made it clear that they wanted their children to know about both religious traditions, especially Christmas trees, said Debbie.

'His mother is watching me all the time. If I have a little cold or a tummy ache she thinks I must be pregnant. But,' Debbie insisted, 'I want to have my baby in the USA and not so much because of citizenship but because it would be my first and I want to be surrounded by my family.'

Irfan got up to fetch us some Seven-Up and I remarked on the fact that the man of the house was serving us. Debbie said offhandedly as if it was nothing special, 'Yes, he does things like that.' Secretly you could tell she was proud that he was different.

While he was out of the room I pounced, asking her how she was finding living in a joint family situation.

'It drives me nuts to be honest. There is no privacy.

'I would kill to have my own kitchen! We have a lady in the kitchen here and when she's working I don't feel comfortable about going in and making my scrambled eggs.'

And then she revealed their latest plans—or was it her own game plan? 'We're waiting to get visa papers for Irfan and then we're leaving—we're out of here!' She checked herself, 'Not permanently of course,' she said, 'but my folks want to give us a reception back home this summer and my sister's getting married. Even when we go home we'll be living with my parents but we'll have the upstairs to ourselves. Right now I'm terrified of getting a job here and then we'd have to stay.'

'You don't want to stay do you?' I put to her.

'Right now,' she said, 'I'm just so homesick that I'm ready to go and never come back. But we've talked about it and I said I'd be willing to come back and I mean that. In a few months we'll evaluate our situation, if he doesn't like it, we'll come back, but right now I want to go home, and if we do come back we are going to try and get our own flat. His parents understand, but I still feel incredibly guilty about it all.'

'Don't feel guilty,' I said. 'Whatever else you feel, put away the guilt.'

'I can't help it, he's been away from his mom for so many years.

'A couple of weeks ago I was crying every single day—I felt miserable and suddenly it dawned on me that I was just homesick and there is nothing wrong with that is there? But I don't want his father to find me a job here and then I'm cornered.

'I said to Irfan, "I've made enough sacrifices for you. I've got the bangles and the shalwar kameez and now it's your turn!" By the way, he didn't know he was supposed to buy me gold bangles for the wedding and his sister went shopping with me and we had to get the biggest bangles in the whole city because I'm so big boned.'

'So you're happy to work in either country,' I said to Irfan as he re-entered the room carrying a tray of soft drinks.

'I was initially thinking to start my working life here in Pakistan with support from my family and then maybe move to another country,' he answered, 'but now that Debbie is getting home-sick—' he broke off. 'Did I tell you she's learning Urdu? We don't expect it but she wants to do it.'

'I'll do anything to please his mother,' said Debbie. 'I know it broke her heart when I came into the family, that is, before she met me. Every now and then I go to her and tell her, "I need a big hug" and I get a hug. She misses her daughter in the US too, just like I miss my mom.'

'One thing we can't understand is why Debbie won't ring her parents more often,' said Irfan. 'She's allowed to make a call any time she wants, but she only does it once a week and we can't understand why she doesn't want to talk to them more. When I'm away from my parents I want to talk to them every day! Is the difference because I'm a family-oriented person?' He didn't say what the alternative was but I didn't think it could be too flattering.

'It's an American thing,' said Debbie. 'I'm independent now.'

This seemed a good moment to talk about dependency, a very Pakistani trait. The family is paramount of course and there is a chain of dependency with links in place to make sure that happens.

Debbie was impatient at the lack of independence she saw all around her and which she found difficult to live with. 'Young people don't get pocket money so they never learn how to handle money or how to budget. Men in their twenties and thirties go to their fathers for money whenever they need cash.'

'It's the big issue with us and we talk about it all the time,' they admitted.

'When I was a teenager, I got $50 a month and I was in charge of my school lunches, clothes, make-up, and *he* still goes to mummy and says, "We're going out for a pizza can I have some money?" and it is perfectly acceptable to everyone, but me! Over here that's how you do things—it's expected but I tell you it's driving me nuts! We have savings of our own but they won't let us use the money! What about when we have kids? Are they going to run to daddy all the time?'

'I don't worry about money,' said Irfan, 'Debbie handles everything.'

'Yes,' she said, half affectionately, half in exasperation, 'Pakistani men are spoilt.'

Irfan told me with pride that many Pakistanis who go to America stay there, 'but with Debbie it is the other way round,' he boasted. I wondered if he realised how much she wanted to live in the States.

'How do you work out your decisions as a couple?' I asked them both thinking back to Ayesha in Lahore and how she'd hooted with laughter when I'd asked a similar question.

'We discuss everything through, just like we're doing now over whether to stay here or go home.' They sounded like two obedient children answering their Sunday school teacher.

'We've both had job offers already from firms in Islamabad,' said Irfan.

'Yeah,' said Debbie. 'I was just telling her,' she told him, 'that I wanted to get out before I got stuck here. We were planning to stay here originally—sometimes men aren't good at noticing and that's when you have to use the tears.'

We talked about the foreign wives' association. Debbie had never gone to a meeting. She was worried by the generation gap. 'Whenever I see white ladies around town they all look twenty years older than me. They're not going to remember what it was like when they first came over here. They seem very straight,' she added. 'I heard that they had a doll exhibition—a doll exhibition, I ask you!'

There were times when Debbie just wanted to burst out and do something wild, like run down the street. She longed to break out of this shell she found herself in, the shell of the good, quiet decent woman.

She showed me the photographs of her Pakistani hen's party. By the look on her face it had been a terrible ordeal. 'We couldn't talk to each other, they were singing songs I couldn't understand; I didn't even know if I was supposed to be clapping along or if I was supposed to be crying. I just didn't understand my role.'

I looked at her wedding photographs. She looked like a glamorous, ornately dressed, stunned mullet.

But despite all the years of waiting and the compromises she'd made and would continue to make, Debbie, part of a new generation of brides, had floated down to Pakistan on a silken parachute and made a soft landing.

✻ ✻ ✻

Many years ago however, a tribe of women as strong as Amazons, settled in Pakistan. They came from every corner of the globe when they were young and in love and when they believed that true romance conquered everything and could change the world. Some of them fell out of love—sometimes for a day and sometimes for ever. Many lost their health and saw their youth fading away like old photographs in an album, but they clung on stubbornly through the days of unbearable heat, through the pregnancies they faced with only strangers by their side, through times they laugh about today, but which caused them terrible pain and often temporary breakdown. Through long years of voluntary exile they kept hold of their identity—against the odds—knowing that it could easily disappear, as it sometimes did.

Their greatest enemy was a hopeless feeling of being trapped and they fought it at every turn. These women belong to an earlier age. Now a younger generation of foreign wives looks at them critically and sometimes with the cruel impatience of women who feel the power of their own sexuality and are inclined to dismiss older women; they think them conservative, and in some ways perhaps they are; but they endured what often seemed unendurable and they learnt how to wait.

'They're not going to remember what it was like when they

238

first came over here,' Debbie had said to me and I remember telling her how wrong she was.

With due respect to Debbie and all the Debbies to follow, the older brides were tougher. They were certainly less self-absorbed, but then again it was a different world and a different Pakistan thirty, forty years ago. Women's self-images were also different: in the West we were still years away from the polemical writings of the second wave of Australian and American feminists, the Germaine Greers, the Betty Friedans and the Gloria Steinems.

As I went from city to city, from Karachi to Lahore from Lahore to Islamabad and north west to Peshawar, I kept trying to meet these women, these foreign wives, as they are called. And I wondered if a foreign wife ever stopped being a foreign wife? Was it like being an immigrant: 'Once an immigrant always an immigrant', no matter how long your length of stay, no matter how strong your commitment to your adopted country.

They all knew how to keep secrets. Under the surface, things were not always what they seemed. I could only guess at the rules and the reason for what now and then seemed to be a ritual of pretence. They'd had plenty of practice at being patient. In my mind I called them 'women in waiting'. What had they been waiting for? Were they still waiting after all these years?

Marguerite learnt how to master her impatience but she still stumbles, even after thirty years, she told me. She was the most flamboyant and dramatic of all the women I met, as if she still couldn't rid herself of the dust lying on the boards of the theatre stage she used to tread in London in the 1960s. But the curtain came down on her budding career (she'd been offered a scholarship at The Old Vic and was a regular repertory player) when she met this dashing stranger and as she said, not so much in regret, but more with a shrug at the inevitability of it all, 'The pull of the stranger was too strong for me'. She simply couldn't resist him, and all her other New Zealand friends sharing digs in

Peter Finch's cellar flat did nothing to encourage her—after all this was London in the Swinging '60s.

'Right from the start it was a strong sexual attraction—such a powerful magnetism and I thought to myself, "I'll have to be careful here," when I saw Riaz's cheeky grinning face.' They met after his sports car ran into the back of her girlfriend's scooter. But right from the start he chased her and he didn't let up for a minute.

So swept away by their feelings were they, that they never discussed her acting ambitions which went on hold—temporarily she thought.

'He told me he must go back to Pakistan to help get the family business on its feet. How was I to know it would take twenty-nine years!'

Her voice still had the rich timbre of the actor and resonated with feeling as she swept her dark blonde hair back from her face. I had the strange feeling that throughout my four-hour visit Marguerite used me as an actress uses an audience, reaching out, projecting herself into my imagination as she wanted me to see her: a charming, slightly eccentric, woman in her fifties; a woman capable of great passion, who'd thrown away a promising dramatic career for love. She had all the mannerisms of a once beautiful woman who never stopped playing a role she knew to perfection.

Finally, she said, they were married in London but not before a dramatic last-minute flight by her brother to bring her to her senses. Only then did she really begin to understand prejudice. Before this she thought the English looked down on her New Zealand origins and hadn't thought much about what Riaz was going through—he looked Italian to her. 'He looks much browner here,' Marguerite said to me, as if I thought that mattered.

So they married in London and she put her dreams on hold—

240

temporarily on hold, she believed—and she had her beautiful babies. And then after a few years came the call to return to Pakistan.

They drove overland through Iran and through the Khyber Pass with their two children and her first impressions of Pakistan were wonderful. The first words she heard were, 'Madam, would you like a cup of tea?', and she thought to herself, 'this doesn't seem so bad after all!'

Finally they arrived in Lahore and she found herself welcomed by her new father-in-law who announced, 'You are my son's bride, therefore you are my daughter'. Only then did she learn that Riaz had 'forgotten' to tell his father about their marriage three years earlier and had waited until the very last minute. Even then the news was filtered through by his cousins, she said.

Marguerite became part of a large extended household of seven brothers: some married with families, three unmarried sisters and a large nest of aunts and cousins as well. Oh! and of course, she said, there were children running everywhere!

'On and off there were about twenty to twenty-five people, and for the first time I felt trapped!'

She caught my eye and paused dramatically.

'My dear! Here we were, all crammed into this old house, no air conditioning and my husband, whom I felt was starting to neglect me, would literally throw cold water over me whenever I complained of the heat!

'I spent one month sitting with the women on the floor cleaning spinach leaves—you know how they do them over here— everyone loves *parlic* as they call it, and you have to prepare mountains of the bloody stuff! Anyway there I was sitting with a group of women I couldn't understand, cleaning tiny spinach leaves one by one, when all I really wanted to do was grab a knife and go chop, chop, chop . . .

'I told his brother Khalid, "I can't stand it . . . sitting on the floor cleaning these bloody spinach leaves one by one [I couldn't help it and started laughing]; flies coming in from the open drain outside, five mosques all calling their azans through the open windows, leaky taps and slime on the bathroom walls. I hardly ever saw Riaz who was working in the family carpet factory till 10.30 every night.

' "I can't live like this," I told his brother, "What do I do?" "Get a job," he said and I did, and I found that my standing increased for now I was contributing to the family coffers.

'I used to wonder about the women and all the jewellery they were wearing—all those gold bangles jangling on their wrists when I couldn't afford five rupees for the baby's powdered milk. I thought all this preoccupation with jewellery unproductive because the young men were saving to get married or saving to buy jewellery for their brides which meant skimping on eggs or other food.

'But they are a proud people, and the family came through all the hard times; those years are all behind us. Look at us now,' she said smiling, throwing her arms wide open. We were sitting in yet another beautifully furnished, extremely large sitting room decorated in white and gold with matching brocade sofas scattered around. Her home was in Gulberg, an affluent area of Lahore and she told me triumphantly that they lived alone with just their own children! The way she flashed her eyes I knew she'd battled to win this concession. Of course her carpets were the most exquisite I'd seen, although at first we both steered away from the question of child labour, until she assured me, without my even asking, that there was no-one under the age of fifteen in *their* factories. 'At last,' she said, 'a home of my own.

'But we're jumping ahead,' she told me. 'There were stormy days at first, especially while we lived with his family.

'Sometimes I would pack my bags and Riaz would beg me to stay. I wanted to go back to London after the first ten months and we started fighting over who would keep our youngest son. Things were at a crisis and that's why he took me back to London for a holiday. I was just skin and bones: I was sick and not eating much ... I couldn't get used to the heat and the food and the water. They were hellish times. Well we went to London for five months but I didn't like some of his Pakistani friends there who'd married English girls; the men were rough types and a lot of them were uneducated and from remote villages.

'I thought long and hard about things and one night, walking along by the Thames, I decided to give Pakistan another go. But let me make one thing clear,' she said, 'I was not entering a relationship with Pakistan—I was certainly not being drawn into Pakistani culture—I had a love relationship with this man and I was committed to him.

'We returned and again I noticed a marked change in Riaz's behaviour as soon as he was back in Lahore and with his family again. Little boys would bang on our door in the morning and he wouldn't say a word. When I argued for a place of our own near by, he would tell me, "They won't understand".'

But she was happy with her work at the international school in Lahore where she taught drama and English and she began a little theatre club where they performed plays. The babies were growing up and the family business was expanding with branches in Copenhagen and New York. Their living arrangements improved by the mid '70s although it still meant living with two of his brothers until they got their own rented house—but that was paradise.

But she never learnt the language and I think she made the decision quite ruthlessly, as if she'd calculated that this would mean a surrender of some kind on her part which she couldn't bear. 'I was not entering a relationship with Pakistan,' Marguerite had told me with steel in her voice. Nearly thirty years and just a few kitchen Urdu words—it seemed a shame.

In the mid '70s however, she tried once again to escape. 'How about me?' she said to Riaz. Marguerite was nearing forty. 'I've given you all these years, made all these compromises and now it's my turn.' The chance to pick up a scholarship and go to San Francisco for a year to study drama teaching to update her skills had somehow fallen into her lap.

So off they all went to San Francisco: Riaz, Marguerite and by now three little boys—the eldest was ten. She enrolled and started going to classes and seeing all the latest shows. 'I felt deliriously happy and Riaz had the chance to visit the New York branch of the business, but it didn't last long. The men in my life,' she declaimed, 'didn't like San Francisco at all. "We want to go back home; we want to go back to Pakistan!" Riaz said to me, "You can stay here, but I don't want to stay. This way of living is awful." And of the course the boys wanted to go back with him. What could I do? I thought, I can't live without Riaz—I was devastated but I'd had a few weeks and I knew I could still cut it on the stage and in the workshops even though I was much older. I felt proud of that.'

'You must love him tremendously.' I said to Marguerite. She chose not to hear my question.

'I'm no saint,' she said slowly, 'but gradually I began to see Riaz's handicap, his feelings of insecurity in the West. He feels threatened—after all he only knows carpets. And then there's the discrimination. I can understand that, I know what it's like when you're never free of people looking at you and just staring, staring. You don't know how many times I've longed to stand up, jump on the table and do the can-can—give them something to really stare at,' she giggled and then her mood changed.

'Since that time in San Francisco I've only ever been able to escape for holidays. As the business prospered I could go now and then with the boys to New Zealand and even though I hated leaving Riaz I've always enjoyed those times—I have a sense of place when I return to New Zealand.

'And now,' she said slowly, 'over the last ten years, I've become more and more fascinated by Islam. Strange for the first twenty years, I had no interest. No-one ever suggested to me that I become Muslim, but in the mystical expression of Islam, in Sufism, at last I've found peace. Islam has ninety-nine expressions for God and I find that so appealing.'

She started telling me with great enthusiasm how she'd begun reading the Qur'an and how she'd dismissed the Marmeduke English translation for the more liberal translation of Yusaf Ali. Islam became self-realisation for her although she never bothered with the ritual.

'Finally, after all this time, I could see the significance of coming here. As a child I always wanted to know "the peace that passeth understanding" and that is so similar to the Islamic concept of going to a place beyond human understanding,' she whispered in exaltation. 'You know what I'm talking about.' But I didn't and I felt I was cheating her in some way.

'Foreign wives,' she said, 'are women with a foot in both worlds. We don't let our husbands' families down. We don't speak out publicly because we don't want all the gossip going around. Some women make it and others don't.

'A lot depends on the position and wealth of your husband and whether you live independently. If the husband is too emotionally dependent on his family it is very hard on the wife for he's not used to standing alone. And here the young men grow up so slowly; the older males keep control and don't want to hand over. It keeps the younger men dependent.

'I'm resigned to not escaping,' Marguerite said. 'But we've come a long way. I began with twenty-five people in an old house and now we have our own magnificent house built just how I've always dreamt of it. My boys are wonderful and I keep myself busy.

'An ex-nun once accused us. "You foreign wives," she said, "you've all sold out". She thought we were pretending to be happy, "faking your happiness," she called it, but each case is different—we all cope in our own fashion.'

When all the children have grown up, and there is only you to think about, doesn't it become tremendously lonely then? I nearly asked her, but then I realised that is hardly ever the case in Pakistan: there will be daughters-in-law, there will be grandchildren—the family will always be there.

❊   ❊   ❊

'I hope I don't die here,' said Kamila, whose name used to be Robyn before she converted. 'But If I do die in Pakistan I don't want my body sent back at great expense . . . that is not what I want at all.'

Of all the wives, she was the most reluctant to meet me. She didn't want to contribute to a book that sensationalised the lives of women married to Pakistanis, she said tersely. But after listening to me, she agreed to meet me at my guest house. 'I won't promise anything,' she said, 'let's see how we get on.'

'Money is the key here,' Kamila explained. 'If you've got enough money to go back every year if you want, then it's wonderful. I have this dream that my children will marry partners who are scattered all over the world and I'll go and visit them. I think it's only a dream.

'I guess I will probably stay here. My husband will never leave and I will never break up with my husband for that reason, but I hope I have the money to visit my sister back in England.'

Kamila liked to keep busy and preferred working to socialising.

What she said impressed me because of its candour, but I'm sorry to say that if I passed her in the street today, I'm not sure if I could recall what she looked like; short brown hair and a direct, unflinching gaze—that's the only image I have left.

Her husband was a doctor, but an honest one, she emphasised. 'He isn't wealthy. He doesn't have his own clinic and while some doctors are honest and poor, there are others who are very rich. Yusuf works terribly long hours for little remuneration. One day I would like to revisit all my old friends and go on holiday—just alone with my husband—that's all I want.

'I love this country,' Kamila said and her face lit up. 'Pakistan has such potential. But Benazir is all speech and no do, and the country is being milked by everybody who can, all the way down. We live a good life and can buy imported things, but how do other people live on their salaries?' She was the only woman who spoke openly about local politics and mentioned her concern about others less well off.

'I love my job as a nurse educator and that is why I want to work until I'm sixty, although as I said I'd like to spend more time with my husband—we still get on very well.'

'In a way I'm disappointed with myself. I don't see the beggars anymore. And I suppose I've restricted myself by telling myself that I can't do anything about corruption in Pakistan, except personally and I teach my children the same, but I still feel guilty that I'm not doing more. But it's so hard being idealistic any more when you meet people socially, and you know they're creaming the top off. It's sad, so we just stay within our own circle of friends.'

Smiling, sunny Helga whose observations were never unkind or thoughtless, met her husband forty years ago in Salzburg. 'He was the first Asian person I'd ever talked to,' she said. 'He came to Austria on a study tour. I met him through my girlfriend and never ever expected to see him again. But after he sent me flowers and I sent him a thank you note, we began corresponding while he was studying in Germany and he visited Austria now and again,' she smiled and gave a little shrug, 'and then after two years we decided to get married.'

Had they ever discussed religion and where and how they would live? 'Oh yes,' she answered. 'We discussed many things by letter. What would happen if we had children was one thing we needed to resolve, and so we decided that if we stayed in Austria, then the children would be brought up as Catholics, but if we stayed in Pakistan they would be Muslims. My husband never minded really and we felt they must have a sense of belonging to whatever country they called home.'

'Your husband must be an unusual man,' I said.

'Yes, he's very tolerant,' she said simply. 'We have always believed that it is better to be a good person than to try to prove that "my religion is better than yours". It's so unimportant because all these religions come from God. I never converted myself, because my husband never cared, but I have a dear friend whose husband and in-laws insisted and my friend still feels unhappy, she had a strong religious upbringing and now she feels she is nothing and her identity is lost. Then again,' said Helga, 'I have friends here who became Muslims after twenty years out of conviction, but to force a person, that is very hard.

'I tried to prepare myself before coming here all those years ago in 1958. I read many books, but they were the wrong books, so when I reached Karachi I was amazed to see such a modern city. All the books I'd been reading were about Peshawar and I was expecting a frontier town, but Karachi was so much bigger than my Salzburg. We were comfortable and my husband's friends made me feel welcome. It was so funny at first,' she said, 'because

I couldn't understand anyone's English with the Pakistani accent, you know and they couldn't understand my very strong Viennese accent. So my husband would translate their English for me, and he would translate my English for them. The fact that both of us had no relations to worry about made things a lot less complicated and I didn't have any in-laws interfering. We are still in contact with those people who came to the airport to meet me forty years ago.'

Helga is fluent in Urdu and saw it as a sensible thing to do, to learn the language of the country you have adopted as your own.

Helga was lucky, she thinks, that her husband's relatives were in India. 'Husbands want to please their mothers above anyone else,' she told me. 'The husbands try to keep them happy because their mothers are already very upset because the son has brought a foreign woman into the family. Husbands do not side with their wives against their mothers,' she cautioned me.

'Living with a joint family is never easy and often the in-laws are not nice to the new wife. You make the best of your life, because once you have children it is not easy to leave—you can't pick up and go so easily.'

We both knew that custody laws favoured the father who under Islamic law was the guardian of his children, especially his sons, although the mother was usually given custody of the children until they grew older. There had been some cases where judges had awarded custody to the mother, but there were times when the court's decision was never implemented.

I told Helga that she was one of the few women who displayed a real fondness for Pakistan, others were more resigned to living here.

'Oh no,' she protested. 'I think you're wrong. I have lots of friends—Hilda and Beate for example—and all are very happy here. Of course sometimes we do grumble, but we would do that no matter where we lived.

249

'It may be different with the young girls of today who seem to lead such luxurious lives, especially the Americans. Their expectations are very different and they take all modern appliances for granted like air conditioning, television and cars. When we first came, forty years ago, we had no fridge, no car—but nobody in those days had such things.'

'But the women of your generation,' I pressed her, 'do you think most of them are happy?'

'Yes, I think so. They wouldn't want to go back.'

I asked her to tell me what she liked so much about Pakistan.

'There is no pressure here and time doesn't matter. Anyone can come to my house at any time they like and we'll sit down. In Austria people are so intent on working, you get caught in this pressure, organising what you must do next week, the plans you must make. No time for family and friends. To have children in this country is wonderful and of course you do have house-help, that gives you more leisure time. You must have help. If you are poor here your life is very difficult—you'd better go home. Your happiness can depend on your husband's circumstances.'

I asked her about women who married men without wealth or prospects.

'They don't stay,' she answered. If parents can't help the young couples, life is hard. In Austria and Germany you can get a housing loan and pay it back over twenty-five years. Here you must have the whole sum. It's only recently that bank loans have come in but you need a lot of collateral. If you want a car you must pay for that in full and of course you must have air conditioning with the heat. Housing rentals are high as well. Running air conditioning is also very expensive and local salaries are not high so it is a tremendous outlay for young couples at the beginning. So they need a family with wealth behind them.

'But the key to happiness here, in my opinion, is linked to your friends. I feel comfortable with the foreign wives because they have the same problems, but I have a lot of Pakistani friends too.

'But,' Helga warned me very seriously, 'there is one thing you must watch out for. Do not make friends with what we call "proper foreigners", that is foreigners with no Pakistani partners—no commitment to staying here.

'Now we are all married to Pakistanis, but if you have girl-friends married to non-Pakistanis it will cause trouble.

'The real foreigners, whether diplomats or business people are here for the quick buck.' It was a strange idiomatic expression coming from Helga. 'In two or three years they make all this money, buy expensive carpets and jewellery, but they have a different outlook and they never settle down. It is easy to make friends with them, but it will only make you dissatisfied with your own life. And then they get so many allowances! You know, it's a funny thing but Islamabad is regarded as a hardship post—fancy that!' she exclaimed. 'I think it is one of the nicest capitals in the world!

'Years ago I had a friend with daughters the same age as mine and she put them in the American School here. Her husband was in business and he could afford the expensive fees. But my children said, "Mummy they have changed. Now they criticise everything about Pakistan—this is dirty and that is filthy. They only criticise and we don't want to be friends with them anymore." These children living here all their lives were now looking down their noses at Pakistanis, such a pity,' she sighed.

'Children should know where they are at home. Our children are Pakistanis, what else should they be? They are not at home in Austria. Even though they speak the language they are not at home there.'

I asked Helga if her children had married Pakistanis.

'Yes,' she answered. 'We organised semi-arranged marriages for both our girls. This family saw my daughter at a wedding when she was eighteen and then some friends suggested we meet with them, but I said no, she is too young. Two years later they approached us again through the same friends—you never go to anyone directly you know. You go through your friends and your friends' friends—quite an involved ritual. As your girls grow up you start to get calls from friends who say they want to drop in and bring someone else with them. And you start to get suspicious. I became an expert and I could smell them. My husband was no help. He said, "It's ladies' business, don't get me mixed up in it."

'And the girls can be terrible. They will come out with the most amazing excuses why they don't like someone. One young man came with his parents and the girls couldn't stop laughing when they left. The poor boy was wearing white shoes and the girls were falling over themselves laughing.

'Then one day my daughter said she liked this young man and they were engaged for two years and then married. I would not let them date but they saw one another before the marriage, I found out later. She has an MA in English Literature and they live in London near his parents but in a separate household.

'My other daughter had many proposals too. I'm not showing off, but my children are tall and people here like tall girls.'

'And they like fair girls, don't they?'

'Yes, they like dark hair and fair skin.'

'Did you ever sense any problems because they were children from a mixed marriage?' I asked Helga.

'A friend told me I would have problems, but I found the opposite. They are local girls you see,' she said in a matter-of-fact tone. 'They are Muslims and they speak the language. No, there have never been any signs of prejudice from local people. If someone is telling you that, it is not true. And,' she smiled gracefully, 'my observations are long term remember. I have been here for forty years.'

Helga, like every other woman I'd spoken to, believed that

certain factors gave intercultural marriages a chance of evolving into happy unions: the husband's circumstances, the wife's career skills and whether she worked outside the house and most importantly whether or not they had a separate household.

' "Of course we'll live alone," says hubby overseas, but when he arrives home, he reverts back into an obedient son, he returns to his unmarried status and follows his mother's wishes. Young wives should never forget that,' Helga continued.

'There are other trouble spots,' Helga laughed, 'but they can be worked out in the long run, although at the time they become giant obstacles in your mind and you fret and even lose sleep.

'Differences in bringing up children, for instance,' she said. 'Child care is often done by little child-servants. It is not the mum-in-law or the sister-in-law, but the ayah system. And the child rarely sleeps in a bed but is usually carried around—this is customary—and if the child is awake it is still carried around and never left to its own devices. Little nine or ten-year-old girls carry out the work and parents think they are doing the child a service by always having someone in attendance, solely there for the child. And then you find that they are speaking a dialect and not proper Urdu and the child is getting fed all these superstitions. I know of cases,' she said, 'where the little girl stays in the same room when the baby is sleeping in case it stirs.'

'So a baby, or toddler is never alone?'

'No, it is never alone and not encouraged to play alone or even sleep alone, and I think it is a bad thing for the personal development of the child,' said Helga, 'for they grow up never being content to be by themselves or never knowing how to deal with it—seeing it as a terrible thing. I was very careful that my children were brought up with the security of being surrounded by people who loved them, but also being able to develop as individuals.

'I tried to find a middle way.'

Helga has been in Pakistan for forty years and she has thrown in her lot with the country and its people willingly, as she explained to me. Other women she has observed seemed more inclined to accept their lot philosophically. They were not here by choice and many stayed in unhappy marriages because of children, or because they had no work skills. 'But as they grow older most women make their peace with living in Pakistan,' she smiled at me. What was their secret?

'Women in waiting', I have called them. Waiting to have a house of their own; hoping their lover would turn away from his extended family to them—yes, in some cases even waiting to 'escape'. Even strong-willed Marguerite, who'd refused to enter a relationship with Pakistan, had found a spiritual home within Islam.

But perhaps it was simpler than that. Perhaps their secret had everything to do with family.

In the early days of their married life many wives had found themselves trapped inside an extended family their husbands refused to turn away from. And so the new bride tolerated the joint family and the joint family tolerated the foreign wife.

The years went by; the women finally developed a sense of belonging by creating and guarding their own 'extended families'. Surrounded by their Pakistani children and their spouses and their grandchildren, was this how they finally made their peace with Pakistan? Or was it only a truce?

CHAPTER 10

Chanan

✻   ✻   ✻

Muhammad Abbas missed his wife Khulsoom although his loneliness was hidden in the heart of his noisy, extended family where a man was never on his own for long. The children of Muhammad Abbas were old enough to know that loneliness and being alone were not the same, but they could not stop their kind, soft-eyed father from grieving for their mother, even ten years after her death.

At first the children pleaded with him to remarry, to take another wife and become a husband and father again. But now it was clear to all his relatives: his sisters and his brothers, his cousins and uncles and aunts in the village and nearby towns, that Abbas would remain a widower for the rest of his life. Such a shame, everyone said; he could easily take another wife, a man not yet turned fifty. 'How could I possibly take another wife?' he would say with a sad half-smile on his face, when one of his four sons or three daughters raised the subject with him yet again.

255

If the truth be known, some of his friends even secretly envied Abbas: envied him his romantic, steadfast love, even his melancholy, for a woman whose face they sometimes had trouble recalling. Their wives however, remembered her well, remembered the good housewife, the even-tempered woman who smiled and sang as she worked; they remembered her as a young girl, hair neatly plaited under her dupatta, as they walked together by the canals giggling on their way to school. They sighed, wishing that their husbands might show a little of the tenderness that Abbas felt for his wife's memory.

Muhammad Abbas had lived all his life in Chanan, a large village in the heart of the Punjab, just off the famous Grand Trunk Road of Kipling fame—the old Mughal highway between Islamabad and Lahore. The immediate family consisted of his four brothers and their wives and children, and his four sisters—at least until they married, and joined their husbands' families in nearby villages.

After his father's death, Abbas became the most senior member of a fluctuating household of between twenty and thirty souls; a benign figure who ruled together with his four younger brothers, Azam, Abdul Ghufoor, Abdul Aziz and Muhammad Tariq. Usually relations were intimate and cordial. The brothers made their decisions together and kept their money in a joint account at the Habib Bank. Lengthy discussions took place before any major purchase—a piece of land, a television set, a trip abroad—was decided on. Usually they reached a consensus, but not before talking it over with their wives in the dead of night when the children were fast asleep and they enjoyed some privacy at last.

But now and then a cold wind might blow through the household for a day or two, if a brother felt slighted over some incident or piece of gossip and turned his back on one or another of his brothers. On these occasions sulking, rather than shouting, soothed wounded pride.

Tensions and quarrels were always difficult to accommodate in the joint household because the silence affected the brothers' wives as well, although the children were usually immune from adult childishness and continued playing together. Only once in the family's history had there ever been a 'Great Silence', as it was called; one which lasted for three years before the rift was healed. Sisters-in-law at the water pump and in the courtyard could not talk to one another—at least not while their husbands were watching. Women's quarrels on the other hand, were like sudden storms which soon blew over and were forgotten, like the quarrels of their childhood when as sisters and cousins they had all played together. But usually the family functioned as a singleminded unit with little room for the desires and selfish whims of the individual.

Planning was in decades, from one generation to the next. Over the years the family prospered, and rose from relatively modest beginnings to a position of comfortable respectability in the ranks of the lower middle-class, running two medical dispensaries and increasing the family's economic wellbeing by exporting sons and brothers to work overseas. For the last sixteen years Abbas had supervised the rise of the family as his father before him, content to watch over his new grandchildren and plan their ascent in the world. Sometimes late at night he talked to his dead wife, with the radio switched on so that no-one could hear; telling her how their children had grown into hardworking young adults, and of the latest grandchild. In many ways Abbas was just like his father Anwar, happy to remain at home, leaving others to discover and explore, to confront new ways and begin to change.

Muhammad Abbas's father and my father were brothers. My

father's money sent from Australia had helped buy the land and build the house in Chanan, complete with hot water and sanitation. Refrigerators and upright gas stoves (which were never used), radios, cameras, cash and a flood of electrical items found their way to Pakistan for nearly sixty years. My father took his duties as elder son and brother seriously and letters and sustenance flowed across the Indian Ocean and across the dusty plains of the Punjab like a life-giving blood transfusion.

The last time we had met was nearly thirty years earlier. Abbas, the first of his brothers to marry, and his silent bride Khulsoom had two young children and everyone lived in an ancient mud-walled house without electricity and indoor sanitation, where the buffalo ate their bales of green grass and straw at night in the courtyard, where hot water for my shower was carried in a bucket to a wooden shed and where a special wooden-throned toilet was built for my use on the flat-topped roof to spare me the indignities and embarrassment of using the fields like everyone else, for there was no toilet in the house.

After neighbours were observed loitering on the roofs of their own houses, a screen was hastily found and my bowels and I were left alone in purdah.

I woke up on those cold November mornings snuggled under a warm quilt after sleeping like a princess on my comfortable string bed, in the room reserved for me alone—an unheard of luxury—with wooden shutters which closed tight over iron-barred windows and hard, cracked cement floors.

Just outside the front door of the house was a tiny alcove where the women of the house squatted over fires, slapping *parathas* in their hands and stirring curries thick with buffalo ghee, onions, fresh green coriander and masala. I remembered their curiosity and their indulgence of my unorthodox ways. They were 'good women', but what was I? I was my father's daughter and that was enough.

Since the 1880s a male of each generation of the family—a father, brother or son—would one day begin to feel restless and vaguely dissatisfied with the small world surrounding him. My paternal grandfather, Fateh Muhammad (Dean was the surname he took on his arrival in Australia) had begun the family tradition of seeking one's fortune far away from the River Jhelum, travelling south across the 'black sea' to the green coastal plains and outback desert of Western Australia, more than 100 years ago. My mother's father, a Kashmiri (who by strange coincidence was also named Fateh Deen: same name, different spelling) about whom we know little, but who was of the same generation as my Punjabi grandfather, was also dreaming of making his fortune at about the same time. As a child I liked to imagine that they may have even sailed on the same ship; one grandfather (Dean) disembarking at Fremantle in the west, while the other (Deen) sailed east to Melbourne. Sadly I have no memories of either man.

Men of my grandfathers' generation joined the ranks of Muslim travellers, settling in Australia, in Canada, South Africa and other distant places. They came from an undivided Indian subcontinent, from an undivided Punjab ruled by the British, long before the modern political inventions of India and Pakistan. My grandfathers joined hundreds of other eager, shy, young men who travelled in ones and twos along dusty roads, clutching their British passports, ready to sail across oceans for the adventure of a lifetime. Times were hard in the Punjab and families were large; there was not enough land and other means of sustaining families must be found.

When I was young I used to believe that had they foreseen the loneliness of their lives, or imagined the bitter racist jibes that would be flung in their faces or whispered behind their backs as they clung to the margins of tolerance, they would still have made the same decisions, but now that I'm older, I'm not so sure.

After years of hard work, my Punjabi grandfather saved his money and sent for his village wife who joined him after innumerable bureaucratic delays (one family story relates how he eventually petitioned Queen Victoria), and so it was in Western Australia and not Chanan that my father was born in 1905. My father's mother hated her life in this foreign land of *Angrezi*, English people with yellow hair, pale skin and dull eyes. We know little about this sad lonely woman, only that she remained in purdah, leading an isolated existence with no other female companionship, for the other Muslim men who came never intended to stay and were either single or left their womenfolk at home. It is unlikely that she understood one word of English, making her imprisonment complete, as if she was buried alive. Therefore it comes as no surprise that she and my father returned to the warmth of the Punjab when he was still a baby. There my father remained until his mother died, when as a young man of twenty he returned to his father's side in Australia.

Before my father left on his great adventure in Australia, the Chanan relatives tried to ensure the tall, handsome youth's return by betrothing him to a young, good-tempered girl—a plain girl, but pliable and obedient. After a few years, they thought, he would come back to the placid ways of Chanan, marry and resume his place in the household. But the years went by and Abdul Majeed did not return. Forty years elapsed before he came back, and when he did, it was in triumph as the local boy who'd made good, with photos of his house, his shiny car, his business and of course his wife and children, and a pile of presents which filled two suitcases. He returned like a rajah and held court like a rajah. Everyone scampered around to do his bidding, but he was a reasonable tyrant and asked only for parathas for breakfast and *sooji halwa* every day.

But what had happened to his village sweetheart all those years ago, we used to pester him as children. And how had he met our mother? Nearly forty years before his triumphant homecoming, my father attended an Eid celebration in Melbourne and met my mother.

My mother had grown up in Melbourne in the suburb of Carlton, the only daughter of the Kashmiri Deen who'd travelled through the Victorian countryside with a horse and cart as a hawker. Incredibly enough he married an Australian widow with ten children who, before she met him, used to take her unruly brood around Australia as a vaudeville troupe of 'genteel' lady singers.

My father fell head over heels in love, and momentarily turned his back on tradition, risking family honour to wed the creamy-skinned, hazel-eyed beauty.

But his family in Chanan stood by their errant brother, and his younger brother Anwar saved our honour by marrying my father's betrothed instead. She became the mother of my cousin Abbas. I remember her as a motherly, smiling woman, usually barefoot, who massaged my shoulders and my feet in spite of my protests and who cooked my favourite dishes.

My father's once-in-a-life indiscretion provided me with enough ammunition for a lifetime, for when he started muttering about the virtues of arranged marriages and traditional ways, I would look at him in pseudo-bewilderment, 'But Daddy, you made a love marriage and I'm only following in my father's footsteps!' It was then, so my mother swears, that he began the annoying habit of grinding his teeth.

To try to understand love and respect between husband and wife in Muslim societies is to look into a private, dimly-lit world where overt signs or demonstrative overtures are banned. It was only when my father was in his late seventies that I came to truly understand my parents' secret world when I stumbled across some passionate love letters written by my father, a few months earlier, while he was overseas travelling alone. This man

I had only seen through the eyes of an impatient daughter
chafing under his control was a true romantic, a poet-lover, but
only my mother knew this.

So through a chain of circumstances, my family life became
rooted in Australia and not in Pakistan as might have been the
case. I have no regrets.

✳   ✳   ✳

My mother always believed that my father spoilt his younger
brother, my Uncle Anwar, by sending him regular remittances
and continuing to support him for what turned out to be an
entire lifetime. Even during the 1930s Depression, my father
managed to send a few pounds sterling home from the desert
goldfields of Boulder and Kalgoorlie where he struggled to estab-
lish a herbalist shop and where my sister and I were born. I on
the other hand could understand my father's feelings of being
torn between two families. I think he suffered enormous guilt
that Australia became his home and that he had witnessed the
trauma of Partition and the birth of Pakistan only from a
distance.

On my first trip with my father to Pakistan I grew rather
fond of my Uncle Anwar. Few words passed between us, for he
had no English and I had no Punjabi or Urdu, but he would
pat my head, which I lowered respectfully, and smile in a curi-
ously absent-minded way, nodding gently over his hookah as he
sat listening to my father who had immediately resumed older
brother status and had a thousand and one tales to spin—from
hunting kangaroos and emus to riding across the Nullarbor Plain
on a motorbike.

Many years later I realised that dear Uncle Anwar was indulg-
ing his opium habit when he drew the fumes from his hookah
deeply into his lungs and smiled dreamily into the distance. For

a lot of the time he was really off with the fairies—or in this case the djinns. But as my father told me sternly (with only a hint of embarrassment), elderly people in Pakistan often smoked opium as a painkiller for their arthritis. And Uncle Anwar certainly looked older than my father, although he was five years younger, in spite of his blue-black dyed hair and moustache. Nobody was ever permitted to criticise Uncle Anwar, not while his big brother was around.

Uncle Anwar had stayed at home while my father followed in his father's footsteps. Sixty years later the pattern repeated itself when Abdul Ghufoor third in line, left for New Jersey and his brother Abbas remained behind. Why Ghufoor chose the USA and not Australia remains a mystery to this day, but I have always suspected that it had something to do with finding it easier to enter the USA as part of a group of young men who huddled together under tarpaulins out of sight when the ship docked and then were smuggled on land when the coast was clear. The answer is no doubt buried in one of the letters my father received month in, month out which filled an entire chest: letters the rest of us could never understand, including my mother, who longed to find out all the Chanan secrets and just how much of our savings my generous father kept sending home. My mother stubbornly refused to understand my father's dual obligations. She fought a rearguard action for most of her married life, trying to prevent him from responding to all of his brother's requests; worried that all their assets (which she had helped accumulate) would disappear, leaving nothing for their own children. I think she was really jealous that my father divided his love as well as his wealth.

Anyway, my poor cousin Ghufoor was unfortunately caught by the authorities who sent him packing and only years later did he set forth again, this time legally, and now he is the proud possessor of a Green Card. The tall handsome seventeen-year-old that I recall is now in his mid-forties with a receding hairline and a tired, lined face. He has joined the ranks of the millions of migrant workers who contribute well over three billion dollars to Pakistan's economy every year—nearly two million Pakistanis work in the Middle East alone. They are now a modern industry and Pakistan's main source of foreign exchange.

By a strange coincidence, the migratory birds were all returning to Chanan within days of each other. The first to arrive was Abbas's eldest son Farid, back from the United Kingdom, the next was Ghufoor from the USA and I came last, as befitted a woman, an honorary male and someone who likes to make an entrance.

❊   ❊   ❊

I arrived on an intercity bus and alighted at the Jhelum crossroads with too many suitcases and a dreadful headache brought on by hours of non-stop Bollywood video music ringing in my ears. Afraid that he would miss me, Abbas had been waiting at the bus stop for two hours. He'd hired a Kombi van to carry the crowd of people—all men—who wanted to be the first to welcome me.

Ten years had passed since my father's death and there was much to talk about. Four of the five brothers spoke English, but their wives—those shy, gently-spoken teenaged girls I remembered from many years ago, now respectable portly matrons, far more dignified than ever before—had forgotten most of their English, however we hugged one another and communicated through smiles, words and photographs. But no matter how hard I tried during my stay, I would find myself locked into the world of my male cousins, who ate with me, gossiped with me and took me on guided tours, while their wives stayed at home gazing wistfully after us. I felt like a traitor.

Built fourteen years ago, the family house formed a large U shape with a flywire-enclosed verandah and a courtyard big enough for a cricket match. The house rang with the noise of the four families housed under its roof. The house was larger than it seemed, which was just as well since each family seemed to have at least four or five children as far as I could make out, for they never stayed still long enough for me to count. There also seemed to be four separate cooking areas and four bathrooms. Two small detached houses had been added to the compound, one for the widowed Abbas who ate with a different family each night, and one for visitors.

As I was regarded as family, I was given a large room in the main house which also had a dining table and eight chairs. Throughout the day, unless I closed the curtains hanging in front of my door, people visited me; they would drop in and sit on the bed and chat. Only when I closed my doors did people keep their distance and it was an action I tried to avoid. My quarters were pleasant with cream walls and old calendars from 1991, which must have been a good year for plump, smiling Japanese babies advertising the goodness of powdered milk.

All four wives maintained separate hearths and while they prepared their own meals, they exchanged dishes with one another and visited throughout the day. The brothers must have learnt early in their married lives that harmony survived in the beehive, and conjugal rights were not at risk, if the women kept their independence. The separate kitchens and dining areas seemed a sensible arrangement. After a few days Abbas reminded me that each couple was waiting for me to take lunch or dinner with them and there was some confusion as to why I was not observing this custom. Hastily I made amends and began my rounds.

Life had certainly changed and it was more than electricity, modern sanitation and running hot and cold water. 'We' had come up in the world and this change was linked to the new house and the new generation who had gone overseas and prospered. Farid, for example, who owned a small chain of children's clothes shops in the East End of London, had married an English-born Pakistani girl who worked with him in the shops and now had two children. Ghufoor had won his Green Card and in another year expected his wife Naseer and his five children to join him in New Jersey where for ten years he'd been manager of a large supermarket. Money now found its way back to Chanan from three continents, for other relatives worked in Germany and Denmark.

A greater awareness of the world outside the village cannot help but introduce social change, and what had taken place in Chanan was happening throughout rural Punjab. Looking outside the village meant working your way beyond the confines of local culture. But although new value systems may trickle slowly into the cracks, women are usually the last to be affected and often slow to change. Material change does not always mean that values, especially the values that restrain women, are changing. The 'kitchen culture' they internalised as young girls remains a powerful influence and they cling to what they know best, but their daughters are already receiving more education than their mothers did, are no longer wearing the burqa and know of their fathers' world through school and television.

The signs of material prosperity were more obvious. All the women of the household now used a local tailor, a woman who came to the house and made their outfits; there was a sweeper woman who came daily; there were barbers for the men and drivers for rented cars; and the rooms were now furnished in what passed for modern style with dressing tables and wardrobes, although the old-style metal chests were still used. Nobody churned the milk, for the buffalo I remembered had disappeared: buttermilk, ghee and yoghurt were brought to the door—

everyone thought this was progress, especially the women. My relatives now outsourced.

And there were other more subtle changes. The women were not in purdah and the burqa which I'd remembered my cousins wearing had gone completely. I have a very clear memory of walking outside the old mud-walled house with three burqa-clad women, one of whom (I think it was Naseer, who later married 'New Jersey Ghufoor') had walked into a brick wall she'd been unable to see through the small meshed grill of her robe. Now the young women walked outside in the bazaars and the markets with just the dupatta scarf—not even the longer chador which was the usual compromise between the scarf and the 'tent'. Most books I'd read led me to believe that lower middle-class families who were making their way up the social ladder tended to place a lot of importance on purdah in all its forms, including segregation, but obviously we were different. The women of the Chanan house did not work outside and had never done so—a source of pride to the brothers. They lived what seemed to be the normal life of a Punjabi housewife, busy with cooking and household chores as well as preparing for special celebrations like the dozens of weddings which took place each year, and of course, childcare. 'We' had not graduated to the ayah system of childcare used by the upper middle-class, and babies and toddlers were picked up and treated with open affection by both men and women who spoilt them outrageously.

Yet the routines were placid and I thought of how the young girls, in spite of better education, were still internalising a world of domestic knowledge and behaviour, learning roles which did not empower them although they may or may not have found them personally rewarding. Learning how to cook and iron, how to look after their hair and their skin and a thousand similar lessons were one part of their female heritage, but they were also learning more serious lessons by observation: lessons on submissiveness, self-sacrifice and unimaginativeness. Watching the special relationships between mothers and sons on television and in real life, girls begin their training by being devoted to their brothers, satisfying their needs before their own. The reality of many women's lives is that they find companionship, affection—even respect, through the emotionally charged relationship they nurture with their sons.

And what did young boys learn?

I spent lazy days sitting on a charpoi out in the courtyard. The heat was increasing and so were the flies already in training for summer; they seemed nastier than the Australian variety I'd grown up with. I watched the girls dress one another's hair and exchange bright lipsticks; they had plenty of face and hair creams and perfumes although I was pleased to see none of the skin bleaches one saw advertised in magazines, potions guaranteed to whiten your skin and make you a desirable bride. 'Little Hanifa', Abbas's daughter and my namesake, never seemed to tire of dragging out a large metal chest and rummaging through swathes of material she'd been given. She told me she already had fifty-two different outfits as part of her trousseau. She also loved showing off her jewellery.

One of the brothers told me in an aside, 'This is how we keep our women quiet. Buy them their pretty bangles and earrings; let them admire one another,' he laughed. I felt as if I was being initiated into the male fraternity.

'You're a man with education, you ought to be ashamed,' I lectured him half-jokingly. But of course he wasn't. Who passed on to the boys the folk wisdom that jewellery was a female tranquilliser? Not their mothers and their sisters, I hoped.

One afternoon, towards the end of my stay, Farid and his big
sister, 'Little Hanifa', took me to inspect the Tariq Medical Hall,
a lucrative little money-maker in nearby Dinga, which Uncle
Anwar (with the help of my dad's remittances) had established
in 1955 and named after his youngest son Muhammad Tariq.
The small dispensary had gradually expanded over the years and
Farid, a pleasant young man with a well-groomed, shiny moustache and laughing eyes—doing very well for himself in London
everyone said—explained that the family had recently bought
the shop next door and had big plans for expansion. Under
Uncle Anwar's indolent supervision the brothers had all served
their time working at the dispensary. Now Abbas contented
himself by taking a back seat and with 'New Jersey Ghufoor'
overseas, the three remaining brothers were left to run things,
helped occasionally (if the spirit moved him) by Abbas's youngest son Mahmood, a silent, sulky-faced youth, spoilt rotten,
given to taking to his bed if denied anything—which seemed to
happen every second day.

The small town of Dinga was only a few kilometres away
from Chanan and as we drove past crops of wheat, mustard seed
and vegetables, past the rows of orange trees, the fields and
byways were alive with large, sturdy black oxen grazing or rolling
in small mud-holes or ambling in front of quick-witted herds-
men on their way to the river, for the pleasures of wallowing in
the water which they cannot live without. The roads we bumped
along had been washed out by storms years earlier, leaving the
unsealed road pitted with potholes. Money provided by the
government to repair the roads had disappeared long ago into
private pockets.

My eye was caught by three prancing white horses with beautifully decorated saddles and reins. The horsemen were wearing
long shirts, vests and baggy Punjabi trousers. Sitting tall and
proud in the saddle, the ends of their coloured turbans waved

in the breeze as they trotted by the side of the road, carrying long lances in their hands. Horses and masters were returning from the annual district horse show where everyone gathered to compete for prizes and relive the glory of the Punjabi cavalry tradition which still provides the Pakistani army with most of its fighting men.

The road to Dinga was thronged with horse-drawn tongas, still the most popular form of transport in rural areas although their days in cities like Lahore are numbered. Wearing the distinctive Afghan headdress, transient Afghan wood cutters and their families sat outside straw huts. On the outside walls of many of the mud houses I saw dung cakes drying, ready to be used as fuel.

We arrived at the Tariq Medical Hall in the heart of Dinga's Raja Bazaar which, in spite of its grand name, turned out to be the most fly-ridden bazaar I'd yet seen anywhere in my travels. The Tariq Medical Hall at first sight appeared no more than a dusty, windowless narrow shop. But once inside the cavern of the shop, it seemed to go on forever. Dusty medical treasures were stacked haphazardly, spilling over the counters and shelves.

Outside the Tariq Medical Hall, the noise of the Raja Bazaar raged around us like live theatre. I was grateful that all the flies were infatuated with the sides of mutton and beef hanging on hooks for sale at the open-air butchers or clustered on the long pieces of sugar cane (inadequately covered by green netting) waiting to be crushed into a delicious, wickedly unhygienic drink. Thank God the flies were too busy to enter the Tariq Medical Hall, or was it the sight and smell of potions and pills, unguents and hypodermics which put them off? But in spite of the dust and the flies the bazaar was full of energy and good humour—it was like a whirlpool, sucking in every item of news and gossip. It was a masculine world.

Muhammad Tariq, who stood smiling behind the counter,

told me all about the diseases which come like clockwork every summer, just a month away: diarrhoea, dysentery, respiratory illness like TB, and malaria.

'Next month will be bad,' said the youngest of the Chanan brothers. 'Summer brings with it the dirty water and of course most of this area still has no sanitation. The illnesses peak for about four or five months.'

During the bad months the brothers would see as many as 150 patients a day.

Chemist shops or pharmacies as we know them in the West, do not exist in most of South Asia. Doctors are few in number and thousands have emigrated elsewhere, taking the 'brain drain' to epidemic proportions—besides most people cannot afford doctors. Instead people put a lot of trust in their local dispensaries and in Pakistan you must have a certificate as a qualified dispenser to run one. The magic piece of paper gives you the right to translate prescriptions and sell medicines and drugs. It becomes yours after a one year, full-time course at a government hospital under the practical supervision of qualified doctors, where you also learn how to stitch wounds and give needles. I was impressed by the brothers' industry but sorry that I had missed the lady doctor who called at the dispensary to see female patients once a week for the fee of RS 100 (US$3), half the usual price.

The following day we drove off on another local adventure to the Pakistan International Airlines (PIA) office in Kharian, a much larger town than Dinga, to reconfirm my air ticket. Farid and Abbas accompanied me and this time we drove a different route and Abbas pointed out a large village of Shias—three or five thousand people, he said, as we drove past the Shia mosque with its traditional black flags flying outside. Sometimes there were tensions between Sunnis and Shias, but everything was quiet at the moment, said Abbas.

It was at the Kharian office of PIA that I was almost 'felled' in the name of purdah. Although we arrived early enough, the office was full of men sitting around with glum looks on their faces waiting their turn—more than forty men, sitting with arms folded, just waiting, coughing and clearing their throats. Other, wiser men were coming and going, tearing a ticket from the dispenser and retreating, knowing they could return in three or four hours and still find themselves in line.

The ticket officers were going about their business in that deliberately indolent fashion which seems endemic throughout the Indian subcontinent, a style impossible to shift, but one which makes you want to run amok with a machete lopping off heads right and left. Suddenly one of the bored officials glanced in my direction. In a harsh voice he told me to 'Go to the women's room.' At first we were puzzled until I noticed that I was the only woman present. So I turned obediently and went in the direction he was pointing, only to find that the 'women's room' was a wooden chair in the corridor between two offices where men brushed past every few minutes. I was modestly dressed in my shalwar kameez, and had made sure that my dupatta was in place and even wore my sunglasses to give a double purdah effect—but really this was too much!

'No!' I said to myself and returned to the main office again, noting that somehow in this altercation Abbas and his son had vanished.

'Go back to the women's room!' I was told, so I turned on my heel and again retreated.

Five minutes later I sneaked back again.

This time, eyes flashing, he snarled at me, but one of the waiting men rallied and found a spare chair for me and so I sat to one side like a leper, although I noticed a wave of sympathy run through the seated men who were all horribly embarrassed by what was taking place. They were men, I told myself smugly, who knew of a world outside Pakistan.

Where were my relatives? I wondered. Time passed and the work tempo had not changed. I realised that I might spend the entire day waiting in this hell hole.

Suddenly I had an idea and when Farid and Abbas poked their heads inside the office to check on my progress, I called out, 'Let's go!'

I was about to conjure up a 'sorcerer's device' known as *sifarish*, which means to call in a favour, or in polite parlance, to call on someone of influence to intercede on your behalf. In Karachi, weeks earlier, I had met a PIA senior executive who amazingly had once met my father in Perth. 'Take my card,' he said. 'If you need any help, here I am.'

I rang this kind man from a nearby office and within ten minutes everything was sorted out, and by the time I returned to the PIA office, a much chastened ticket officer, bowing and scraping and offering me cups of tea, proved that such a thing as customer service did exist in Pakistan. The waiting men didn't seem to mind—it was a victory for all of us. I noticed some smiles and like to think they approved. Everyone in Pakistan, even BB, needs someone, somewhere, sometime to intercede for them; with a policeman, a doctor, an immigration official—poor people especially need sifarish.

On the way home I asked Abbas why there were so many small brick kilns with smoking stacks everywhere you looked.

'Ah,' said Abbas, 'When the men finally return from working overseas, they are only interested in building mosques as monuments to their piety. Everywhere you have these mosques which are almost empty and are only half-filled on Fridays when jumma is held. While they are still overseas the men send their dollars or their deutschmarks home so their families can tear down the old mud wall houses and build new brick houses.'

'Like you have done,' I said.

'Yes,' he replied, 'like we have done.'

According to some reports less than two per cent of total remittances sent by migrant workers are put into agricultural or industrial investments. Mosques and houses; houses and mosques were the priority—and of course repaying money borrowed so that a son or a brother could follow the yellow brick road to the Middle East, the USA or another land of wish fulfilment.

When the men are away, the women grow more confident and begin to grow like strong vines taking in the air and reaching for the sunlight. Throughout the Punjab there are many households—some people say whole villages—where the husbands and sons have become remittance men, leaving wives and mothers to take on new challenges.

There is a neighbour across the lane who, they tell me, does everything herself. Maleeka Begum is her name and while her husband is away in the Middle East, returning home only every second year, she is the head of the family and handles the reins of authority with a light but telling touch. Maleeka Begum now makes decisions she has never before been called upon to make: the purchase of buffalo, her daughter's wedding and the construction of the house—all the things which men claim as their birthright and normally do.

But even tall, sharp Maleeka bows before her brother, leaning on him in times of need and showing him respect, for everyone knows that a brother can never be replaced. Who lent her the money for the doctor when her son was ill and who found him work in Lahore? Who arranged the loan for her daughters' dowries?

One day I spied her cutting grass for her buffalo on a piece of land at the back of our house. 'Doesn't that land belong to you?' I asked Abbas.

'Yes,' he said with a helpless smile on his round face. 'I once planted fruit trees and started a little orchard just for our own use. But it failed because all the young boys used to raid the mango trees I planted and there was nothing left for us. I don't mind if Maleeka Begum takes the grass for her buffalo,' he finished off in his mild voice and I was sure that Maleeka knew that he knew, and was pleased that he turned a blind eye to her escapades. I wondered if his largesse had anything to do with Maleeka Begum's childhood friendship with his dead wife Khulsoom.

∗　∗　∗

The Chanan extended family seemed to function well (although everyone may have been on their very best behaviour). But many of the middle-class feminists I'd spoken to seemed to accept the nuclear family as the ideal model; one that would be an antidote for all of their domestic unhappiness. Yes, I could see that a joint family arrangement could oppress and inhibit, but were there no positives?

When I spoke to Naseer, the wife of 'New Jersey Ghufoor' she told me she was not looking forward to living 'the American way', as she put it. She wanted to join her husband but was frightened of the notion of living alone without the support of her sisters-in-law and her relatives. Ghufoor had been away for twelve long years, coming home only once a year. She shrugged helplessly and that single movement showed how much she had missed him over the years—her husband, the boy she had hoped her parents would choose for her. Naseer and Ghufoor loved one another dearly but they had grown into middle-age away from each other. But at least in the village Naseer was never alone and her feeling of abandonment was lessened. The women shared the domestic work and childcare; older relatives were not left to fend for themselves—all of this was revealed to me in Chanan.

But soon there would be change and I wondered if the household would ever be the same? Naseer and her five children would go to New Jersey in a year or so. 'Little Hanifa' was to be married and would move to the town of Sarai Alamgir to live with her husband's relatives.

And what of Muhammad Tariq and his family? Just before my arrival a quarrel had broken out and it seemed that the rift was not yet healed. Tariq's wife wanted her family to leave the village of Chanan and its quiet ways to live with her sisters and their husbands in the grand capital, Islamabad, and who could blame her? Abbas was not pleased; he was not pleased at all, but by now was sadly resigned to the break-up of the family.

But I thought Abbas was unduly pessimistic, for something would always draw the migratory birds back to Chanan. Some of the brothers had wandered off to seek their fortunes in other lands and their sons would continue the custom; others were content to remain behind, but I had the strangest feeling that one day when their desire for the material goods of the outside world and prosperity had been sated, they would eventually return to Chanan. Perhaps they would build a mosque as an act of piety and in remembrance of their parents buried in the local cemetery close to the wife of Abbas. It would not surprise me to one day see four elderly brothers once more living under the same roof, quarrelling gently, treating one another now and then to 'silences', and once again the women of the house would be united.

CHAPTER 11

Zainab Noor

* * *

The torture of Zainab Noor was a story I baulked at putting down on paper for a very long time. When I finally kept my promise and tried to find ways to describe what happened to her on that terrible day in February 1994, my mind protested and dragged me down into a dark place. Quite simply, the words refused to come.

Zainab's narrative radiated an almost unbearable intensity. I try to use the word 'unbearable' sparingly these days. When you meet women who have lived through the 'unbearable' you learn to feel ashamed.

By the time I met Zainab Noor in Islamabad in April 1996, she had almost become a forgotten woman. Two years earlier her sad, waif-like face featured everywhere on the covers of magazines in Pakistan. The whole country was in shock and even the Prime Minister, Benazir Bhutto, felt moved to intervene.

The story of Zainab Noor is also the story of another remarkable woman, Shahnaz Bukhari, who carries the nightmares of too many women in her head. She is now marked for life and in her dreams descends into a world where death is something women pray for.

Zainab sat with her young son, Muhammad Kaleem, on the worn floral sofa in Shahnaz Bukhari's untidy lounge-room in Islamabad. They sat close together. Zainab held her son's hand tightly, and while it was hard to tell who was comforting whom, one could sense they were used to consoling each other.

Zainab's enormous dark eyes followed Shahnaz wherever she went, scared the older woman might disappear. She was a whisper of a woman, fragile in appearance, a woman used to waiting in the shadows for something to happen. We waited in silence for Shahnaz, who had brought us together, and even now was trying to create some space in her crowded day to join us. Without her we were lost: she linked our worlds together as interpreter, friend and mentor. To Zainab she was also the woman who had saved her life. She called her *baji*, or older sister, and her eyes lit up whenever Shahnaz entered the room.

Kaleem was a beautiful boy of eight, whose eyes were made extra lustrous with black kohl. He was as neat as a button in his brown checked shirt and trousers, his hair glistening with oil, combed away from his face—he was the image of his mother; there was no sign of his father in his face, which must have comforted Zainab. Kaleem seemed unnaturally quiet and much too still for a child his age. But I made him smile by recording his voice on my tape recorder and playing it back for him. In a small clear voice, he explained in Urdu that he was eight and that when he grew up, he wanted to be a soldier in the Pakistani army. Finally when Shahnaz joined us—all the while shouting instructions over her shoulder to her daughters—we sent him into the next room to play. We wanted him out of harm's way so that he couldn't hear what his father had done to his mother.

Our protection was more symbolic than real; those huge eyes had seen too much. I watched him through the glass doors, sitting solemnly on the floor playing with the tiny Matchbox cars I'd bought in Australia, knowing I was bound to meet families with children in my travels. He looked like a child used to playing alone.

'Salaam alaikum,' Zainab began. 'And peace be upon you,' I answered, 'Wa laikum salaam.'

She married her husband when she was fourteen. Their marriage was organised on the basis of the customary practice of *watta satta* or exchange marriage. In such an arrangement a brother and a sister from one family marry the siblings of another family, but according to her mother, her husband's family never kept their end of the bargain and refused to send a girl to marry one of Zainab's brothers.

Her husband was much older and had already married and divorced one wife. He came from a religious family. Qari Muhammad Sharif was his name. The title Qari means one who recites the Holy Qur'an. He was the imam of the village mosque and because he was also an *Hafiz-i-Qur'an*, one who has memorised the entire Qur'an, he was given great respect. He also used to teach the children the Qur'an the old way, by rote. No doubt he was a stern disciplinarian like most madrassah teachers.

Zainab's family earned a meagre living by working in the fields of a rich farmer in Attock, a village near Peshawar in the North West Frontier Province where she was born.

Like many young brides she endured what she described as the normal jealousy of her mother-in-law; she would cook and clean and do everything asked of her but as soon as the son stepped into the house, his mother began complaining that Zainab was lazy, that she did nothing all day, and then the mother would stand back and watch while her son beat his wife, and he beat her very badly, she said.

'For eight years, I was married to this man,' she said softly, keeping her eyes fixed on her lap while Shahnaz held her hand. 'The first few weeks of our life together were all right, but after this time there was never a single day of peace that I remember,' she paused and added with dignity, 'although I gave him a beautiful son.'

Qari Muhammad Sharif was actually her first cousin. He was the son of her mother's eldest sister. The mother-in-law who egged her son on, was also her aunt.

I listened to yet another story about an older woman who incited attacks against her daughter-in-law, instead of protecting her. There were households where women wreaked some kind of twisted revenge, who felt their own suffering was validated by watching younger women enduring the same treatment handed down to them long ago, when they were dreamy, soft-eyed brides. After a lifetime of waiting, the wife becomes a mother-in-law, finally gains a little power and they wield it with a meanness of spirit that is heart-breaking. They cannot break the cycle. The slave becomes the slave-master.

On visits home to see her parents, a pattern developed where Zainab would refuse to return and her husband and his family would come after her. 'Send her back to us; we won't do it again,' they would cry. And their entreaties always won the day. But as soon as she returned, the cycle of abuse began all over again.

'He knew my parents could do nothing,' said Zainab while Shahnaz added, for my benefit, that the Qari knew his power was absolute because her parents were too poor to protect their daughter, while his parents were more influential. They had the ear of rich men in the village. Such men find it useful to have an imam in their pocket.

'He thought he was god on earth,' Shahnaz explained. 'The man was an ignorant mullah; he thinks it is in the Qur'an that

there is one God in heaven, while god on earth is your husband.'
She gently coaxed Zainab to carry on.

'There were four brothers in the family and all of them were
mullahs, a family of mullahs,' Zainab said, returning to her story.
'They were not poor, they were better off than most.'

I asked her if the other brothers were also unkind to their
wives.

'They beat them, but not too badly,' she answered, and a
vision filled my mind of a stern tribe of men all cut from the
same cloth, who had never learnt to behave towards women
according to the Islamic principles which they liked to boast
governed their lives. In Bangladesh I'd seen them as ruthless
political figures or puppets out in the streets, yelling slogans,
pronouncing fatwas and forcing the way towards a total Islamic
state—I'd never thought of them as husbands and fathers before.
Everything I heard about the brothers fed my antipathy towards
these kinds of men.

Life became worse when Qari Sharif insisted that Zainab
persuade her mother to organise another marriage—this time
between his youngest brother and Zainab's youngest sister. This
was his wish and he expected obedience.

'I would not agree,' Zainab said, 'because he was still beating
me and why should I deliver my sister into the hands of such a
family?'

By now they were living alone, in a house next to the mosque
a long way from her parents. He kept pressing her and finally
it was too much for her to bear and she gave in. So the marriage
was arranged and the *nikah* ceremony took place although the
bride remained with her own family for the *rukhsati*, the sending
of the bride to her husband's home, had not yet taken place.
Zainab immediately regretted what she'd brought down on her
sister's head and she found the strength to defy her husband by
secretly sending word to her mother, begging her to get her sister

divorced immediately and at all costs not to send her. 'Don't join her to this family,' were her words.

He never forgave her for defying him. He locked her inside the house and took their son to his mother's to live. He visited Zainab once a day to give her some food.

One day she escaped from the house for a short time and enlisted a friend's help. Perhaps it seems strange to the reader that Zainab didn't run away, but an illiterate rural woman cannot travel alone, even if she is veiled or completely draped in burqa. Such women do not control their own personal space; they have never learnt to enjoy simple freedom of movement as a right. Decent women do not roam without their husband's permission. It is not always the binding of women's feet, like the old Chinese custom, which prevents them from fleeing: there are other ways of crippling women, other customs and social taboos and a vast cauldron of domestic knowledge kept bubbling by the women of the different generations. Gossip, folk tales, superstitions, tales of the exemplary conduct of the Prophet Muhammad's wives, popular sayings and other oral traditions, handed down by grandmothers, ayahs, aunts, girlfriends and teachers. They constitute a value system that keeps women shackled as surely as chains and fetters.

Her friend's husband went to the Qari and said, 'Stop what you are doing! Stop the beatings! You are supposed to be a religious man and you preach in the mosque. Why then must you be so harsh to your wife? I warn you,' he said, 'if you do not stop beating her, I myself will escort your wife back to her home.' It took a brave man, a kind man, to interfere in the life—in the honour—of another man who was not even a relative. There is a saying which is well known to all: 'What happens inside the four walls of a man's house is his business alone'.

Qari Muhammad Sharif felt disgraced by this upbraiding and decided he would punish his wife for her disobedience; he would teach her a lesson she would never forget. He forced her to lie down on the bed and tied her arms and legs to the railings at both ends. Then he inserted a metal rod into her vagina. We know that he attached electric wires to the rod which he then attached to the main switchboard, although at the time Zainab couldn't see what he was doing because he covered her face with a blanket. The electricity was off because it was that time of day when load shedding occurred. Then he lay down and rested on another charpoi and waited for the electricity to come on so that his wife's re-education could begin.

'Suddenly the lights came on. I started screaming and that is all that I remember.'

Shahnaz believed that he continued torturing Zainab because a whole day and night passed. 'When she first gave her evidence,' Shahnaz told me, 'Zainab said that whenever she screamed too much, he turned off the power. Praise be to Allah I think she has forgotten that now.'

The next morning he went to the village dispensary and bought some ointment and some kerosene oil which he gave to her. Later that night he took her to the local hospital but there was no lady doctor on duty, and naturally she couldn't be examined by male doctors. As is the custom, he described her symptoms and told the doctor that she had fallen on top of the kitchen fire and burnt her internal parts. The doctor could not speak to Zainab nor could he ask her any medical questions.

The doctor gave him some medicine and sent them away.

By the next day Zainab's stomach and genitals were swollen and blistered and she was admitted to the local hospital for six days until the staff told her husband to remove her and seek help from the Rawalpindi General Hospital. As they went from hospital to hospital he threatened her. 'Don't tell ... I will kill your son.' By now he must have been frightened.

I hoped he was frightened—I hope he had a foreboding of the horrors of a Pakistani prison.

After two days at the Rawalpindi hospital, the doctors operated—her condition was critical—and when they opened her up and saw the extent of her internal injuries they realised that the accident description on her admittance sheet was false—what they were looking at was not a case of external burning. She was in a coma for two days and when she awoke they questioned her; she finally told the truth because she believed she was going to die and wanted them to save her son.

We stopped. Zainab's eyes glistened with tears and she showed signs of distress. She also had difficulty sitting in one position for too long because of her injuries.

Shahnaz stroked her head and I did my best to distract her by admiring her pretty earrings and she smiled at me and told me they were fake stones and not at all expensive, that she'd purchased them only last week at the local Sunday bazaar. I was upset that I had unleashed her demons, but Shahnaz seemed unworried and I reminded myself that she'd been involved with Zainab's case for two years now; this was not the first time she'd helped Zainab tell her story. Shahnaz was a clinical psychologist; she would never allow Zainab to be hurt; this was the only way she knew to bring attention to Zainab's plight.

Her daughter brought Kaleem back into the room where he sat once more by his mother's side—they were safe again and when she looked down at her son she smiled, smoothing his hair which was still as neat as it had been when we sent him off to play. I wondered if there would ever be room in Kaleem's life for another woman or whether the emotional bonds he was now forging with his mother would make a relationship with any other woman difficult.

Later that day Zainab and her son returned to the hospital where they lived in a tiny room. Shahnaz had tried her best to persuade Zainab to stay and eat with us but she politely refused.

I had just asked Shahnaz to continue Zainab's story when her eighteen-year-old daughter, Samia, came in with the news that a mother and a daughter were on the doorstep seeking help and what should she do? Clucking and sighing, Shahnaz bustled into the adjacent dining room which, strewn with files and clippings, also served as her office. As she left the room she yelled at her daughter to stay and keep me company.

Samia had been with her mother on the day when they saw Zainab for the first time. This meeting with a woman even the doctors thought was dying was to be their indoctrination into a world they never knew existed. Now they often make the hospital rounds together, following up suspected cases of homicidal stove burnings which are gaining publicity for the first time in Pakistan.

Four terrible weeks had passed since Zainab's 'accident'.

'In the beginning it was just awful for me to go into these hospital rooms with my mother and see all of these women, most of them dying,' she said. 'I started helping my mother with Zainab Noor and that was like . . . the end of the world. I don't think there's any form of torture which goes beyond that!' Her young voice quivered but she didn't look away.

Inside my head, a voice shouted that she was too young to witness these nightmares—she was just eighteen for God's sake! How old was she when she began? Sixteen? She should be out in the sun laughing with other young people, licking ice-creams, eating pizzas and window shopping, not walking from ward to ward with her mother, listening to the screams of dying women—whose faces had melted so that their chins were frozen to their chests and you could see their teeth through pieces of their jawbone. I had forced myself to examine Shahnaz's photos of women whose features had been burnt away so that only the expression in their eyes showed that they were human. But part of me understood why her mother was involving her. What would I have done if I'd been her mother?

I dragged my mind back to what she was telling me with difficulty. 'There was this woman on the bed,' she said, 'lying in a third-rate general ward with ten other patients, some maternity cases, some of them with broken legs—just a general ward. She would have died within two days if we hadn't found her. Zainab hardly weighed anything—twenty kilos. Her legs looked like sticks and her insides had melted out. My mother started to faint and they took her outside. I couldn't move—I just stood looking at her. I was in shock. A nurse came in with a large bundle of cotton wool—like a huge slab of ice. She opened Zainab's legs and she placed her hands inside her, like this,' she said and she showed me, and then she just pulled out this mass of cotton wool.' I was beyond feeling sick. 'And there was water and blood and all sorts of fluids coming out of this huge hole and I couldn't move. I'm glad my mother didn't see that, you know, because she's seen too much and sometimes she wakes up screaming in the night. She dreams that she's on fire.'

I didn't dare ask Samia if she woke up screaming in the night too. But her efforts to shield her mother moved me. And to this day I still remain unsure if Samia really understood the vileness behind what she saw week after week—the act of betrayal played out in every one of these crimes when a man sets fire to his wife, his sister or his sister-in-law—and of the older women who often aid them, refusing to give evidence against their sons. Did it really matter? I was annoyed with myself for trying to intellectualise human suffering. Samia had witnessed women dying in agony in hot, dusty, wards with no drugs or specialist treatment—what was the point in speculating whether she understood the psychology of the betrayal behind the attacks?

Before she left the room, Samia told me she wanted to return

286

to her studies in the USA, take up law and then come back to Pakistan—she made it sound like a day of reckoning. I sat listening to the murmur of Shahnaz's voice in the room next door and the soft unmistakable sound of a woman crying.

While I waited for Shahnaz I worked my way through a pile of newspaper articles about cases where women were set on fire by relatives who later claimed stoves had burst, setting the woman on fire—despite forensic evidence showing this to be impossible. These crimes are usually motivated by dowry demands or so-called acts of indecency and/or disobedience. They are rarely prosecuted because witnesses (often a mother, mother-in-law or another relative) refuse to give evidence.

I became fixated on dates and place names and all the minutiae of events. I had developed my own way of coping with the stories: it kept me busy, helped me reach out for some sliver of rationality—kept the visions of flames and burnt flesh at bay.

From the press clippings I also pieced together a rough chronology surrounding Zainab's case. In the middle of February the doctors who operated on her realised something terrible had happened to her and with the help of women doctors and nurses persuaded Zainab and her mother Sharaf Noor to speak out. This was a rare occurrence. A police unit stationed at the emergency ward of the hospital was notified and this time justice moved swiftly. They took Zainab's statement and arrested her husband on 21 February. He confessed at the police station, although on his release three days later he withdrew his statement.

A doctor leaked the news to a reporter and on 9 March a story appeared in the paper—it was the day after women's groups in Islamabad had held their annual march to mark International Women's Day. Shahnaz rushed to the hospital and her organisation, the Progressive Women's Association, gave a press conference and women's groups throughout Pakistan swung into action and began lobbying the Prime Minister to personally intervene and order a special investigation.

They also raised funds to pay for Zainab's drugs and her hospital expenses which were 500 rupees a day, less than US$20, but a fortune for her parents.

Four days later, on the 13 March, Benazir Bhutto visited Zainab at the Rawalpindi hospital and immediately issued orders that she be transferred to the Pakistan Institute of Medical Science, an elite private hospital in Islamabad. All expenses were to be met by the Prime Minister's Office. Eleven days later Zainab was taken to London by her doctor and her mother, to receive the artificial system that she would live with for the rest of her life. Again all expenses were met by the government, which also awarded her mother one lakh rupees.

Following Zainab's return from London in June, her husband's trial began. The doctors' reports, submitted as medical evidence, found that three major organs had been totally destroyed: her reproductive organs, and her urinary and bowel tracts.

Under the PM's orders and because of the incredible hue and cry throughout the country, the Punjabi Court had moved quickly. Qari Sharif was found guilty and sentenced to thirty years' rigorous imprisonment plus a heavy fine. The judge, Justice Khawaja Mehmood Ahmed, regretted he could not impose a more severe sentence under the Pakistani Penal Code, but his hands were tied.

*　　*　　*

I said at the beginning of this story that Zainab had become the forgotten woman. Her health is much improved but she is still not completely healed. Now she faces other problems and there is only Shahnaz to help her, to intercede on her behalf, to use her magical sifarish.

Zainab wants to divorce her husband and gain legal custody of her son who under the law can be returned to her husband's family. Given the circumstances this is unlikely but it hangs over her head; she frets and doesn't know what to do, for legal costs are beyond her means.

Shahnaz told me that while it is not unusual for a mother to receive custody of a child, often the court's decision is flouted and the child is not handed over to the mother by the husband or his family. The family may be influential, or wealthy enough to bribe whoever is waiting in line, and in Pakistan the lines are always long. Zainab doesn't trust her husband's family because after his arrest they did everything in their power to settle matters out of court and brought the influence of important locals to bear on her parents. She is worried that they will move on her son. According to Shariah law, the father is always the child's guardian and often the mother must hand over a son to the father when he turns seven.

But there are other problems. Because of her health she cannot return to village life—the dust, the water, the lack of sanitation, all mean the risk of infection is too great—she needs clean surroundings and air conditioning. She cannot even afford colostomy bags. They come ten to a packet but are expensive so at present she re-uses them three or four times before throwing them away. The hospital now threatens to evict her—they need her tiny cupboard of a room, they say. She doesn't want to leave—where can she go? She would like a job as an ayah, looking after children—yes, she smiles, she would like that very much. At present she does a little work at the hospital and her son attends the hospital school. Zainab, who is now just twenty-five, weighs less than forty kilos. The city people who were so moved by her story have forgotten her and there are ridiculous rumours circulating that she has a well-paid job and a government pension. Shahnaz showed me another letter addressed to Benazir trying to rekindle her interest in Zainab. I wondered what BB's response would be—would she even get to read the letter?

Just a few days earlier, on 4 May 1996, Benazir Bhutto had been declared the most powerful woman in the world. Journalists from the *New York Times* and the *Australian* had compiled a list of the hundred most powerful women in the world and Benazir Bhutto had topped the list. Power was defined in terms of the political power, financial power or personal influence they exercised in public life.

As I read the article and looked at the beautiful face of the PM, draped in the inevitable, but flattering, white dupatta—a carefully controlled and nurtured image that the cameras loved, I was shocked, and then a feeling of irrational rage swept over me—everything I'd tried to keep suppressed while hearing Zainab's story—journalistic whims in downtown New York and Sydney are far removed from the reality of what happens in Pakistan. BB might appear to be the bastion against fundamentalist values in Pakistan to the outside world, but her coalition government seemed helpless to implement social or economic reforms. I read that journalists had selected BB because, according to them, she had made effective use of the power she inherited to lead a nation with a population of 130 million and a nuclear capability!

A caveat told readers that the list reflected power rather than achievement.

Years ago BB had promised three specialist burn units for government hospitals; an end to the country's illiteracy by the year 2000; the repeal of discriminatory legislation ... it is always interesting to watch from the sidelines and observe how mythologies are constructed. Benazir Bhutto, I felt, had personal courage and political stamina aplenty. But watching Pakistani politics from afar, it wasn't difficult to predict that BB would soon face a do or die struggle from a disillusioned electorate.

✳   ✳   ✳

Shahnaz is a trained clinical psychologist who works night and day for no salary on behalf of the growing number of women she finds in hospital wards or who beat a path to her door.

Throughout the four days I spent with her, she worked at a feverish pace: hospitals to visit, lawyers to telephone, submissions to write, police to liaise with—she had developed a good working relationship with the local police in Islamabad and Rawalpindi, she told me. There were many burn victim cases pending and she was the linchpin holding everything together, trying to create a whirl of publicity and haul in legal resources. I felt that I was witnessing a 'one woman show' and her highly emotional involvement made me uneasy—why I couldn't exactly say, but I was concerned with more than signs of an imminent break down.

'No, sweetheart,' she cried out dramatically to me once, 'Foreign Aid is international beggary!' Her energy, her colourful outbursts, were so passionate that I nicknamed her "La Bukhari", because as I explained to her, she had the intensity of a flamenco dancer. She laughed loudly. 'La Bukhari,' she repeated, and I could see she liked the name.

'La Bukhari' wants to set up a centre for homicidal burn victims with sterile areas, air conditioning, masks, gloves and oxygen. Everything points to an increase in these cases and public hospitals presently lack proper burn centres and women dying from burns to 40, 60, even 90 per cent of their bodies with flies infecting their wounds, lie next to women with TB or broken legs.

'In the name of Allah,' cries La Bukhari, 'let them die in peace!' She has built up case histories of more than fifty victims from just two hospitals in the Islamabad area. At present she receives on average nine enquiries, all dealing with violence, a week. Her list explodes many of the popular notions of the Pakistani family as the all encompassing place of protection for women. Some families prey on young wives.

'The woman I spoke to this morning,' said La Bukhari, 'is frightened for her daughter, but she cried, "What else can we do with our daughters in Pakistan? We have to give them in marriage! There is nothing else."'

'Her daughter is being beaten by her mother-in-law and sexually harassed by her brothers-in-law. When the young wife— she is only seventeen—appeals to her husband he answers, "As long as my parents are alive, everything is in their hands, including your wishes."'

Because finding any time alone with her was becoming impossible, I pushed La Bukhari into a taxi and took her to lunch at the Marriott hotel. As we drove through the streets of Islamabad, the red bottlebrush trees were in bloom and the capital reminded me of Canberra with its small shopping centres, green trees and gardens, and the Margalla Hills in the distance. If there was poverty in Islamabad it was well hidden away or confined to its twin city Rawalpindi. The weather was unseasonably humid and we were in for a thunderstorm.

Shahnaz has often been threatened by the families of those she defends but refuses to employ chowkhidars to guard her house—there are no servants at all. She employs a few volunteers who receive an honorarium and this comes out of her own pocket.

'I don't need guards,' she laughed at me from behind her

glasses. It was the laugh of a reckless woman who seemed to be running her own personal fortunes into the ground but who couldn't stop herself.

'There's an army of builders working next door and if I need protection, they would rush to help me. And so would the guards from other people's houses.' She seemed to have her own Neighbourhood Watch on hand.

She smiled one of her cheeky smiles which didn't quite camouflage how tired she really looked. Her face was round, and a little pasty-looking, her long hair tied carelessly back from her face was still wet from the shower. This was a woman who after meeting Zainab Noor three years ago, felt compelled to analyse her own comfortable middle-class position. She hated what she saw—it seemed an insult to all the women dying from burns, and so she had crossed over and taken her daughters with her—none of them would ever be the same again.

When Shahnaz walked, she bounced and left a trail of papers behind her. When she left a room it felt empty and drained of life. She joked incessantly—it was a household with a lot of shouting, a lot of laughter and bantering back and forth with no sham concerns about status. Laughter was like a moat, encircling the house to protect everyone's sanity. The girls teased her and called her the slave-driver.

* * *

In Pakistan, Bangladesh and elsewhere in the region it is widely believed that the family is a benevolent institution which protects its women. For many women across society this is a fallacy with dangerous repercussions—but it is a persuasive mythology and we all fall under its spell from time to time.

While the women's movements in both Bangladesh and Pakistan have raised awareness of violence against women in all its forms, and are vocal against the issue of polygamy, they rarely criticise or examine the mythology surrounding the family and the idea that marriage ideally protects women. Women feel protected within families even though daily violence may be common. The family is regarded as an almost sacred institution and a bulwark against moral chaos and social disintegration.

Perhaps that is why many Pakistanis refuse to believe what they are now reading in the newspapers. 'How can this be possible?' they ask. 'How can a husband, or son, or brother, or mother-in-law do such a terrible thing?' They prefer to believe it was an accident. And many stove accidents do take place, but not as many as they would like us to believe as Shahnaz's statistics and hospital monitoring now proves. The insularity of the educated classes blinds them.

In the closing remarks the judge made when handing down his sentence at the end of the trial, he was reported as saying that Zainab had lost her honour. 'Honour,' he said, 'is like the lustre of a pearl and once gone it can never be regained.' The learned judge was wrong. Zainab Noor never lost her honour. Her husband lost his; he has thirty years hard labour to regain it.

CHAPTER 12

The Living Law

* * *

HOTEL POLICY
Guns cannot be brought inside the hotel premises. Personal
guards or gunmen are required to deposit their weapons with
Hotel Security.
We seek your co-operation,

—Hotel Management

The Pearl-Continental Hotel in Peshawar is a building of five-
star luxury and good taste. The soft purr of air conditioning
mingles with the well-bred voices of the local staff who stand
attentively behind marble-topped reception counters, their mod-
ulated voices a testimony to Western-style training. In the
thickly carpeted foyer of this shrine to opulence stands this
elegant gilt-framed sign for all to read.

The message is succinct; the warning implicit. Men plus
weapons equals violence. Within the hotel, there is an atmos-
phere of wealth and decorum. Lounging comfortably in plush

295

armchairs, foreign experts and overseas businessmen hold court. The experts are wooed by locals who by now know when to smile, when to laugh and when to leave. Outside the real Peshawar is raw and masculine—in keeping with its history as the dusty frontier capital of the North West Frontier Province (NWFP) and gateway to the Khyber Pass and Afghanistan. For two thousand years Peshawar has stood in the way of advancing armies marching through the Khyber Pass or through the Punjab; it has been taken and retaken countless times and it has always survived.

Less than sixty kilometres away in neighbouring Afghanistan, the wandering Taliban boys carry their *jihad* forward like a psychopathic Children's Crusade. And in the towns they conquer, among the second line of casualties, are women forced to give up their jobs and cover their faces to bolster the wounded egos of educated young militiamen without jobs, whose paper qualifications have not fulfilled their dreams of a better life. They become full-time professional revolutionaries in someone else's country and would have us believe they do all of this in the name of God. The fundamentalists' latest diktat issued by the Department for Promoting Virtue and Preventing Vice, orders women to 'walk quietly' and has banned the wearing of white socks, denounced as 'comely'.

The NWFP is not cut off from events in Afghanistan. The border separating the two countries has more to do with the modern nation state than past history and the reality of tribal life. For thousands of years tribes, clans and nomads have followed ancient trails and attended ancient gatherings which recognise no barriers. In modern times smugglers seem to cross the border whenever they like. The Pathans (tribal and urban) live on both sides of the border; they speak the same language, believe in the same customary practices and tribal laws and are famous for their feuds, their fighting and more recently for holding as hostage the occasional rash tourist who thinks the Khyber Pass is still as accessible as it used to be in the '70s.

In the chaotic streets of Peshawar surrealistic signs entreat us to SMILE and SAY NO TO POLLUTION! while a policeman wearing a gas mask directs traffic. STAY CLEAN AND GREEN, reads another, and all around us are dust and dying trees. The city planners have gone mad. This is the NWFP, where in some districts literacy rates are as low as six per cent. Who is reading the signs?

But in the middle of all this, a strange thing happened to me in Peshawar: in spite of the confusion I began to see things more clearly, to understand how agonisingly slow the process of change is. It was tough going: the contradictions were more contradictory, the complexities more complex, the answers far removed from a feminist textbook.

Peshawar summed up for me the enigma of Pakistan. It is a place where middle-class women appear to have 'everything' while nothing seems to change for lower-class women; a country where the female Prime Minister, the most influential woman in the world (said the West), could not improve the quality of life for those at the bottom; where some families restrict their daughters' lives out of love and ignorance and others from blind obedience to laws that celebrate male control. It is a society with nuclear capacity where camel and buffalo outnumber farm machinery—a land where nothing is as it seems. And the strong hand of customary law and religious conservatism which dominates the unruly society of the NWFP was revealed in every story I heard.

The living law is everywhere in Pakistan—even foreign wives and educated women growing up overseas can't avoid its touch. Customary laws and practices are powerful, more powerful than the statute laws of the High Court or constitutional laws of Parliament, more powerful even than Islamic beliefs.

The living laws are deeply buried in the nation's psyche, but in the NWFP they aren't even just below the surface. Just west of Peshawar, for instance, Pakistani law gives way to tribal law in the tribal areas of the north-west.

Pakistani women's groups like Shirkat Gah and the international network, Women Living under Muslim Laws (active in Bangladesh, Pakistan and other countries), are conducting research on the informal laws which imprison women. Customary practices such as arranged marriages (in their different forms), karo kari, *khoon baha* (blood money), bride price and dowry, inheritance, customs regarding a woman's mobility and segregation—there are hundreds and hundreds of customary laws, many of them in conflict with the statutory laws of the land and even the Shariah, or religious laws. The institutions which protect and teach the living laws are powerful—the family is one of them; feudal and tribal structures are others.

The living laws stretch back through history and combine with feudalism and tribalism and a broad South Asian culture within the Islamic faith. Women are left with only a small space in which to manoeuvre, and some are better equipped to do this than others. Add to this the culture of poverty and everything it entails and only then do you move closer to understanding the marginalisation of women in South Asia and how patriarchal control over women is maintained.

'I can sympathise with women who are tired of the slow rate of progress,' a professor from Peshawar University said to me. He was a kind man, a progressive man, proud that his university had five women heads of department—but he was no fool: he knew what still needed to be done, especially in the field of adult illiteracy where short-term programs, under-resourced and short-lived, had him at his wit's end.

'But this has to be tempered with the realism of the situation,' he told me. He was a great admirer of Kemal Attaturk who shaped Turkey into a modern society and tackled the country's literacy problem in the 1920s.

'We need structural change not quick fixes! We must move towards a quiet revolution. A wristwatch is still working even though you can hardly hear it.'

*   *   *

My search for a Mona Lisa in Pakistan proved disappointing. The guest houses I found were more like small hotels: clean and efficient but without character. But in Peshawar I was invited to stay with a family and immediately my luck changed as I tapped into a new vein of women's stories and experiences.

Salma Ali Khan and her husband Ali were an agreeable couple in their fifties whose married children now lived overseas, leaving them with time on their hands and a spare bedroom. I enjoyed living with them. I badly needed a respite from a heavy diet of horror story marriages. If this was a typical picture of middle-class, middle-aged life in Pakistan then it had a lot to recommend it, for I was looking at two people who respected one another and treated each other with a loving kindness.

Ali Khan came originally from the state of Orissa which after the 1947 division of spoils fell to India, and Salma was a Punjabi who'd lived in Peshawar for twenty years now and loved her adopted home town dearly. They lived productive lives. Ali was a slim, observant man, quietly dressed and quietly spoken, who kept fit by running up and down the outside staircase of the family home thirty times a day, stop watch in hand.

Salma laughed at Ali's regime and like most Pakistani women of her generation was at peace with her comfortably rounded figure. She led a full life, working voluntarily with various women's and children's organisations and, more recently, preparing for a Masters degree in Urdu Literature. They were well-matched and in an undemonstrative way, devoted to each other. As he sat reading the papers and drinking his tea after a day at the office, Salma would talk about her activities and the next wedding function on their social calendar—it seemed a calm idyllic life.

Weddings are the single most important social occasion in Pakistan—they mark the alliance of families and clans as well as individuals. I asked Ali Khan how many *validas* they'd attended so far that year. More than twenty, he thought, and the season was not ended, though with a hot arid summer just around the corner, weddings as well as trees, shrivelled in the heat and families preferred to wait for cooler winter weather.

Towards the end of the wedding season most men were fed up with the celebrations and tired of running into the same people; they would rather stay at home watching television— especially cricket. But a Pakistan without wedding receptions was like an Australia without the great Aussie barbecue. They were both important social rituals, one dominated by rich foods, the other by alcohol while both favoured gender segregation as the best way of having a good time.

＊　　＊　　＊

We smiled nervously at one another; it was one of those impromptu meetings thrown together very quickly the night before by a friend of Salma's. But they were special women and it was important for me to meet them. They were women who actually went out into the villages and small rural towns—as opposed to women who just talked about women who went out to the villages. They were plainly spoken, unsophisticated, practical 'doers', not the glamorous, urban women from 'good families' I'd met in Lahore, Karachi and Islamabad. We sat in the lounge of the women's centre, nursing our cups of tea, eyeing one another furtively.

Meraj and Rehana looked alike and could have been sisters. The *hijabs* they wore, like a nun's habit, revealed only the contours of their faces, making it hard to distinguish between them physically. They believed that this 'invisibility' gave them their own personal space or freedom from the gaze of men. 'We are judged by our words and actions and not by the shape of our bodies or our faces,' they told me. Their argument was similar to Western feminists who analyse the impact of constant sexual scrutiny on women's lives—until they begin to age, they note wryly.

Ameena was a Filipina married to a Pakistani. She'd worked with Afghan refugee women and seemed different from other foreign wives I'd met; she gave no sign of regarding Pakistanis as 'the other'. And then there was poor Alison—well, poor Alison stood out like a sore thumb and was ill at ease in her new clothes and surroundings. I felt sorry for the vegetarian from London who'd only been in meat-eating Pakistan for seventy-two hours and was reeling from jet lag and culture shock. She remained silent and sleepy and I concluded that our discussion must be part of her induction course.

Rehana understood that Western feminists were often critical of the slow pace of change. She told me about her training course at Sussex University where all the feminists were quick to give her their materials on sex education, eager to 'convert' her. 'Yes,' she said. 'I was shocked because you know in our culture we don't discuss these [sexual] matters.

'Our problems are different from those of the West. They continually talk about equal rights—they don't seem to understand that we have our rights at home, at least at the domestic level; but our problems are more basic. If we don't have enough to eat how can we talk about liberation and going out into the streets? They come from industrialised societies and have no understanding of history or the process of change and what it involves.'

'You know that slogan,' Meraj interjected. "What do we want? Change! When do we want it? Now!"' Everyone giggled except Alison, who seemed to have missed the joke.

We talked about my visit to Bangladesh and the problems women faced. 'The same here! The same here!' they interrupted excitedly.

Rehana said, 'People need to understand the context of our work; the society we are a part of—they have no idea! Here in the NWFP less than six per cent of the women are literate— marching in the streets is ridiculous for us. It may be part of the Bangladeshi political culture, but here, with our tribal background, it is ridiculous for us—it would only be counterproductive.

'Most of the time we come to Meraj for advice. She is more religious than we are,' she said, looking at her friend. 'Will the mullahs say it is against Islam, is what we usually want to know. If it is, then we don't have a chance and we have to work out ways around this.'

'I was not always religious,' Meraj explained. 'When I was younger I believed I had no rights and I was rebellious against Islam. I hated all these restrictions placed on me. "If Islam is so cruel towards women then I will rebel against it,"' I used to say.

'I came across a book which cleared the myths away and I started to disagree with my parents and show them where they were mistaken in the Qur'an. I began to understand the historical and social context of the birth of Islam and now I am fully convinced that Islam gives you general guidelines. It does not restrict you; you interact in your own way and there are no barriers between you and Allah.'

'We should not see the mullahs as opponents,' argued Meraj.

'The secret is you must work with them; you must woo them. You can do nothing without their co-operation. When we go into villages we always work with existing groups and any of the traditional collectives used for harvesting or conciliating neighbourhood disputes.'

'I don't believe in confrontation either,' said Rehana. 'Last month we were holding Meena Bazaars [women's fairs] at village level and the men, or rather the elders, had given us approval—or so we thought. But one of the men, when he saw women from other villages arriving, he ran to the fields and yelled "Come quickly! All the women are joining together!" Now this created big problems for us! The man who'd originally given us permission started shouting and told us to leave and never return.

'We were worried because a year earlier we'd also started a school for girls, so when things started getting sticky we asked them, "Do you want us to stop the school as well?" "No," they said, "we want the school." Here they were yelling at us and ordering us to leave, with this old man brandishing his pick axe at us and shouting. There was violence in the air, I can tell you.

'We'd had to talk to them for so long over such a long time to get permission to start the primary school. "What do they need education for?" they said. "They are only going to get married!" But then a year later, in the middle of this fiasco, when we said we'll close it down, they said no, they wanted to keep it.'

Meraj blamed herself. 'We had mistaken their hospitality for agreement about holding the Meena Bazaar. They were just being polite. We were to blame because they hadn't fully understood that strange women from other villages would be coming. You always need more time and longer talks,' she said patiently.

Ameena had been quiet till now. She believed a lot could be learnt from the experiences of international refugee organisations over the previous decade. Refugee women from Afghanistan were also hemmed in by the unwritten laws. She told us about a landmine awareness program in Afghanistan called 'Operation Salaam'.

The Soviets in their day had planted thousands of landmines. Operation Salaam focused on women and children because they were the ones most affected—they were the ones hit by the landmines as they worked in the fields and carted the water while the men were all away fighting. Of course they didn't know what a landmine looked like. There were twenty different types; even one which looked like a butterfly, which attracted children.

'Now the problem was how to reach the women?' said Ameena. 'The Afghan men were very strict and would not even permit the women to gather for a meeting like this. The organisers spoke first to the men of course, who seemed to understand the benefits and would probably have agreed, but the mullahs were dead against it. "We cannot allow our women out of the houses; we cannot allow them to be exposed to foreigners and other men."

'We worked out a plan. We asked the men to choose the most respectable house, out of the village, and let the women gather there while the men sat altogether outside as guards, with their rifles next to them. The women who would conduct the training, even foreign women, would have to cover themselves in burqa until they were inside, but even then were expected to dress modestly in front of the local women. The women who started this mine awareness program were all Canadian; here they were straight from overseas into a remote village in the hot months of May and June and they agreed to wear the shalwar kameez, it wasn't easy for them by any means, *and lives were saved*,' she emphasised. 'You see it all rests in how you co-operate. Once you start co-operating with the men then you can reach your goal, but if you get on your high horse and say "I'm

not going to wear that terrible tent! It's against my principles"—
and I've heard that from many foreign women—if you go down
that road you will fail.'

Story after story unfolded. 'Going through the children is a
good way to reach the women,' said Meraj, 'and of course,' she
smiled, 'talking about stoves is the real ice-breaker.'

Special fuel-saving stoves were originally designed for Afghan
refugees, but then used in the villages of the NWFP. 'Small
stoves that women squat in front of to cook—not your grand
big Western models,' Meraj laughed when she saw my face. 'We
used the stoves to get into the village and then talked about
health matters and sanitation. This "camouflage" was great
because health is always linked with family planning in the villagers' minds and this is not at all popular in Pakistan—it's seen
as very threatening. So whenever they see us enter a village, the
word goes round that the "Stove Women" are here.'

❋　　❋　　❋

Dining at the Peshawar Club, on the open lawn, with a hot
wind stirring the leaves and a full moon staring down, was a
scene straight out of a John Master's novel of life in British
India, when officers and their wives dined there to the strains
of music from the officers' mess. Those days are long gone, the
only reminder the attentive waiters in white uniforms. The table
linen and the cutlery had fallen on hard times and pink gins
and whisky were *haram* and nowhere in sight. Now all the faces
were brown and the buildings a little worse for wear with undis-
ciplined children running around as their parents dined al fresco
at a club which used to be off limits to 'natives' unless expressly
invited by an officer or high ranking bureaucrat.

I was taken to the club by Salma and Ali, long-time members.
We arrived to find not an empty table in sight. A tall man in

his sixties who was sitting alone, poring over a pile of documents, immediately stood up and insisted on giving us his table. Ali Khan whispered that he was none other than the Prince of Chittral. He wore his long shirt, vest and baggy cotton pants with panache. They told me the Prince spent much of his time engaged in court battles against the government, fighting them over compensation for his lost hereditary wealth which had vanished into thin air when Chittral joined Pakistan in 1971. He carried himself with authority and as I watched him out of the corner of my eye, I saw him gazing around at everyone quite benevolently, as if we were there for his amusement—and perhaps we were.

Just then a smartly dressed, confident-looking woman in white waved in our direction and strode across the grass to join us. Rushda looked like a real 'daughter of the soil' (meaning she was born in the NWFP). She was tall, with a fair complexion and reddish brown hair cut in a severe geometric style. Her family were wealthy feudals of Pathan origins. The way she wore her clothes suggested she'd spent time overseas—perhaps it was the colours or the designs, but she stood out and I noticed that other diners stopped to stare at this woman holding centre stage.

Her father was a colonel in the army and she came from a village which her father practically owned, she said, as all the inhabitants were his tenants and he ruled over them with the same mentality of feudal lords everywhere. No-one could speak against him—if they dared, they'd be evicted.

Years ago, she and her sisters had caused a scandal by walking out of their father's house in broad daylight, so that everyone could witness their act of rebellion. Like many from the officer corps, the colonel wanted a marriage alliance with political connections for Rushda, but she refused and her two younger sisters walked out in sympathy. Instead they went to live with a married sister and a sympathetic brother-in-law. Now she lived permanently estranged from a father who had disowned her. 'We made a new joint family,' she said.

But what Rushda really loved talking about was their family retainer, the long-suffering Anani, who'd been with the family for thirty-five years or more. While we waited for our mutton kebabs and pilau, she regaled us with stories about the family maid and I gathered that she dined out regularly on these anecdotes—all of which seemed to be at the expense of her illiterate, religiously devout family retainer, turning her into a figure of fun for our amusement. Rushda's mother had rescued Anani after her husband died when Pathan custom dictated that she marry her brother-in-law. Instead she had chosen to run away and throw herself on the mercy of the nearest feudal family.

And then almost without pausing, Rushda began talking about a completely different woman, an Afghan woman who had passed out of her life ten years or so ago. She had no idea where this woman was, or whether she was still alive. She spoke of this woman with an understanding and respect very different from the Anani anecdotes. The story was set towards the end of the Afghan War in the late 1980s. The impact of the Afghan War on Pakistani society, through gun running and international drug trafficking, has had devastating effects over the years. There are still 2.2 million Afghan refugees in the Peshawar region alone.

'I met her when I was working with the International Rescue Committee,' said Rushda. 'She was trying to set up a school for girls here in Peshawar. There was a lot of resistance from the Afghan fundamentalists and she needed our support. She wasn't fluent in English and I helped her with some translating, and that is how we became friends.

'I didn't know there could be women like her,' she said simply. 'She used to talk about her time in prison when she was tortured by the Soviet interrogators. They drove nails into her fingers, pulled out her hair and half buried her in the snow for hours. They were after intelligence secrets because she acted as a courier between the different Mujahadeen factions and organised the intelligence networks. She never gave in.

'But once the war was ended another battle began and this time she used Islam as a weapon. When the fanatics confronted her and threatened to kill her if she tried to start the girls' school, she said to them, "I won't start this school if you can show me in the Holy Qur'an where it is written that education for females is forbidden." And of course we all know that the Qur'an tells you to travel to China if necessary in search of education and knowledge and they were forced to leave her in peace.

'But what really broke her spirit, something the Russian prisons could never do, is what happened after the war ended. The men she had fought beside, turned against her. I don't think it was anything personal, you know, it was because she was, after all, a woman. She had played an equal role to the men in the war, she had been involved in physical combat too—but now it meant nothing.

'In the post-war period all the Mujahadeen factions organised a large Shudra Council.' (*Shudra* is an Arabic word meaning consultation and is still often used as a traditional way of reaching consensus.) 'Now,' continued Rushda, 'My friend wanted to be a member so that she could represent women's voices on the Shudra. They turned her down, so she went to Islamabad to present her case, thinking that her old comrades in arms could not refuse a personal plea.

'They told her bluntly, "You can't be a member because God doesn't want women in these positions", and when she protested they said, "If He really wanted women to be in a position of power or decision making, He would have sent a female prophet as well".

'She answered that it was women who gave birth to prophets.

She pointed out that if there were male prophets, then there were also male *Shaitans* or devils. She pleaded with them, but they turned her down.' Rushda paused to sip her drink.

These were the 'freedom fighters' who could do no wrong when they were fighting against the Soviets. They were freedom fighters then—today they are fundamentalists.

She had fought alongside them, been imprisoned with these men ... Her sense of betrayal, I thought, must have been immense. And then, from out of nowhere, I remembered, and a terrible feeling filled the pit of my stomach. I said nothing. I sat and listened.

Rushda continued her story as the moon moved behind the dark hills. We sat listening with just the clink of soft drink bottles and the tinkle of cutlery as the waiters cleared the tables. Most of the guests had already left. We were alone except for the Prince of Chittral still at his table reading his documents, looking up now and then with a smile, gazing absent-mindedly at his surroundings, listening to his voices from the past while we sat drinking our cardamom tea, mesmerised by Rushda's story.

'My friend told me,' said Rushda, 'That this is the plight of women everywhere. When they really need you, they smile their false smiles. You fight and you take care of the country, the fields and the children; you get blown up by the mines, you watch your country become a land of widows and orphans.

'There was no recognition for what she'd done. She'd fought Russian tanks, been captured and tortured ...

'She never ever regained her health,' Rushda added abruptly.

'No, she didn't,' I said.

'There was no brightness left in her face; you could see the emptiness in her eyes whenever you talked to her.'

'Yes,' I said.

'I had a chance to go with her into Afghanistan but I didn't take it. I think this is something we women do to ourselves. We have a lot of strength but we don't believe in ourselves enough. But her influence on me wasn't completely wasted, I like to think, because at that time in Peshawar we were having a lot of bomb blasts in schools and the shopping areas (this was in 1986 and 1987). All of a sudden we were getting the brunt of the Afghan War and I started waking up and became involved in more intense refugee work.'

'When was the last time you saw your friend?' I knew the woman's story was not yet over.

'In 1987,' she answered, 'and then we lost touch after that. Then one day I heard she'd been killed. We rushed to check the rumour with Afghan friends. They told us that she was alive and in fact the whole family had emigrated.'

But she continued to talk about her friend as if she was really dead. Ten long years had elapsed. We fell silent.

'What was her name?' asked Salma gently. It was time someone asked the question; the woman from Afghanistan deserved the dignity of a name.

'Her name is Jamila and she lives in Perth,' I said.

*   *   *

From Peshawar to Perth seems like a mystical journey from the old world to the new. You dream of making a fresh start, a new life, but clutching at your coat-tails, refusing to say goodbye, is your past, and you know you will travel together: language, lifestyle, values, culture and memories.

Peshawar, the dusty, inland, most northern centre in Pakistan; a town of bazaars and caravanserais, where generations of soldiers have marched and regiments have fallen. A place marked by violence and tragedy.

And Perth, the capital of Western Australia, on the Indian

Ocean side of an enormous continent—another dusty, arid country, where most of the population huddles together on the green east coast—perhaps the most isolated city in the southern hemisphere. Perth, the sparkling town of supermarkets and car parks—where tribes worship the cult of the sea, and the holy trinity of swimming, surfing and sailing. Peshawar and Perth: contrasts of the head and the heart. And Jamila, to take such a step into the unknown—she must have been desperate.

That night in Peshawar we sat stunned by the strange set of circumstances that had brought Jamila into our lives.

I first met Jamila three years earlier. Friends told me about an Afghan woman living in an outer Perth suburb—try to meet her, they urged.

I only met her twice in all, and by then she had changed so much that there was little trace left of the woman Rushda had once known—even the depressed, bitter woman she had last seen in 1987. By the time our paths crossed six years later, Jamila had aged, but it was not the passage of time which had altered her appearance, which turned her prematurely into an old woman. Despair had pulled her down into a dark place where memories played no part other than to taunt. Her spirit was dying; I could do nothing. Although the picture painted by Rushda had been of a woman who had survived torture, there must have still been trauma—at the time I met her I knew nothing about this part of her story.

I remember driving to her house in a nondescript working-class suburb on the outskirts of Perth where bus services were inadequate and the houses all looked alike in that strange Australian style, where even the ugliness of suburbia is disguised by sunshine, blue skies and eucalyptus trees. Even a less well-off suburb, by Australian standards, doesn't really seem deprived against a back drop of clear blue and gold. She and her family were living in a square brick veneer bungalow, next to a house

311

that looked the same, next to another house that looked the same ... Even the old cars parked outside looked alike.

Nobody answered when I knocked on the door. I knocked again and a curtain moved in one of the front rooms. The door part opened and a muffled voice said 'Yes?'

I identified myself. Slowly the door opened and a woman dressed in a dark coloured shalwar kameez with a black dupatta over her head allowed me to enter. The house seemed dark and silent as if nobody lived there. All the curtains were drawn and no natural sunlight was allowed to enter. The woman's skin was sallow and she looked unwell with dark rings under her eyes. Her hair was badly dyed a harsh blue-black colour which had left visible marks circling her forehead.

For the two or more hours we sat together, she talked mainly about her past life. Her teenage son acted as interpreter; although I thought it was not really necessary, she thought her English inadequate and it seemed to give her some relief to have him by her side at first, but after a while he left and we were alone.

I remember her words very clearly. Later I was able to repeat them word for word to Rushda that night at the Peshawar Club. 'I'm like an old chair,' she said, 'and one day I expect to be thrown outside in the rubbish.'

She had come to Australia as a refugee. Because of the fighting taking place among the different Mujahadeen factions, her life was in danger and she feared for her family's safety and so she had come here to Australia, although by the time we met, she must have realised the mistake she'd made in coming to Perth of all places. The woman who'd fought in her country's war, withstood torture and defied the mullahs to open her girls' school was dying. But it was a slow process.

Day after dreary day, she stayed at home alone in the heartland of suburbia with no reason to get up in the mornings other than to face her depression. 'I feel I am in gaol,' she told me. Twice a week a tutor from the State Adult Migrant Services arrived to give her an English lesson. She wasn't confident enough to catch a bus on her own to the classes held in town— she wouldn't have enjoyed sitting down with others whispering silly answers to silly questions. The skills she had used in Afghanistan were of no use to her in Western Australia. Perhaps if she'd gone to Melbourne or Sydney where the expatriate Afghan community was larger in number she might have found work of some kind.

She showed me letters given to her by nineteen different Mujahadeen leaders and I now understood that these were the same men who betrayed her once the war was ended. Worn pieces of paper with signatures and official stamps testifying to her contribution, she clutched them to her as a reminder that she was still alive.

And I wondered how you wrote a reference for a freedom fighter.

She pressed other letters into my hands, letters from international refugee committees testifying to her outstanding work with refugee women in Afghanistan—even one from the Agha Khan—but now she was a refugee herself. She badly needed help. A few Australian university women were trying to assist her but until her English improved nothing much could be done.

We arranged to meet again, but the next time I returned, she met me at the door with no sign of recognition; she was clearly distressed and under the effects of some medication. She could not remember that I'd just spoken to her twenty minutes before on the telephone.

I left and that was the last time I saw her. I heard later that she went back to Pakistan for a short while but after that I lost track of her. She slipped away from me just as she had disappeared from Rushda's life.

*   *   *

My stay in Peshawar was drawing to a close. Soon I would fly to Karachi and home to Australia. I'd asked Salma to tell me her story, but she insisted that her life was uneventful. 'Nothing remarkable ever happens to me,' she answered.

'Everyone has a story,' I said, trying to persuade her. I knew that Salma had a secret, one connected with Bangladesh, for the more I talked of Bangladesh the more melancholy she became.

'I wish I could see Dhaka again,' she sighed and that was how I finally learnt that Salma had spent four years studying at a girl's college in Dhaka in the 1960s.

They were fascinating years for the sixteen-year-old Punjabi girl when she found herself living with Bengali girls, at first as a stranger, and then as a beloved friend at a time when Bangladesh did not exist.

She could speak no Bengali at first, only Urdu which did not endear her to the Bengali-speaking students and teachers who cherished their own language and detested the brand of cultural imperialism they were facing from their big brother in West Pakistan. She had never heard of the 1952 Language Movement, when the Bengalis had resisted the imposition of Urdu as the only language of Pakistan.

'Strange, everything was so strange at first,' she said. We sat quietly together with only the fan clanking overhead. I don't think Salma had thought about Bangladesh for many years; it seemed a lifetime away.

'This was a part of Pakistan,' she told me, 'but it was so different. I didn't feel welcome and there were so many cultural differences. Small things I suppose, but at the time they seemed huge to me. Teachers were called apa (elder sister), not madam; they didn't say "good morning" but "Salaam alaikum".'

She laughed. 'And the funniest thing was that they learnt by rote and it was such a noisy way of learning! Whenever there was an exam the whole hall would be buzzing as the students recalled the answers aloud—the same way they'd learnt them. You couldn't concentrate—but if you were stuck for an answer, you could always listen in!'

The way Salma talked about her Bengali friends, it sounded as if they came from a different world. The differences were historical and cultural, yet in those days the two wings were supposed to be united as one country. West Pakistanis at the time generally looked down on the Bengali language and culture: 'they' were different; 'they' were alien. But Salma grew to love her time in Dhaka and later she passed this on to her children.

Yet it was clear to me that the young Salma did not understand what was happening around her at the time. She did not realise that East Pakistan was asserting its 'Bengaliness'. Many of the cultural differences she noticed: the sari; the bindi (or red mark on the forehead); the songs celebrating Bengali nationalism (especially the songs of Tagore which were later banned)—these were acts of political dissent. And in the final years of East Pakistan thousands of women took part in the demonstrations.

'I think we in the Western wing were trying hard to become Westernised. I admired the way the Bengalis respected their own culture. And oh, my dear,' she laughed, 'the Bengali passion for politics! From what you tell me they're still at it, while we have spent so many years under martial law, that we have become immune to politics; much more cynical—we have not participated in politics the way they do in Bangladesh.

'That has always been their way from what I remember. It is so sad, we never believe that anything we do will have any impact.'

Salma even met her husband Ali in Dhaka in 1964, when she was eighteen. From her photos you could tell she was an exceptionally beautiful young woman, the kind of beauty you see in Mughal miniature paintings and prints.

Young sisters are always on the lookout for brides for their brothers. A whole network of young girls, even today, sift out suitable candidates from 'good families'. In a society where there is no dating and gender segregation quite normal, finding a suitable match can be a problem for a young man's family. Even today weddings are an ideal marriage mart where a young girl can be sized up and even her parents are on view, their manners watched, their jewellery assessed, signs of good breeding or vulgarity weighed up.

Now Salma, knowing the traps that a young girl might fall into if she wasn't careful, told her girlfriends in Dhaka that she was already engaged—a white lie to keep them at arm's length, she thought. Her mother had warned her never to visit any home with a marriageable son.

But by the time she returned to West Pakistan for holidays, her mother had already received a letter from Ali Khan's family proposing a marriage, but Salma wasn't keen to marry. Her own mother had found herself married to a man who already had a first wife, a man content to keep two wives in the one household. But her mother had refused this arrangement, insisting on her own household.

Finally Salma and Ali met in Karachi when he visited her family home, but she still didn't trust men, she said, although her mother was completely won over.

'I do not want you to be forced into this marriage,' Ali told her one day. 'I will make up an excuse for my parents—I'll say you are too short or too tall. Don't worry, I will make up an excuse, nobody will blame you,' he repeated.

'His gesture melted my heart. He was the perfect gentlemen and he has not changed in all these years. He is still the perfect gentleman,' she said and we smiled as Ali walked into the room.

They were married soon after her Dhaka studies were over and moved to West Pakistan. And then came 1971 and the war with Bangladesh and she felt so depressed, she said. Because of the heavy censorship they received only one side of the story. She grew silent.

Two hundred thousand women had been raped. These were the Bangladeshi Government figures that I eventually unearthed. And while there are some who may contest the official estimate, the magnitude of what took place is clear.

But at the time Salma knew nothing about the army atrocities.

'When did you learn the truth?' I asked.

'About ten years after the war ended,' she answered. 'I saw a BBC documentary. And then I remembered my student days and I recalled that they were unhappy with us: I remembered all the things that were wrong.'

She read me a poem written by her daughter, Shadab Zeest Ali Khan, now studying in the USA. One verse in particular stayed in my mind.

A year later I will be born
in a country that was cut in half,
because its own two wings kept it from flying.

Postscript from Dhaka

*　　*　　*

January 1997　Little has changed at the Mona Lisa over the last twelve months—the house of men, as I once called it, remains as predictable and as contrary as ever. Devout Saleem still performs miracles in the kitchen; Gupta, the old fox, continues to bully guests and the chowkhidars sit guarding the green gates from the world outside. Molly Mac, my old adversary, and Scott the anthropologist are long gone, but there are new guests to distract and entertain me. Everyone rushes to meet me, to tell me the latest news—I am back where my journey began and feel at home again.

But outside the gates life has moved on. Six months earlier the hartals, the protests and demonstrations finally forced the BNP Government to step down and elections were held. Voter turn-out was high, with an unprecedented participation of 80 per cent of women throughout the country. Voter education campaigns targeting women organised by NGOs had born fruit. And there is more good news: the people of Bangladesh have once more turned away from religiously-based political parties and Jamaat-i-Islami lost fifteen of its eighteen parliamentary seats across the country. Religion belongs in the mosques and at home—but not in politics—was the message the ordinary people delivered.

The Widow and the Daughter have now changed places: Sheikh Hasina, leader of the Awami League, is the new energetic Prime Minister and Khaleda Zia is languishing as Leader of the Opposition with a new series of hartals planned for the winter.

Pakistan also has a story to tell of political change. Benazir Bhutto has been ousted for the second time in her career after being dismissed in November 1996 by her former ally, President Farooq Leghari on charges of nepotism, corruption, economic mismanagement, undermining the judiciary and failure to end the terrorism in Karachi. In the months following, Bhutto campaigns desperately, maintaining till the end that 'The people of Pakistan love me . . . I brought glory to Pakistan'.

But in spite of her confident rhetoric, the omens always looked dark. Six months after being named the most powerful woman in the world, photographs appearing in newspapers and magazines told a different story—the unthinkable had happened and Benazir lost control of her carefully nurtured image. Gone were the glamorous photos of the most powerful woman in the world, an immaculate white veil over her gleaming coiffure. Instead shots appeared of a tired woman with shiny nose and lanky hair with scarf awry—the love affair with the camera, and perhaps even her romance with Washington, seemed over. A few months on, elections are held amid widespread voter apathy (only a 30 per cent turnout) and Muslim League politician and wealthy feudal-industrialist, Nawab Sharif, is chosen as Prime Minister, his second time in office—this time with a two-thirds majority in Parliament, large enough to change the laws he wants to change, unlike his predecessor. Nawab Sharif, not Benazir

Bhutto, will head Pakistan later this year as it celebrates fifty years of Independence.

Political survival is as ephemeral for women as it is for men in this part of the world and I wonder how these shifts in leadership will affect women, if at all.

There is more news waiting for me. The voice of my friend Shahnaz in Islamabad finally reaches me. Zainab Noor has obtained a divorce from her husband and been awarded custody of her son Kaleem—they are at last safe and the nightmares are starting to fade, I am told. This is the news that matters to me more than the rise and fall of the 'political Begums'; the personal and the political intertwined.

Sitting once more inside my zenana verandah, ready to do battle with the cockroaches which seem to have grown bigger in my absence, I sip chai with my Bangladeshi friends who are curious about my time in Pakistan and call on me to make comparisons between the two women's movements. I try to marshal my impressions. I explain that the women's movement in Pakistan reflects the diversity of Pakistani society: a society fragmented by class, culture, language and ethnicity, as well as the divisions between rural and urban, and tribal and feudal. In Bangladesh, the Bengali language and culture, the strong links with rural life and a more buoyant feeling of nationalism, give the appearance at least of binding the women's movement closer together; disagreements and tensions are not immediately visible. Pakistani women activists, in comparison to Bangladeshi women, do not submerge their personalities into a chorus of collective voices—they soar like operatic divas. But their strong voices falter now and then; decades of political instability and Islamisation programs have worn them down. They continue the struggle, refusing to give in, but their movement lacks the optimism that characterises Bangladesh's movement. Pakistan's NGOs seem to be replacing the women's movement rather than feeding it.

But still the women's organisations in both lands listen to one another's voices and Pakistani women have reached out attempting a reconciliation for what passed a quarter of a century ago when Bangladesh was struggling for its independence. In a statement issued in March 1996, the Women's Action Forum of Pakistan apologises 'to the women of Bangladesh that they became the symbols and the targets in the process of dishonouring and humiliating people'. The letter goes on to deplore systematic violence against women, particularly the mass rapes by the military: '. . . We must judge ourselves as history has already judged us.' The letter is endorsed by a number of Pakistani women's groups, but still no official apology from the government.

In both countries, national identity, history, class, culture and other factors make nonsense of the idealised image of the 'Muslim woman', that single definition of Muslim womanhood used to describe women in countries as different as Morocco, Algiers, Egypt, Turkey, Iran, Bosnia, Malaysia, Indonesia and the South Asian region.

But now it's my turn and I ask my friends to tell me how the Yasmeen case is proceeding. Slowly, like all these cases, they reply. Four or so witnesses are called each time the case is scheduled, but on every occasion one or more witnesses are missing and the proceedings are further delayed. Three years after Yasmeen's death only twenty-seven out of fifty-four prosecution witnesses have given evidence and the people of Dinajpur are losing faith in the judicial system. The three former policemen remain in Rangpur Central Gaol near the court house.

They tell me that the Yasmeen case was used by the Awami League in the last elections and that posters with photographs of Yasmeen's body lying on a police van were plastered everywhere. But in spite of these efforts, the BNP candidate was re-elected in Dinajpur even though it has always been an Awami stronghold and remains so, they inform me. But a different political chemistry was at work during the last election and rumours swept through Dinajpur that Awami, if elected to government, would put a stop to smuggling activities. As many of the local people live off smuggling, they voted on this occasion for the BNP.

Yasmeen remains an icon of the women's movement, but there are many 'new Yasmeens'. Last year in the port city of Chittagong, a young Hindu girl, Seema, was raped while in police custody and sent to gaol where she died. Police tried to portray her as a prostitute, just as they did with Yasmeen and the case against the accused policemen was dismissed for lack of witnesses. People in Dinajpur say that Yasmeen's case will meet the same fate. They say that the police force and the local administration in Dinajpur continue much as before.

And the trial of writer-in-exile, Taslima Nasreen is still pending. My curiosity with the enigma of Taslima Nasreen will probably only be satisfied if one day I follow the trail of Taslima to Europe and finally meet her ...

I sit and watch the passers-by, knowing I am invisible and that no-one can see me. I think about the bangles which encircle women's lives: the politics of family relationships and the silent laws, systems and beliefs propping up ancient institutions; I think of religion, of poverty and patriarchy and how women are tired of being invisible.

Perth, August 1977 A verdict has been handed down in the Yasmeen case. The three policemen have been found guilty and received death sentences. Journalist friends who prophesised that the charges would be dismissed are amazed. The rule of law has prevailed in spite of their misgivings. My women friends are euphoric ... it's a great victory for the women's movement.

No-one has any news of Yasmeen's mother, Sharifa Begum.

GLOSSARY

*   *   *

apa	elder sister—respectful term
azan	call to prayer
bhai	brother or mate; friendly term used between men
bindi	red dot on forehead traditionally worn by married Hindu women
burqa	long covering from head to toe. A mesh insert allows the wearer to see
chador	shawl-like covering
chowkhidar	guard or security man
djinn	genie or spirit
dupatta	light scarf worn with shalwar kameez
Eid-ul-Adha	Festival of Sacrifice
Eid-ul-Fitre	Festival at the end of Ramazan
fatwa	scholarly opinion from a religious expert on a point of religious law
Hadith	saying, act or tradition of the Prophet Muhammad
haram	that which is religiously prohibited or forbidden
hartal	traditional political agitation popular in Bangladesh and the region, involving marches and strikes
haveli	a house for women similar to the Arabic idea of harem
hijab	head covering
imam	leader of prayers; official attached to mosque
Insha'Allah	'God willing'
jihad	a struggle or fight to bring about an Islamic order—either an internal struggle with the self or an external one
jumma	Friday communal prayer
kafir	unbeliever or infidel
karo kari	honour killings
lakh	a unit of 100 000

lathi	*stick used by police*
lungi	*sarong*
madrassah	*religious school*
maulvi	*generic term that includes well-versed religious scholars and theologians as well as some half-educated imams and mullahs who teach and officiate at religious festivals*
muezzin	*the man who calls worshippers to prayers*
mujahadeen	*freedom fighters*
mullah	*usually religious official or leader based in village; gives religious advice, teaches Qur'an and plays role on various religious days; today often derided as unscholarly and rustic*
pir	*mystic guide*
purdah	*custom in some Muslim and Hindu communities of keeping women in seclusion; may also refer to the wearing of the veil and/or keeping women out of the public domain*
purdah nashin	*the veiled, secluded woman removed from public gaze; often in the past idealised in literature*
Qari	*one who recites the Qur'an professionally*
Ramazan	*month of fasting*
Salaam alaikum	*'Peace be with you'—greeting*
salish	*village council*
shaitan	*the devil*
shalwar kameez	*trousers and loose tunic worn with dupatta*
Shariah	*the Law or entire corpus of rules guiding Muslim life; derived from diverse sources including Qur'an and Hadith*
Shia	*believe that the legitimate succession of the caliphs derives from Ali, the Prophet's son-in-law (husband of the Prophet's daughter Fatima), cousin of the Prophet and the fourth caliph*
shudra	*literally 'the consultation', deriving from the commendation to Muslims to consult together and reach consensus*
sifarish	*to call on someone of influence to intercede on your behalf*
Sufi	*one who practises the mystical tradition of Islam*
Sunni	*majority division within Islam who accept the entire first generation of Muslim leaders as legitimate, in contrast with Shia who accept only Caliph Ali and his descendants*
thana	*police headquarters or local government office*
Wa laikum salaam	*'Peace be upon you'; answer to the greeting Salaam alaikum*
waz mahfil	*religious gathering*
zamindar	*traditional term to describe wealthy, influential landowner. Land reforms have reduced their influence and their holdings.*
zenana	*secluded women's area*
zina	*fornication, sex out of wedlock*